Business, Commerce, and Social Responsibility

BUSINESS, COMMERCE, AND SOCIAL RESPONSIBILITY

Beyond Agenda

Richard H. Reeves-Ellington

and

Adele Anderson

The Edwin Mellen Press
Lewiston•Queenston•Lampeter

Library of Congress Cataloging-in-Publication Data

Reeves-Ellington, Richard H.
  Business, commerce, and social responsibility : beyond agenda /
Richard H. Reeves-Ellington and Adele Anderson.
    p. cm.
  Includes bibliographical references and index.
  ISBN 0-7734-8442-6 (hardcover)
  1. Business ethics. 2. Free enterprise--Moral and ethical
aspects. 3. Organizational behavior. I. Anderson, Adele (Adele
Kathy) II. Title.
HF5387.R44   1997

                                             97-37725
                                              CIP

A CIP catalog record for this book is available from the British Library.

The Edwin Mellen Press
Box 450
Lewiston, New York
USA 14092-0450

The Edwin Mellen Press
Box 67
Queenston, Ontario
CANADA L0S 1L0

The Edwin Mellen Press, Ltd.
Lampeter, Ceredigion, Wales
UNITED KINGDOM SA48 8LT

Printed in the United States of America

For Bunny, Charlie, and Zola,
and in memory of Lum.

Contents

Contents

Illustrations

Foreword:
Returning Cultural Propriety to Commerce

One of the most exciting trends afoot in both the theory and practice of management is the renascence of interest in economic embeddedness. Recognition of and attention to the extra-economic dimensions of our marketplace behaviors—the interpenetration of economy and other cultural institutions—is driving much current disciplinary advance and shaping much enlightened intervention. In an era of globalized markets, when increased contact among cultures escalates the opportunity for ethical conflict, the need to chart the moral geography of business activity has never been more pressing. The authors of *Beyond Agenda* undertake just such cartography in this intriguing and provocative volume.

Richard Reeves-Ellington and Adele Anderson present us with a cultural ecology of corporate social responsibility. Because managers are inevitably behavioral engineers or social architects, and because management is often an ethically invasive procedure, theorists and practitioners desperately require a framework for evaluating and humanizing the impact of business on people whose lifeways are touched by the corporation. To build such a framework, to facilitate the "reintegration of business and society," Reeves-Ellington and Anderson explore the "moral tasks of practice" in local markets and workplaces around the world; the United States, Japan, Bulgaria, Latin America, and Indonesia are given particular attention. Their anthropological perspective of ethical encounters between firm and folk, grounded as it is in field work and library, makes compelling reading.

The authors describe two approaches to ethical systems. The "agenda" approach, a top-down imposition based on "formal, uniform mechanisms" of authority, views actors as statistical aggregates and is insensitive to context. The approach emerging from "cultural interpretation" is a bottom-up enterprise that recognizes individual agency as locally situated and views actors as particular personalities. The former regime is a deontological one often favored by Western corporations. The latter, a teleological one, is more likely favored by many anthropologists. Integral to the authors' position is their discussion of leadership styles in such companies as Apple Computers, The Body Shop, and a pseudonymous multinational, Pharmco. Transactional leaders guide organizations that follow a "business" model and adopt a bottom-line attitude to social responsibility. Transformational leaders, who share characteristics of the shaman, guide organizations that follow a "commerce" model and push beyond the bottom line, to embrace an employee and customer welfare attitude to social responsibility. Through illuminating anecdotes and extended case studies, the authors explore the practical implications and consequences of each ethical approach.

What is perhaps most satisfying about this volume is its relentless return to a stakeholder orientation toward corporate social responsibility, and the authors' emphasis on the need for a vision constructed jointly by those whom strategy will touch. Anthropologically informed managerial practice seeks solutions appropriate to the needs of local, as well as organizational, culture. Everywhere around the planet, we are witnessing a dialectical engagement between cultural hegemony and cultural pluralism. As the forces of homogeneity and heterogeneity contend, managers who adopt a posture of cultural propriety will most likely negotiate radical change in the best interests of their stakeholders. Motivated by a corporate vision that is tempered by an intimate, locally rooted understanding of lifeways, and a profound respect for the integrity of traditional social structures, these managers recognize that an ethics grounded in cultural ecology makes good business sense. Cultural propriety is not simply sound intuition, nor is it relativist cant. Reeves-Ellington and Anderson show us how the stance is developed, tested, and refined in field settings that are collectively the touchstone of anthropology and management alike.

Empowerment is among the greatest challenges we face in the new millennium. Beyond concerns for humane management, consumer satisfaction, and sustainable development, we must discover ways to improve the life chances and quality of everyone caught up in this latest wave of economic transformation. A cultural perspective reminds us that the words "ecology" and "economics" derive from a common root (-*oikos*) signifying "household," that all markets are local and that each is comprised not of "others" but of "selves," and that consequences of our managerial decisions will be the less unanticipated and unintended for our ethnological due diligence. Social responsibility is a shared obligation among stakeholders. Reeves-Ellington and Anderson demonstrate the managerial value of cultural wisdom, and our understanding of ethical decisions is enriched by their demonstration.

—John F. Sherry, Jr.
J. L. Kellogg Graduate School of Management
Northwestern University

Preface

A foolish consistency is the hobgoblin of little minds.

—*Ralph Waldo Emerson*

This book is directed primarily to those professionals, scholars, and students who are concerned about doing business responsibly within contexts that are globalizing, yet also culturally fragmented. We address in particular those who find the idea of social responsibility worrisome because they can identify many examples in which its dictates conflict, and they know these dictates refer for their legitimacy to competing sources of authority. Our goal is to bring anthropological insights to the cultural and moral aspects of business, with an ultimate aim of enabling people to work more effectively toward a reintegration of business and society.

As with many human endeavors, when people in business feel the weight of their responsibilities, they often seek a simplifying framework. They hope this will help them resolve the many human complications that come with their work. In other times and places when social institutions were less formal, specialized, and rationalized, human economic competition could certainly be morally complicated, but cultural heterogeneity was addressed in less subtle ways. Such contexts produced durable, yet flexible, moral guidance and a convincing source of identity, but the same mores often excluded outsiders from recognition as part of the human community and sorted insiders arbitrarily, and sometimes brutally, into unequal statuses.

Despite what we might like to believe, social science and theories of management have fallen far short of equipping us for the demands of social responsibility in late modern times. When the source of moral pressure becomes unbearable, authoritative directives and simplified sources of guidance have great appeal. Simplification harks back to the earlier models. People may turn to older or newly adopted cultural or religious traditions, personal missions, or political ideologies, or they may just look for more rational frameworks for pursuing business dealings. Those people not in an easy position to command a wide variety of resources find it particularly difficult to smooth over the dissonance between the informal and personal space of their cultural mores and the day-to-day formal requirements of complex organizations and society. Inquiring deeply into social responsibility in particular situations can make a person's actions appear self-contradictory even on those fortunate occasions when the person is convinced they are trustworthy and valid.

Organizations of business add more layers of consistency problems, and when they intersect with national and other sectoral boundaries, the pressures multiply further. Business organizations are often one thing to their stockholders, another to partners, another to parent companies, and still other things to subsidiaries, suppliers, and varied sets of employees and customers. One kind of response to all this inconsistency is to shed personal responsibility and make business-at-large the villain. Another is to locate blame in other persons inside an organization or in another sector of society, perhaps in capitalism as a system, or in modernity as a whole. Through blame, people can, whether they are powerful or not, adopt *moral* powerlessness and proclaim a kind of modified innocence of the self, attributing responsibility for poor outcomes to one or more external sources.

The authors do not propose to try to relieve people of their experiences of inconsistency. We would prefer to accept contextual tensions as a necessary source of creativity, discovery, and adaptation, rather than try to reduce them by applying a new set of nostrums. Such pronouncements would only add to the existing welter of defining and counterdefining of jural and moral prescription. Therefore, we provide no procedural advice for the solution of particular classes of problems, no specific mental exercises, no new social agenda for responsible business. Instead, we view responsibility from an anthropological perspective. This book represents an attempt to think differently about responsibility and business in ways that move beyond agenda.

To do this, we have had to enter a less-developed terrain in business responsibility, a cultural space in which moral suasion rather than authority finds center focus. Personal responsibility and cultural interpretation are the primary elements in this space. Accordingly, we discuss responsibility through cultural interpretations rather than from structures, institutions, and rules. In the later chapters, we use illustrative material to raise questions of moral and business issues at several different levels of organization and analysis. These questions have been important to us, two practitioners with graduate preparation in anthropology who have practiced outside the academy for the majority of our work lives. We challenge the academic, jural, and politicized connotations that have become so pervasive in discussions of social responsibility. By themselves, they are insufficient to the moral tasks of practice. Culture, as holistically understood, provides a richer, necessary, and long-neglected ethical basis for personal interpretation and action. We believe that practitioners, scholars, and organization leaders can only take on greater personal responsibility by gaining better awareness of culture. It forms the basis for their own and others' valorization of ethical actions in activities of buying, selling, and making.

Existing variations in day-to-day business social behavior and the variability of their interpretation in alternate cultural settings are among the least understood aspects of social responsibility. As increasing numbers of people from different cultural settings encounter each other in business, neither the old mores of outsider exclusion nor the new rules of interpretive exclusion will suffice. Any new, living moral community we discover is as unlikely to derive from legal and political authority as it is to owe its existence to a single, monocultural source.

Those practitioners who stand at the bridgeheads of transcultural business will quickly recognize the kinds of inconsistencies to which we refer. Operating in highly rationalized organizations that straddle incommensurate legal and cultural systems, they must overcome the tendency for purely rational and economic aims to sever their human relationships with trading partners. The business context is not a mere contest between mutually exotic adversaries or opaquely bounded parties. The first thing practitioners must understand is that rules will not save them. The second is that others do not see the world ethically in the same terms they do.

The moral variations and uncertainties of business are important reasons for entering the conversation of social responsibility with an aim of moving beyond agenda. Business globalization will only increase the awareness of differences in interpreting what social responsibility is. Incommensurate social injunctions will continue to press in. Both business and social outcomes will become harder to control or predict than in the past.

A culturally interpretive approach reaches out to the wider business audience beyond corporate headquarters: Despite the popular tendency to aim advice mainly at top executive levels of management, most people whose work, study, and practice involve them in for-profit activities have certain practical limits in the scope of the resources and conditions they can command or control on a day-to-day basis. In the context of these limitations, their need is to learn skills of clear inquiry, mindfulness, and cultural sophistication. To do more than survive for an amoral context, they must obtain tools and skills to expand their receptivity to new avenues for proceeding responsibly amid limitations of various kinds. The conceptual and methodological tools of anthropology can contribute much to this effort. The elements we discuss here have assisted business practitioners with basic tasks of cultural inquiry as they faced novel cultural situations in the field.

Pursuing social responsibility through the sanctioning structures of authority and seeking justice through continuing struggle for needed institutional reforms are essential features of modern civic life. But, the answer to an abdication of personal responsibility will not be found in exclusive resort to agendas. By themselves, they are too limited a moral vision. Pursued without personal responsiveness, they only speed the loss of a holistic integration that traditionally included consideration for social responsibility in all human economic activity.

If members of society want business done in socially responsible ways, they must first educate themselves to be socially responsible. To become responsible, every practitioner must develop his or her own sophistication with inquiry, in live dialogue with colleagues and partners.

Commercial practitioners must prepare themselves to actively look for and respond to new opportunities for becoming responsbile. In doing so, they may at times run the risk of departure from the dictates of one or another agenda, but a desirable result is that options for how to be responsible and *human* are broadened rather than narrowed.

Paradigm, Strategy, and Materials

Using anthropology's qualitative, holistic, and ethnological approach[1] to culture, we employ a number of cultural and organizational concepts relevant to social responsibility in settings that we and others have observed, researched, and experienced across a variety of cultural settings. In all our discussions, we begin from a vantage point of the western European cultural models for late modern business; most of the social responsibility conversation we want to address has begun there. We expand on this perspective to consider alternative views and interpretations of responsibility, first by calling attention to the variability that exists in ethical concepts, meanings, and practices in other cultural contexts, then by framing a working understanding of culture and responsibility, and, finally, by examining some extended illustrations in which responsibility takes varying shapes and appearances.

In the contexts we describe, what social responsibility is will not always be obvious; in some instances, it will extend to social aspects beyond what business practitioners ordinarily assume to be relevant, or even the proper, venues and methods of business activity. We urge readers to pay attention to the material between the lines—the level of organization, the home perspectives of those who interact, the doctrinal or institutional stance the players are taking.

A subtle awareness of between-the-lines context casts new light on the limits of strongly held principles, beliefs, or procedural cookbooks to prevent or remedy irresponsibility. Cultivating the awareness of differences in common practice and their meanings in unfamiliar settings has been a hallmark of anthropological inquiry, a discipline that remains too little utilized in business management and the education of future practitioners.

American discourses of responsibility most often emphasize areas in which it has been lacking; this has been abetted by the increased visibility of bad outcomes with the growth of media communication. Current discussions of business ethics tend to gravitate to extreme and spectacular cases. In most of these, legal and institutional debates frame the questions, and the liability or economic consequences provide the moral of the story. Practitioners are seldom asked to stop and consider what local conditions, doctrinal positions, and features of cultural context figured in the emergence and identification of the problems in the first place. Most discussions of context are dominated by power monologues and focus on bad faith, compromised enforcement capacities, or the need for a more or less complete overhaul of certain cultural institutions, or even of capitalism itself.

The cultural models for the western European business organizations that are now dominant are well suited for this siege approach: The chief responses to charges of irresponsibility have been legal defense, countersuits, lobbying, counterorganizing, or image campaigns of media and public relations. Yet, the more common interpretive basis for taking responsibility at the level of people is that of a positive, long-range commitment to community. Such commitments run throughout the memberships of organizations and their wider communities and would surely be expected to include all a company's stakeholders. This, and not adversity, is a more likely basis for integrating economically oriented organizations with the other structures of society. Neither adversarial nor exclusive actions will move business closer to social integration. These social strategies only drive a wedge between these sectors of society and disempower people as their members.

Sociocultural and interpretive views of business responsibility lack the glamour and finality of courtroom battles, large public demonstrations, and solemn meetings at the formal summits of power. Cultural issues of responsibility are more like preventive and chronic medicine—daily and ongoing, requisite of continuous attention, and holistically affecting all aspects of the lives of those involved. The benefits are not immediately apparent, but only accrue prospectively over longer periods of time. They include no guarantees that a negative event will never occur; they have no visible certainty or finality of impact. They defy simple or categorical analysis of questions of greed, of something not working properly, or of a cataclysmic betrayal of natural order. We even suggest that they have little or no impact on the economic health of most business, at least in any short run. The cultural paradigm we advocate for socially responsible business brings the focus of agency down from larger agendas, either political, economic, or academic, to the mundane activities people pursue in their daily business dealings.

The plan of this book is to define and describe, then to support an outlook and approach to responsibility that may superficially appear skeptical, but is strongly pragmatic, philosophic, and optimistic in its application. Qualitative sketches, cases, and issue reviews focus on the cultural aspects of social responsibility in a variety of Western-run businesses operating across cultural settings. The more extended case illustrations, which begin after the first two chapters, are unlike typical business cases in several ways. They focus on social, not economic, parameters, selectively sampling from a range of organizational levels and situations.

In Chapters 3 and 4, we give extensive attention to the consequences of contrasting leadership approaches and assumptions for the cultural integration of organizations with society. In Chapter 3, these include the cultural features evident in contrasting leadership types at Apple Computer, Incorporated, in the 1980s. The early 1990s ethical controversy surrounding the British cosmetics company The Body Shop is the focus in Chapter 4.

The next two chapters move to the upper middle, middle management, and first-line general management levels of field operations within a multinational pharmaceutical company, which we call Pharmco.[2] Chapter 5 details the revival and turnaround of a marginal and failing region within the Pharmco corporation. Chapter 6 offers a microlevel view of a foreign joint-venture land purchase in 1970s Indonesia.

We think readers will find the examination of these diverse materials to be sometimes surprising, sometimes dismaying, sometimes encouraging, but always indicative of the moral suasion of culture. In viewing business through a cultural lens, we hope to show that the relevance of interpretation for responsible business practice is not trivial. It is a force that can be completely compatible with, but also operates quite independent of, the necessity for prior or conclusive demonstrations of economic impact.

Our reviews often center on actions of individual persons; they include many first-person business experiences of Reeves-Ellington. The group of illustrations as a whole includes business roles from leaders at the top echelons of companies to persons who would be attributed lower status within traditional companies, but who in a number of instances were key to developing positive agency near their organization's periphery, in dialogue with customers and others outside formal company boundaries.

We owe much, in organization methodologies described in Chapter 5, to the influence of a family of pragmatic action inquiry methods. These include *kaizen*, a process of continual improvement now adopted by many business and manufacturing organizations, reflective practice and organizational learning from the organizational behavior and management literature, and selected aspects of grounded theory and participative action inquiry from across several related social science disciplines.

Our core theoretical approach and disciplinary base, however, remain broadly and holistically interpretive and anthropological. We find value, especially for field and midrange organizations, in viewing the social realities of business as culturally constructed. Taking this position figures importantly in how we recognize and interpret ethical and responsible action. Responsibility must operate in the same positive discovery space as entrepreneurism, but it cannot depend for its justification on specific economic results.

People are the only agents who ensure integrity in the ongoing dialogues within and across organizations and cultural traditions. It is they who create the integrity of translation and disclosure of the business value of a relationship to each of the involved parties. For this reason, we also reject the idea of situation ethics because this term implies the participants have no compass or plan and have not made substantial and ongoing efforts to understand their own and others' cultural and ethical contexts. They need this commitment to knowledge and discipline to optimize the realistic and desired dimensions of their business relationships. Without a continuing search for cultural understanding in unfamiliar and changing business situations, business actors are not and cannot be responsible.

We believe socially responsible businesses are those that will anticipate, facilitate, and support the personal agency of their practitioners for integrating organizations with the whole of society. This, more than many formulas now advising for business success or for rules of ethical behavior in business, will have the greatest likelihood of producing desired (and we believe, adaptive) pan-human outcomes. These are the outcomes that all global inhabitants share in common.

The Authors' Context

This project grew out of an ongoing dialogue between two practitioner-anthropologists, one from international business (Reeves-Ellington) and the other from American government and voluntary-sector organizations (Anderson). Reeves-Ellington's more than 33 years in multinational pharmaceuticals took him to 23 countries and included many non-Western and Third World employees, partners, and customers. Anderson's more than 15 years in evaluation, regulatory, and quality consultation brought her close to issues of organizational responsibility, the role of authority and sanctions, and the processes of dialogue between field operations and central governance in a range of human services.

For both of us, the home offices were relatively advantaged cores of production and marketing, while the customers, partners, and other recipients were most often more vulnerable in their organizational position, as well as in their conditions of life. Thus, both of us have had many encounters in which we faced an organization's responsibility as the more powerful agent, and on most of these occasions we have been among the inside parties or observers to transactions.

There were academic research designs in force in some of the illustrated cases, but these were primarily the concern of other collaborators and consultants. Most often, the authors' functions were to produce information, activities, and results for an organization's mission. In our nonacademic roles, we were often customers for academic and consulting technologies brought in by outsiders. We functioned as the interpreters of these inputs, acting as yet a different kind of cultural broker. Now, with our primary roles in higher education, we hope that our analyses and perspectives on these experiences will help others to grapple better with the applied cultural dimensions of social responsibility.

Audiences

We believe there are a number of audiences that can benefit from this book. They include, especially, graduates and upper division undergraduates in international business and applied anthropologists and others in related disciplines concerned with the social impact of business. Thoughtful business practitioners, especially those in charge of field operations in large and transcultural companies and scholars and teachers who prepare future business practitioners also stand to benefit.

An introductory background in business and ethics will be helpful in putting our discussions to use, as will preparation in anthropology and related studies in sociology and organizational behavior. It is our hope to provide an approach that complements and challenges the many fine traditional books on culture, society, and the institutions that support business integrity. We believe there is a need for glimpses of alternate perspectives that are marginal today but may gain significance in business of the future. We hope to provoke a rethinking of frameworks and assumptions about responsibility that remain common in both the business community and the academy.

The authors' native socialization is that of two North Americans (albeit one with many years of life abroad) who have been shaped by European and Protestant backgrounds. This culturally specific heritage, in addition to our educational and professional socialization, surely affects our outlook. The same specificity is inherent in our material, which involves Western-run businesses and spans from the 1970s through the early 1990s, years in which the initial post–World War II multinational explosion and economic growth eventually gave way to concerns about global competition, the regionalization of markets, and the growing asymmetry of wealth distribution. Our belief in the need for reintegration of organizations and society allows for the possibility that this may happen in unanticipated ways. We also believe there is enormous unrealized potential for the cultural contributions of businesspeople who come from outside the Western cultural region and who will profoundly affect business of the future. We look forward to learning through continued dialogue across these sources, and we persist in our outlook of optimism for the pan-human future.

Acknowledgments

A number of our colleagues and friends have generously read, commented, and contributed to our understanding of social responsibility. We would like to thank some early readers of drafts, papers, and manuscripts that became part of this book. They include Robert Chantra, Barbara Reeves-Ellington, Robert Seidel, and M. Estellie Smith. Bernice Kaplan and John Sherry, Jr., were kind enough to read and comment on full manuscript drafts. Special thanks go to Jon Meccarello and Tabisam Javed for their assistance with collection and consultation on several cultural issues specific to Islam, and to Jennifer Burr for library reference help. Adele Anderson is grateful to staff members Alexandra Cutler and Marcello Palazzi of the New Academy of Business, who welcomed her in 1995 as a touring visitor and asker of many questions. As is the case with most efforts of this size, some errors are bound to remain; these are the sole responsibility of the authors.

Notes

1. Ethnology is generally the comparative study of one or multiple sociocultural features across many cultural settings. This anthropological approach uses similarities and contrasts among a broad variety of features, from motifs in symbolic areas such as folklore, religion, and the arts, to comparative studies of politics and social structure. It contrasts as a broad description of anthropological activity with ethnography, a written or otherwise recorded narrative account of a particular cultural setting.
2. Pharmco is a pseudonym that we use throughout this book to denote a group of multinational pharmaceutical organizations in which Reeves-Ellington worked and that formed the business organization context for various projects that we describe.

1
Responsibility's Less-Developed Terrain

Social responsibility in business will sometimes evoke images of admired, civic-minded leaders who accommodate wider social interests along with their successful pursuit of profits. Unfortunately, it more often brings to mind businesses that do not live up to public expectations. These less-desired images include underpaid child and undocumented workers in U.S. garment industry sweatshops; low wages and dangerous conditions in American and joint-venture factories in the Third World; pollution, social disruption, and environmental degradation produced by global energy and resource-extraction companies; and the cost-calculating approach that is often taken to consumer product and service safety.

Blame and enforcement responses have immediate appeal. But another perspective, equally important, has been neglected. It is a more culturally interpretive view of responsibility. Based on discovery, understanding, and acknowledgment of customary and symbolic variations, it reveals what the instances of poor regard have in common. They all reflect prior human problems of social connection and cultural interpretation.

Social responsibility in business, in a positive sense, demands an ongoing, inclusive view of human success. Its premise, usually unstated, is that organizations must integrate with the wider societies of which they are a part. Just what constitutes an adequate and desirable integration, and how or whether this can be achieved by business within current institutional frameworks, have been widely debated issues. This chapter sketches the authors' working position on these difficult issues. We address them in general philosophical and conceptual terms. Specifically, we argue the relevance of culture to ethical interpretations, lay the groundwork for further interrogation of responsibility in business, and prepare the reader to examine responsibility's manifestations in the extended illustrations we will present in later chapters.

We begin with several assertions: Business now can be socially responsible. It can do this only through ongoing, integrative interaction with the wider society. This interaction must extend beyond purely economic transactions. It must happen at the informal cultural level, among the full array of practitioners. Finally, it must be constructed jointly, linking people who are located across the formal borders of organizations. In short, socially responsible business is person based, extends beyond economics, knits together diverse levels of the organization, and promotes personally meaningful linkages with the people outside.

This is our idea of socially responsible business. It does not require a particular agenda or formal source of authority for action to be taken, but it does require self- and other-awareness of cultural patterns and of interpretation as a basis for all socially meaningful actions. Many volumes have been devoted to formal and institutionalized structures that would define rules and procedures to enforce responsibility inside and outside organizations. Millennia of philosophy have resulted in a uniquely Western study of ethics and law. Yet, there remains a large and relatively undeveloped terrain for fostering greater social responsibility. It can be found in the observances and responses to daily cultural interpretations in business activities. Because a sophisticated cultural inquiry involves acknowledging that people will continue to differ in their preferences and habits of discretion, it is also a slippery and dangerous terrain. It deeply involves personal views, identities, power, and the valued assumptions we make about the world and human nature.

Culture-Based Ethics, Modern Agendas

Responsibility as an idea is historically western European in origin, rooted in an older Western ethics that can be traced to classical Greek philosophers such as Plato and Aristotle (Runes, 1970, p. 98). Modern business ethics, derived from those earlier moral philosophies that studied and proposed standards of moral conduct and judgment, was shaped by the events and conditions of its particular cultural history, and retains visible elements of this past in the writings and arguments of modern business ethicists. But, from early to late modern times, business ethics and Western ethics in general have become increasingly mediated by consideration of formal legal frameworks and thus dislocated morally from their specific cultural origins. The authority for ethical responsibility has separated into specialized sectors, evolving to increasingly formalized specialties, just as has occurred with other institutions of society. As this has taken place, legalisms have often come to replace what at one time would have been subject to consensus-based mores.

This has had both good and bad results. Legal enforcement has overcome many cases of severely ethnocentric exclusion and patently inhumane treatment of some people at the hands of others. At the same time, certain advantages have been eclipsed that were inherent in culture-based ethics. Older authority sources have become obsolete, superseded by new and rapidly evolving policies and legal codes. Personal discretion in harmonizing ethical agreement with others appears to have diminished because people are saturated with new information and feel uncertain—they cannot keep up with the latest demands and developments. It is easier to relinquish responsibility to the authority of experts, who can later be blamed if the outcomes are not good. Amid an atmosphere of blame and suspicion of motive, people will find it easier to draw increasingly fine claims and distinctions rather than risk attempting to find the commonalities between themselves and others.

In public settings, moral interpretation is increasingly a matter of a person's politics. In its most politicized forms, social responsibility has become more a code for promulgating competing programs, identities, and claims than for creating and fostering responsible people. Increasingly, it has become a battle of agendas over the definition of social reality. Responsibility viewed only through the lens of agendas will hinder more than help organizations to integrate with wider communities.

Responsibility emerged in public discourse in western Europe during the early modern years of the Renaissance and Enlightenment. Michael Harmon (1995), drawing largely on a 1957 review by McKeon, cites the use of the word *responsible* in the writings of Ben Johnson, John Locke, and, later, Alexander Hamilton, in which the word had positive and active connotations (p. 14).

In later modern times, responsibility often surfaces in discussions referring to its absence, or else it takes the form of ever-finer and more minute calculations of pinpointed liability that someone should incur, as increasingly happens in the legal adjudication of business ethics and responsibility cases. This is rarely satisfying or adaptive for the long term. The Christian philosopher H. Richard Niebuhr (1963) recaptures some of responsibility's earlier positive usage by suggesting that the term be interpreted culturally; he would see responsibility as "the fitting action, the one that fits into a total interaction as response and as anticipation of further response" (p. 61).

This is just the sense in which we refer to responsibility throughout this book. It is an older sense, with great danger for overinterpretation if used with reference to any one exclusive cultural viewpoint, but it offers exhilarating possibilities for a pluralistic reintegration of societies. The best use of this sense of responsibility requires a sophistication about culture and community that has for the most part yet to be achieved in either business organizations or modern society generally. Pursued as an experience of learning, it promises the new levels of social integrity on which pan-human adaptation may well come to depend in the future.

In organizations pressed by internal and external competition, a positive responsibility that relies on people to decide and act on situations together often seems all but unattainable. Why this is so, as Harmon (1995) points out in *Responsibility as Paradox*, has much to do with the limits of the modern rationalizing approaches that have come to dominate the concept of responsibility. Harmon argues, from a perspective that stays completely within the Western tradition, that people must ultimately face the paradoxical nature of their responsibility as a tension between active individual agency and the acknowledgment of answerability to outside laws and authority. Harmon's argument provides an alternative to the increasing devotion of intellectual energies to a competition for airtime among diverse political identities, which have been couched as alternate cultural perspectives and world views. These positions, taken largely within the context of American and western European cultural traditions of discourse, have less to do with culture in a pan-human, adaptive sense than with culture recast as a social and political agenda.

Harmon arrives at conclusions that are both uniquely Western and uniquely suited for engagement with a multicultural world. Both his paradox and his answer, the reflective and responsive exercise of courage in the face of doubt, begin to suggest the outlines of a person-based strategy for responsible transcultural conversations in business.

Social responsibility pursued this way could produce a commerce of exchanges that extends beyond the sheer economic, integrating business with a wider social arena of activity. This integration could far exceed the ill-fitting and irresponsible business metaphors of conquest and colonization, with their mirror images, resistance and revolution. Developing the neglected cultural view would require a more holistic approach to the gaining of livelihoods and a greater faith in social investments. Above all, it would call for acknowledging the uncertainty of power and agenda. Business practitioners must be better prepared to engage the stunning variety of authoritative backgrounds, institutions, and cultural metaphors that exist across organizations and cultures to orient good action. The adequacy of their response in their encounters, how fitting they are to the situation, will further integrate or further separate their organizations from society as a whole. Through their interpretations of differences and rules, practitioners can make themselves more fully human and responsible. Through neglect and blame, they can reduce themselves to rogues and pawns.

Fostering reflection and responsibility at a culturally interpretive level requires more than the injunction to be courageous or even to study extant case materials to try to learn from others' mistakes. Both of these things are surely basic necessities for practitioners, but their chances of success can be vastly augmented with greater knowledge and sophistication in the concepts of culture and the thoughtful and reflective pursuit of learning amid unfamiliar and uncertain conditions. For these tasks, anthropological knowledge and methods for studying culture offer a rich and adaptable body of tools and concepts.

Culture and Agenda as Ethical Frameworks

Anthropological observations of human cultural systems suggest that ethical and responsible behaviors often spring from nonrational cultural and ideational roots. The conscious rational frameworks advanced to explain characteristics of particular societies and economies we see throughout the world have as often followed as formed them, and often exist primarily for their justification. Although we now ethically interpret behavior in public through increasingly formal and rationalized sources of authority, the culturally based alternatives have long existed at a more informal and interpretive level. In order to examine culture's relevance for ethical responsibility, we need to begin with a working understanding of the concept of culture.

Culture

Exactly what culture is has been long debated in anthropology, but most recently it has been recognized as a helpful construct or abstraction for understanding the patterned and interrelated meanings that people attribute to their actions. It includes anthropologists' recognition that people jointly and continually build, coordinate, and reinterpret these meanings across the many dimensions of a social system. While "shared meanings" is surely an oversimplification, it does get at the flexibility of a construct that has helped generations of anthropologists to describe the observable gradients, and the sometimes discontinuous distribution, of various themes, symbols, and other value-orienting motifs that they have found among the societies of the world. In its most encompassing uses, culture has included all the details of technology, social arrangements, and beliefs of a society, yet when it is considered as a system influencing behavior and decisions, certain of its unique qualities stand out. It can be seen more specifically as a shared system of publicly enacted meanings inferred and interpreted from the particular events that occur among people. (C. Geertz, 1973, and Keesing, 1974, have provided extended examples and syntheses of this interpretive use of the culture concept in anthropology.)

Each social science discipline has had a distinctive view of culture, and in recent decades the emergence of a concept of organizational culture has further complicated its use as a heuristic tool. Our discussion of culture here and in Chapter 2 puts chief emphasis on those kinds of cultural distinctions that can be made across countries and world social regions. For an approach with a holistic perspective, it is important to appreciate these larger and more inclusive and visible sets of difference before considering the finer, more qualified and restricted uses of culture as a term within organizations.

Cultural features shape the way members respond to others and guide and limit their attention so they may select from among a variety of contexts to construct the particular meanings they will need for fitting behavior that is adequate to their commercial relationships. There are reflexive benefits for the cross-cultural observer, who in turn gains a deeper understanding of the home cultural setting. From the experience of other possible interpretations, this observer gains insight into the arbitrariness of many cultural elements that may have been taken for universal. This is also why a qualitative cultural exploration is worthwhile in practice settings that extend beyond the well-worn confines of much Western social science business and management research. To do productive cultural inquiry while working in their own organizations, practitioners will find that they need to draw on the work of other scholars and analysts, but their application of the results will be far different. Practitioners will often need heuristics to aid in thinking procedurally, rather than typologically, for more adequate and creative responses in action. In a business environment of rapid change and multiple cultures, this task is as difficult as any of basic science.

People continually elaborate and reinterpret culture in ongoing interactions with each other. This process of assignment and reassignment of meanings, continual adjustments, and adaptations has been the major mode of creative human adaptation throughout changing conditions for the many millennia of human existence. It provides a powerful basis for achievement of a more integrated life between business and the rest of society.

Agenda

In the late modern context of complex and highly industrialized societies, formalized and increasingly politicized agendas have transformed much of our collective, informal, and culturally based ethical wisdom for a more modern interpretation of public ethics. Agenda as we use it means the programmatic formation and pursued implementation of rational—or at least rationalized—principles; furthermore, it always implies a pursuit of greater certainty, uniformity, and unified control of behaviors and outcomes. In the context of social responsibility, it also carries the connotation of a unified moral position that its authors hold and that they would impose in the direction of actions by others.

Formal and standardized procedures for the improved justice of social outcomes have been an important aspect of the civilizing process. These standards, in the form of laws, policies, canons, and other principles promulgated by recognized authorities, stand as evidence, through their artifacts in extant written and architectural structures, of a recognition that reliance on parochial custom did not result in just outcomes for a diverse civil society. In liberal democracies especially, a more culturally cohesive and homogeneous public ethic of older societal models has largely given way to the rapidly expanding, formalized bodies of procedures and rules. In authoritarian regimes, public ethics may be promulgated through formal structures that bear at least some superficial resemblance to formalized laws and codes with which we Westerners are familiar. But, the background institutions and processes through which they are established are different, as are the variations in which they are realized in public behavior.

The processes of formalization of a public ethic have been relatively successful in Western democracies. A modern utilitarian preference for evaluating them through measurable outcomes on a large scale has also brought about an accelerated obsolescence and revision of various codes, laws, regulations, and grand strategies of policy. It has also set the stage for the intensification of a contest for authority and agenda among the fragmenting and specializing social sectors. Institutions of wealth creation and accumulation pursue their economic agendas, and institutions of regulation and wealth redistribution pursue alternate economic and social outcome agendas. On either side, large-scale and programmatic approaches, usually focusing on economic distribution and outcome measurement rather than local and particular process and engagement, have often resulted in disappointing outcomes. There is a missing element of cultural interpretation in the overreliance on these approaches and measures. In business ethics, this deficiency fuels an endless market for legal manuals and other cookbooks on how to stay out of trouble. In social responsibility movements, it has provided grist for philosophizing about correct attitudes and right values. Too often, the proponents of various positions assume that adequate behavioral response and socially good outcomes will automatically follow if only people will follow the right recipe or join the right ideological camp.

These are the hallmarks of modern, agenda-driven ethics. Their interpretation flows from the top down from a within the relevant jurisdiction and affects subject populations who exist largely in the abstract. The statistical features of these populations may be well known, but they lack a personal relationship or a known cultural connection to the authors of agenda whether they are called constituencies, market segments, consumers, or audiences. Despite scientific sampling, polling, or imaginative extrapolations from focus groups, there is, under agenda thinking, a paucity of sustained give and take. Figure 1 illustrates a visual metaphor for the dynamics of agenda-driven ethics.

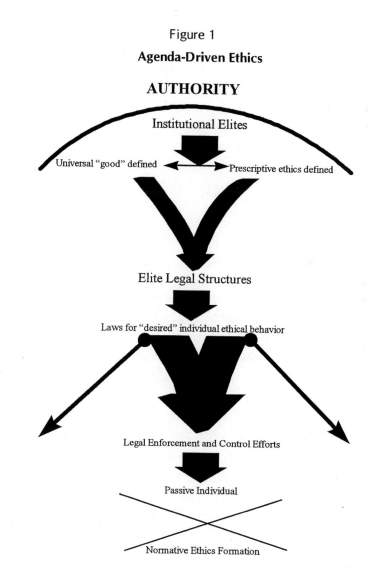

Figure 1

Agenda-Driven Ethics

AUTHORITY

Institutional Elites

Universal "good" defined ← → Prescriptive ethics defined

Elite Legal Structures

Laws for "desired" individual ethical behavior

Legal Enforcement and Control Efforts

Passive Individual

Normative Ethics Formation

The following statement is characteristic of an agenda-based ethic: I cannot legislate attitudes but I can legislate behavior. It reflects less the variant normative assumptions and practicalities of everyday situations than the product of an enlightened, abstract system of thought. Agenda's arbiters, usually an elite, conceptually define the good and set forth the accompanying behavioral prescriptions and legislative structures provide for their orderly dissemination and enforcement. Input to their formation must pass through what Clegg (1989) has compellingly described as the formal circuits of power in social organizations and institutions.

In a successful liberal democracy, these circuits are orderly, rational, and accessible for a large segment of society, yet they do not furnish all the elements needed for social responsibility. In less-democratic and less-affluent social regions, the circuits of power are less pluralistic and allow the elites to buffer themselves from influence by most people in the society through personal and social advantages of wealth, kinship, social networks, or other institutional circumstances. In these settings, however, the cultural and interpretive basis of public ethical behavior is often more visible. Lacking widespread public recourse against abuses, there may be considerably less consistency, even superficial, between rules and conduct at either the elite or the popular strata of society. For mutual survival, the subject populations must often interpret the official ethic much differently in day-to-day practice than was intended by the authorities.

A prevalent liberal democratic response to tyranny in modern times has been to organize formal structures in an effort to enfranchise out-groups by appealing to wider communities of opinion and enforcement. This, too, is an agenda-driven ethical response to unjust social conditions. Advocates resisting tyranny and maldistribution of resources through counteragendas may reach international circles of influence or the educated public with their messages through conferences and media. There, they may challenge the decisions or practices of authorities whose behavior is irresponsible. They often pursue the needed reforms politically through agendas of their own. Economic organizations likewise pursue agendas that will benefit their interests, whether within a state framework or within international frameworks of agreement between companies or nations, or between a company and a nation.

Similar strategies of agenda promulgation, and occasional counterorganizing by subject groups, occur within another arena in the democratic social context—

corporate business ownership and management. Here, the contests of agenda may be between the proposed regulating mechanisms to give a workforce greater discretion over the conditions, processes, and outputs of their work, and the official corporate policies and rules that have been the prerogative of owners and top management. So, these contingents of economic organizations also take agenda form and pursue power over behavior and its interpretation. Many of the obvious counterorganizations involve union movements, which may similarly resort to outside social authority for imposition of social change. But, there also exist within business organizations, among the managerial ranks, less externally visible coalitions with their own strategies of agenda. In either case, the nature of the battle, agenda versus agenda, is basically the same.

When the ethical basis for either social or economic activity is linked integrally with the participants' cultural motifs, the efforts at collective adaptation and change are most likely to be responsible or fitting to the situation. When agenda organizing proceeds only from issues and programs that are visible to and concern only a small segment of those affected, they are less likely to mesh with peoples' everyday experiences. Too pure a reliance on the politics of agenda, when divorced in this way from interactional cultural interpretations, can quickly become an exercise of reified power. It is thereby emptied of potential for a wider and more robust cultural interpretation, even when pursued with the best intentions and interests of the subject population.

Culture-Based Ethics

A less-formal, less overtly political, but more risky source of ethical guidance is afforded by using cultural interpretation. This kind of ethics is much softer and less efficient. It relies on establishing a connection to the particular themes of a given cultural setting related to how its inhabitants view the world. Cultural influences shape people's normative behavior in ways both conscious and unconscious. These interpretive ethical sources, while potentially powerful, are not consolidated and uniform the way the power of agenda ethics is. Their users may experience them as traditional, newly adopted, or personally improved, but the behavioral results of these ethics are always highly interactional because culture exists through repeated encounters; it is not just a concept in people's minds. Cultural norms are not ideal, but subject to ongoing revision; they can be seen operating in public, but do not depend for existence and enforcement on the official public authority of a state or a proprietor. Culture-based ethics are accordingly variable in both form and consistency, and they can therefore be highly unpredictable for large-scale social outcomes. (Figure 2 illustrates our idea of this dynamic.)

Perhaps the key difference between an agenda-driven ethic and a culture-based ethic is that agenda looks to formal and uniform mechanisms of authority to distribute good in general across contexts, while culture relies on people acting for the good in particular contexts. For this reason, we could expect proponents of agenda ethics to be hostile to discussions of culture-based ethics. If they are governing elites, whether of states or of corporations, for example, the agendaists will often view culture-based behavior as dangerously variable and potentially insurgent. It may pose threats to social order, to health, or to security—or to their own practical power (and most often they are correct in this last assumption).

Other agenda advocates, especially those critical of sitting elites, those out of power, or those contending for a better position through legalistic reforms, tend to be equally suspicious of a culture-based ethic. Political agenda critics may also see it as traitorous, but to *their* cause. Alternately, they may view action from a culturally interpretive basis as shortsighted, unenlightened, amoral, or indicative that people are victims of false consciousness regarding what their real interests should have been, if they had adequate education and resources to fight for themselves.

Still others who rely more passively on agenda to provide ethical orientation may simply suspend doubts about the cultural basis of ethics They may feel they are acting by turns charitably, inconsistently, or in other nonintegral ways. It is probable that most people have been largely inattentive, perhaps even cynical, about differences between formal ethics and informal cultural interpretation. Some may have come to inhabit a nonintegral stance more or less permanently.

Most business practitioners, faced with competing institutions of enormous formal and economic power on the one hand, and civil societies with variable consistency and interpretations on the other, are ill-prepared to recognize and come to grips with personal responsibility in these public spheres. They are even less likely to recognize that their ethics are not the ethics of others. Charity, tolerance, ignorance, and imposition are nonintegral stances, as is agenda, because in any of them, the people on either side of the point of action do not inhabit a common moral

Figure 2

Culture-Based Ethics

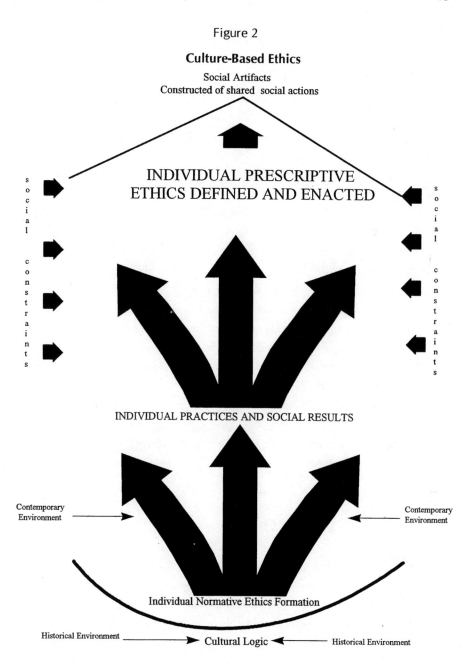

Social Artifacts
Constructed of shared social actions

INDIVIDUAL PRESCRIPTIVE ETHICS DEFINED AND ENACTED

social constraints

social constraints

INDIVIDUAL PRACTICES AND SOCIAL RESULTS

Contemporary Environment

Contemporary Environment

Individual Normative Ethics Formation

Historical Environment ——→ Cultural Logic ◄—— Historical Environment plane. Nonintegrity becomes most dangerous when practitioners trade, market to, and hire others from diverse social regions. This situation is becoming increasingly frequent.

Those in business who press for more acknowledgment of a culturally based ethic, seeking sophisticated and responsible interaction with alternate informal and culture-based sources, can expect to find few friends in any quarter of the most zealously control-conscious, rule-abiding, or rule-challenging public spaces of modernity. Our boss or senior officer is likely to suggest that spending time in re-flection on others' cultural viewpoints will distract us from the policy directives and economic agenda of the business. Our firm's lawyers may tell us it is suspect, too complicated, and they cannot adequately control the outcomes. Many of our socially conscious colleagues will tell us that we should leave the profane and in-herently antiethical world of business and undertake instead social redistribution, or perhaps charity; or that we should formally organize to protest the policies and practices of our industry or organization. Perhaps they will tell us we do not know enough about the social results and therefore have no business interacting at all. We would respond that most practitioners are already interacting, and they can do so either more or less responsibly. This is why recognition and adequate response to cultural interpretation are relevant to ethics and at the same time must occur on the practitioner's own terms. First, it furnishes a way to be responsible while re-connecting to more holistic sources of the practitioner's own humanity, and, sec-ond, business people will not long operate in ignorance of culture without mind-lessly destroying much of the adaptive potential of livelihoods—certainly those of others in the short run and, in a much longer run, perhaps their own.

The Fitting Response

Most of the inspiration that still exists for reconnecting culture-based ethics comes from anachronistic sources—our religious philosophers. Consider the late modern dislocations that rational divisions of labor produce: In the public and secular side of life epitomized by American business, there is consistent division not only in the workforce, but also in the world of ideas concerning what is ethical and responsible. More often than not, people find themselves reduced and fragmented conceptually to become the parts of a rationally divided whole.[1] In business and other work organizations, they may even be called *resources* or *reports*. Some are responsible for some things, others for other things. In America, this has raises tensions with more culture-based norms regarding the autonomy and integrity of the individual. In other cultural contexts, it may well raise even more discrepancies with cultural assumptions of familial or other social arrangements. So far, organizations have dealt with these tensions mainly by producing new layers of legalisms that would create new uniform ways for dealing with difference.

The rational division of labor extends even to the separation between religious and charitable institutions, business-economic organizations, and public governance and enforcement institutions. People in charge of secular organizations tend to look to religious institutions and their leaders to take care of the private and personal parts of responsibility. Thus, moral aspects, especially in the informal-cultural rather than formal-legal sense, are neatly removed from the mundane necessities of running the business.

Messages from religious figures, on the other hand, invoke images that are more culture based. The ambiguity of these images intrudes on the neat divisions, and sometimes further challenges individualism itself. The following particularly beautiful example from Martin Buber (1958, p. 3) illustrates this well:

> The primary word I–Thou can only be spoken with the whole being.
> The Primary word I–It can never be spoken with the whole being . . .
> When a primary word is spoken the speaker enters the word
> and takes his stand in it.

The message is thoroughly Western and is from a source well within the Judeo-Christian stream. As long as it is contained within a private context, perhaps its only paradox is for assumptions about individual autonomy. When we place it in the context of public and secular work, it looks more radical; its much older, communal cultural roots begin to show. Buber's image, evoking relationships in which people might make mutual adjustments and commitments, contravenes all assumptions about convenience, transience, anonymity, disenchantment, and efficiency in human exchange. In secular public, it has an almost embarrassing intimacy.

Yet, in spatial as well as social terms, conditions of more intimate encounter are not diminishing and have not done so in the four hundred or more years since the early Enlightenment. To the contrary, humans' spatial and communicative proximity to each other has done nothing but increase over the millennia. It is the practical mores people adopt to address this closing-in that have been changing. The need for response and ongoing commitments in a globalizing world of strangers, now increasingly thrust on each other, will only continue to grow.

Buber's (1958) message underscores cultural dislocations that are in need of repair in moral and ethical systems of meaning. Niebuhr has commented that "(T)he I in I–it relations is not a reflexive being . . . It values but does not value itself or its evaluations. The I in I–it moves from within outward, as it were, and never turns back upon itself" (1963, pp. 72–73).

The outward push of an exclusively agenda-based ethics is an *I–It* relation. A more culturally specific ethics involves how a person will promote and support survival and benefit along with others who hold social priority. For a long time, this was a local human problem for which the ethical prescriptions of culture always provided specific interpretations. With the one-way expansion and outward thrust of rational systems of meaning, the local human problem has been reinterpreted more globally as a social control problematic. Thus are ethics increasingly dislocated. The attempt to address human problems of meaning and social connection, by their nature subject to variable and context-specific response, will be futile if pursued only by resort to ever-increasing control and rationalization.

This is why we advocate learning to use a cultural lens for a more expanded view of social responsibility in business. That something so apparently simple is so complex and difficult to practice indicates not only the breathtaking variation in cultural diversity, but the large roles that in-group preference and out-group distrust have played in human competition. The difficulty of these issues is evident in the way practitioners and scholars alike struggle with the cultural lens of responsibility. The intercultural communication literature generally shies away from ethical interpretations, and the business ethics literature, reciprocally, ignores or tries to encompass local difference through broad generalities. It is not a question of value-free or value-laden ethics. Rather, the main reason culture is a less-developed ethical terrain is the general absence of distinction between formal authority and informal culture as a web of meanings in live, daily interactions. Live and local interaction requires more work to sustain; it is built up through longer periods of time and is much more variable in its details. Culture has been described as soft and enduring (Moran and Volkwein, 1992), and it remains the major challenge at the frontier of social responsibility.

Human Nature and Moral Community

To become socially responsible, to find the fitting response, requires an orienting image of moral community. This image includes both a sense of a larger whole and a more central point of orientation, which we might think of as a cultural home base. From this home base or perspective, there is some autonomy of judgment and discretion. The interaction of this part-whole relationship becomes a model for interacting with the world, allowing concerns to be addressed as they arise.

The idea of moral community suits a diversity of scales of inclusion. It offers encouragement for people to ask themselves, whether as individuals or parts of other centrally orienting social units: Who is the *we* of which I am now a part, and the other *Thous* with whom I become more whole? In day-to-day practice, this kind of inquiry may be specifically cultural and interpretive and not necessarily a philosophical or religious question in the sense in which Westerners are accustomed to study these specialized subjects. It need not rely on a Western conception of the self as long as it provides a social compass for orientation and discretion. It has the potential for working through an expanding range of social inclusion, not just thrusting outward with one-way exclusions or one-way impositions. It insists on developing the home perspective responsively with successively wider encounters with the outside world. The social space of responsibility expands as attention is given to learning other perspectives, or else the point of its ultimate landscape, a pan-human one, will be missed.

Moral community, the image of an association of people in a social arena beyond the self and, often in transcultural business, beyond the cultural home base, does not necessarily imply that the basis of human ethical orientation lies in any simple, all-encompassing, or deterministic ideal. A more limited idea of moral community often discussed in economic anthropology has been well described by Richard Wilk (1996) in his recent synthesis, *Economies and Cultures*. Wilk presents moral community as one among three models of human nature that anthropologists have used to explain human economic activity. Two other models, the microeconomic or rational self-interest model and the social or political economy model, originated largely in disciplines outside anthropology.

Wilk traces the rational self-interest model forward from the writings of Thomas Hobbes, through Adam Smith, to its later variations within modern microeconomic utility theory. He comments that the key element distinguishing all approaches based on self-interest is that the individual is taken as the basic unit of analysis (1996, p. 37). Americans especially like to associate self, self-interest, and selfishness with the use of individuals as analytic focus, and there is in American public culture much discussion that assumes a dichotomous contrast between what is good for the self versus what is good for the larger community. Wilk shows signs that he may share in this cultural interpretation: He even proposes a selfish-altruistic continuum as a possible cross-cultural analytic tool. But, while using individual persons as units may indeed be Western in influence, it need not lead inevitably to this kind of bipolar continuum. (In fairness to Wilk, he acknowledges that none of the three models he describes is complete in itself.)

The European-educated billionaire financier and philanthropist George Soros (1997) displays a similar tendency to link individualism with economic selfishness. He declares open society (that is, liberal democracy) to be threatened by excessive individualism, which he more or less equates with laissez-faire capitalism. He sees capitalism, in turn, partly following Hegelian interpretation, as potentially bearing the seeds of its own destruction (p. 45).

Our point is that social science theories and measures often contain culture-specific valences regarding what is good for individuals and groups. Although superficially appealing in the rational business environment, they may be a dubious way to explore alternatives to a culturally Western ethic. This caution applies equally to microeconomic self-interest and its chief Western rival, the critical or political economy model of human nature.

Wilk describes political economy as an alternative to microeconomic self-interest in its focus on the way people form groups and exercise power (1996, p. 37). According to political economists, people are still maximizing competitive interests, but as members of some collectivity rather than as self-interested individuals. These collective groups may consist of classes, occupational groups, world-system strata, or other kinds of interest groups. If we rely on this interpretation, however, we face many of the same Western assumptions about human nature that we find with microeconomic individualism. The political economy alternative is still about competitive strife, and it emphasizes the nonintegrative activity of clashing groups. From the viewpoint of ethical applications in business, political economy only expects people to be more or less subject to the selfish masters of a dominating group, or else to act ethically by overcoming their own selfish or unenlightened desires through an uplifting collective struggle for power. Thus, either microeconomic enlightened self-interest or political economy can reduce quickly to agenda politics, public or private.

The alternative we favor, moral community, is rather deterministically portrayed in Wilk's (1996) anthropological account. Too pure a view of it falls short of an adequate description of how people behave, as Wilk argues. But, moral community serves better the cultural lens for viewing ethical and responsible behavior than either of the two other Western-based models.

Wilk says moral persons' motivations are shaped by culturally specific belief systems. Their choices are guided by a desire to do what is right and flow ultimately from a culturally patterned view of the universe and the human place in it. Moral sense is "grounded in a view of the way the world works" (1996, p. 38).

While we can agree that all of a person's choices do not rest only on consideration of his or her moral sense, the constructions that people place on responsibility or on other ethical concepts in their cultural setting do cohere with and tend to reinforce the views they hold of themselves in relation to others and to the world as they perceive it. In other words, in economics as in other areas of social life, responsibility and ethics are culturally constructed. At the same time, there is considerable variability in cultural interpretation. Social responsibility need not exist only in established sets of rules, codes, or assumed oughts; nor does it reside in a single or unified norm or ideal. It links individual people in dynamic and living relationships, and these are subject to variable interpretation. Even the patterns, scope, and conditions for the interpretation vary—the limits of flexibility themselves are found in different contexts within different cultures.

An early task of the student of cultures and interpretation is to arrive at a working home base, a sense of ethical orientation in which priorities of responsibility are at least provisionally identified. This orienting perspective must include not only a sense of center, but also a consciousness of others. From this point, it is the responsible practitioner's task to inquire and respond, integrating the perspectives of the home with new perspectives gained from the world. This enlarging image of an included world, partially known and open to mutual discovery, therefore requires at least the imagination of moral community.

Unlike social science scholars, business Practitioners in the field do not necessarily begin by analyzing and theorizing about human nature and behavior. Rather, they need to discover and begin to recognize its folk models, as Wilk rightly characterizes them (1996, p. 147), and to interact fruitfully and responsibly in terms of these. A practitioner's task is aided by insights from the analyzed data of cross-cultural and organizational studies, several examples of which we include in this book. But, ultimately, overreliance on a priori dimensions and analytic categories may constrain the discovery and the practice of new syntheses and relationships. This is just what has happened in much of American business and the education of managers. In their choice of principles and dimensions of measurement, unexamined cultural assumptions often guide the choices. How people define themselves in daily practice and how power is manifested in these culturally specific choices are often conspicuously absent from the discussion.

Thus, while traditional anthropological descriptions of moral community provide a reasonably good starting point for viewing the cultural construction of social responsibility, our preference for this concept does not mean we can adopt or fix it simply or wholesale any more than we can ignore the presence of self-interest as a motivating element for individuals, or peoples' conscious and unconscious ideologies, or their socialization into the varied ethical outlooks provided by their professional training, occupational status, or employer. All these sources of influence are significant. But, because we are cultural creatures, we need the image of moral community, especially in changing and unfamiliar conditions.

For these contexts, business practitioners will not be well served to consider the moral world only in terms of rationality, competition, and power, as for example, in the reduction of moral and ethical questions as a balancing act. (For example, Wilk characterizes the positions of Margolis and Etzioni this way [1996, p. 39], and the Western metaphor of balance shows up twice in his own reflections: "How, in practice, do people balance these different motivations?" [p. 40] and again: "Most of us live . . . trying to balance self-interest, group interest and moral precepts" [p. 40]).[2] We find the transitive use of the metaphor of balance telling: Often, when well-socialized business practitioners seek to balance things, they only find themselves repeating the too-habitual Western attempt to predict and control—a return to *I–It* relations. We would rather see them seeking first to find their own balance as members of the wider society who also practice in the complicated field of business.

Responsibility and Cultural Norms

People in general prefer to perceive and act on social responsibility and ethics as if these reflect–or ought to reflect–a set of absolute and universal standards. In the context of affluent industrial states, codified rules exist to regulate conduct throughout government, professions, and industries. Those who have worked in regulatory and quality professions know how exacting, detailed, and systematic these standards can be. These standards continually erode under the scrutiny and challenge of competitive and superceding forms and interpretation.

Softer social concepts of similar ideas as they appear in other languages and cultural settings are interpreted and enacted with much greater interpretive variability from place to place and from time to time. Culture is the single most conceptually integrative way to understand these differences. Practitioners must begin to grasp the basis for cultural variations they see, construct their own theories of practice, and test these against experience in a disciplined and guided way. Then, they can gain insight about their own cultural assumptions, obtain a more subtle understanding of cultural appropriateness, and do what is fitting while remaining culturally true to themselves.

As a part of culture, a society's ethics and its other ideas related to what is responsible include certain normative expectations for how its members ought to behave in their dealings with one another. As we suggested earlier, what business practitioners and especially Americans commonly take for standard, especially in its details, is really very specific in both origins and distribution. For example, from an American outlook, a strong emphasis is placed on seeming to be impartial, at least in public: Treatment of people and the standards applied to evaluate their conduct ought to apply equally, or even-handedly, to all with whom we deal. This ideal reflects the American preference for very little power distance (as further discussed below in our discussion of Hofstede's work) between people who have unequal access to resources or social status. The intensity of Americans' socialized affect about our societal failures to realize this norm is reflected in our distinctive history of social movements for rectifying inequalities among social groups, largely through the kinds of agenda strategies we have already described.

So, a current legalistic push to universalize social responsibility in business, coming from American and western European quarters, should not be surprising. David Vogel (1992) also has pointed out that globalization of the economies of highly technological and industrialized states is making business practices more uniform (p. 30). He notes that many American legal norms and standards of corporate conduct are being adopted in other capitalist nations, and he speculates that, in the future, multinational firms may well come to adopt common ethical standards (p. 47). But which multinational firms, whose standards, and the extent of adoption are very uncertain.

Based on current circumstances, it is extremely unlikely that a single set of standards based on American business ethics will become universal. Vogel (1992) observes that considerable national differences persist in how business ethics are defined and evaluated, and even if there could be fairly widespread agreement on a set of principles—which currently is less likely than a more unilateral imposition of conditions for participation—the question remains of culturally varying interpretations in practice. Social responsibility extends beyond the rules for minimum acceptable conduct in business transactions. It may include, in a larger sense, the more wide-ranging and socially encompassing issues of what kind of business is done and with whom.

We have only to look at some of the fractious results of recent global conferences, such as the 1991 Rio meetings on the environment and economic development (Grubb, Kock, Thomson, Munson, and Sullivan, 1993), to see continuing North-South intergovernmental dissent over normative expectations for business development among nation-states. These issues reveal differing agendas and underlying cultural interpretations of governments' and businesses' responsibilities in physical, as well as social, environmental relationships. Related issues over economic and trade concepts, such as biopiracy in the synthesis of pharmaceutical and related substances based on rain forest resources (e.g., as discussed by Raghavan, 1995), or over intellectual property rights, in disagreements that continue both among states and among ethnic groups within states also reflect differing agendas regarding social responsibility.

Given such divergent agendas, will it be possible for business, collectively, to cross the great divides that remain in ethical and responsibility outlooks? If the discussion is limited to a universalizing discourse of agenda, it is not possible at this time, and there is little optimism for the near future. Spokespersons for business have made their own agenda statements, indicating intent and effort in similar directions (e.g., Giscard d'Estaing, 1995), and there is a hopeful rhetoric of global cooperation among nongovernmental and intergovernmental elites (e.g., Boulding, 1991), yet it is nowhere near realization. At the time of this writing, there exists no global moral community in either culturally normative or legislatively uniform terms.

So, despite a welter of international business laws, regulations, and agreements, business practitioners in the field, especially those in multinational and transnational companies, will find little practical help for social responsibility in legislative rule. Meanwhile, they immediately face difficult and important issues that will deeply affect their businesses, their customers, partners, suppliers, and themselves. Yet, actual cultural crossings do occur responsibly every day. It is not that business people exist in some amoral world beyond the pale of rule and regulation. It is just that the crossings require them to engage unfamiliar cultural traditions responsibly within and between differing local contexts. Practitioners working throughout various levels of operations will be as consequential in their response to ethical diversity as the agenda authors who occupy corporate headquarters.

Metaphors and World View:
Cultural Logic and Values Orientations

The responsible business practitioner will need an expanded vocabulary to discern and respond to cultural differences. These differences, while complex, are more similar in adjacent regions and often overlap in a variety of their elements; they may also be seen to be patterned and thematically cohesive ethnic enclaves and within national and world regional settings. There are commensurate differences between these cultural settings and the metaphors people use to understand themselves and the outer world. These world views have both cognitive and emotive aspects. They are reflected in the metaphors of linguistic description and may have variable effects on how experiences are interpreted and perceived. For example, as Schultz and Lavenda (1995) point out, mechanistic cog-and-wheel metaphors have shaped modern thought about the social and moral stresses of a rationalized, bureaucratic, and highly complex, organized life in the 20th century (pp. 520–521, 531–533). Other metaphors have prevailed in other cultural settings. Understanding and interrogating the basis of a person's cultural metaphors can free him or her to more imaginatively reevaluate assumptions, as well as to appreciate the differences between his or her native world view and those of people from other cultural backgrounds. That person can then respond in a more fitting way, following the social and behavioral implications of these differences for better human relationships and more responsible decisions.

The metaphors of a cultural setting also give some indication of the thematic cohesion of the world view. Those who interpret social life after a certain pattern perceive that this coherence makes their actions sensible and amenable to judgment. Practitioners have found it helpful to think of this sense-making as a given tradition's cultural logic. This heuristic reminds them to seek coherence in what may otherwise be a confusing array of behaviors and expression. The ideas and metaphors regarding what people ought to do, how they ought to do it, and what they are responsible for doing can be expected to reflect to some degree this internal cultural logic.[3]

There is, of course, a wide array of roles and statuses, with divergent viewpoints from different positions within a cultural context. Tradition will suggest different perceptions and consequences of the internal cultural logic for the different players in each of a variety of scenes. Therefore, a cultural setting will offer varied opportunities or discouragements to people in their ability and desires to live up to perceived expectations. Behavioral expectations vary within, as well as across, cultural traditions, offering yet another arena of complexity for the newcomer to learn. In Western business, for example, there are widely divergent expectations as to the behavior of a chief executive officer, a vice president, or a brand manager within a single organization. Responsibly navigating among people in these diverse positions is a challenging task even within a home cultural setting, and the business organization is only part of the relevant cultural context.

Perhaps the parameter of greatest interest to cultural learning for responsible business practice is the construct of *values orientations*. This construct, first used by F. R. Kluckhohn and Strodbeck (1961), refers to the transcultural variation in specifically how a cultural tradition guides people in the particular way they will evaluate, prefer, and desire social good for themselves and others. Values orientations are another way of expressing a people's themes related to their world view.

Values orientations are a more specific and complex pattern concept than values, which we popularly hear discussed in the sense of moral preferences and priorities. At a recent scholarly meeting, Uichul Kim, a scholar whose research concerns values orientations on the dimension of individualism versus collectivism, was asked by an American audience member to comment further on "Korean cultural values." Dr. Kim's brief response was that basic human values are the same everywhere: All people desire to survive, to have adequate food, to be secure, and so on.[4]

Indeed, this is what social science researchers usually mean by values. Values orientations differ in their specification for cultural arrangements of *how* people are to perceive, acquire, allocate, and set priorities for these universally desired qualities and states. This is where cultural difference resides in relation to values. Values orientations are the modifying aspects for how to reach what humans value as good and desirable.

Values orientations are complex, but definitely patterned and discernible. Reeves-Ellington has found that business practitioners in the field have benefited from thinking about them as an interplay of three kinds of cultural elements: (1) the normative values that together can be seen to form the cohesive cultural logic that we described above; (2) prescriptive social ethics, the social knowledge of insiders who guide and interpret their actions in accordance with this logic; and (3) the most visible part of the cultural set, artifacts, which are comprised of outward physical and symbolic manifestations such as dress, architecture, office layout, seating arrangements, and other visible parts of the context (Reeves-Ellington, 1995b). To act appropriately, newcomers must become aware of all three spheres as indicative of values orientations. Cultural logic, social knowledge, and artifacts provide direction to the cultural context, ethic, and reflection of a peoples' particular view of the world. Toward the end of this chapter, we illustrate, in a brief profile of a field experience of doing business in Japan, how this three-part model worked.

Among the best-demonstrated scientific constructions of values orientations, acknowledging a patterned cultural logic, is Hofstede's work using social psychology measures in cross-national surveys of organizational and national culture (e.g., Hofstede, 1980; Hofstede, Neuijev, Ohayv, and Sanders, 1990). For Hofstede, cultural differences are vividly reflected in peoples' normative attitudes about their social relations—their evaluations and preferences about what behaviors and qualities they expect and accept in day-to-day human interactions. Hofstede has identified a number of social-psychological dimensions along which differences in these preferences can be systematically measured across different countries throughout the world.

A particularly useful example of differences in values orientations is illustrated in Hofstede's empirical construct of power distance. He defines power distance as "the extent to which the less powerful members of institutions and organizations within a country expect and accept that power is distributed unequally" among people (1991, p. 28).[5] Hofstede explains how, in his survey norms, the power distance data can also be seen to vary by class and occupation; one cannot compare engineers from one country, for example, with secretaries from another (1991, p. 29).

In relatively high power distance places such as France, subordinates' attitudes are in general highly emotionally reactive to power differences in the workplace—these feelings can even polarize, creating differences between those who adore and those who despise their supervisors (Hofstede, 1991, p. 36). The 19th century political economy theorist Karl Marx came from Germany, which Hofstede finds in general to be a low power distance country. Hofstede claims that a low power distance affinity can be seen in Marx's assumption that the exercise of personal power can be transferred to a system, that is, that power should yield to law (Hofstede, 1991, p. 41).

Whether or not one agrees with such a reading of Marx's personal value orientation to power, Hofstede's cross-national and cross-organizational studies, for his dimensions of national culture particularly, have withstood a number of critiques and revisions. As Peterson and Smith report (1996, pp. 3–4), despite broad critique and subsequent alternative formulations, Hofstede's comparative work on national culture dimensions remains the seminal model for this type of analysis in social psychology for over a quarter century (see also Smith, Peterson, Leung, and Dugan, 1996, p. 5).

This is all fine in theory, a practitioner might respond, but merely appreciating in the abstract that differences do occur in value orientations as part of a world view and that social knowledge and artifacts proceed from and signify an informing, basic "cultural logic" does not in itself help us to get through a business day, much less find common moral ground. To grapple with social responsibility as an individual in a multicultural world, one has to be able not only to "read" the alternate texts of culture, but to actively interpret and act on them. The first step will indeed be how to use cultural knowledge to get through a business day. This is the topic to which we now turn.

A Cultural Learning Model

As Clyde Kluckhohn first pointed out, the members in a particular cultural context define and determine which parts of their social life are important in cultural terms (1951, p. 10). They do this in response to survival needs and over long periods of time, building sociocultural systems that are complex and adapted to particular environments. Business organizations, as a particular kind of human sociocultural system, require sufficiently coherent information exchange for their economic survival in a competitive ecology. Thus, they too must find a coherent set of common moral and ethical meanings that allows them to deal responsibly with partners, customers, and hosts.

Different national traditions in business interaction are the best places to see the way this accommodation works. Among the three heuristics we have identified (cultural logic, social knowledge, and artifacts), social knowledge provides an accessible and essential doorway to understanding the moral and ethical basis for human action. Bound by peoples' world view, and grounded within normative orientations (the cultural logic), social knowledge comprises the desirable ideal toward which people act, the collective "oughts" of a cultural setting (Hofstede, 1980, p. 53).

But, social knowledge is not accessible immediately. It is not the first thing visible when encountering partners in new cultural situations. Artifacts are usually the most immediately visible thing. In a cross-cultural encounter, whether between subcultures of different American organizations or between the cultures of two similar organizations from different countries, these elements will most often be accessible in the order illustrated in Figure 3.

Figure 3 shows levels of orienting data for people who must deal with other partners across cultural boundaries. They make the user aware of possible differing interpretations of visible symbols and behaviors, and of reactions to one's own behavior, in the encounter. This model assumes initial transcultural contact at the level of the most obvious and visible difference, the outward artifacts. Users gain a social interpretation for better comprehending those artifacts by empirically inquiring through practice and feedback in actual situations. After discussion of experiences and comparisons of outcomes, they may gain an understanding about the cultural logic that forms a basis for the more superficial expectations and appearances. This cultural learning model thus offers a progressive learning sequence. The model permits its users to become more conscious of their own cultural logic, as well as that of others. They can then discuss their understandings, and, should they wish, they may undertake conscious efforts at adjustments and change.

The importance of an interaction and inquiry involving all three kinds of elements can be illustrated in an example, below, that shows the limitations of knowing elements of world view and cultural logic alone. The importance of viewing all three kinds of cultural elements in practice cannot be overstated. While cultural logic answers the

Figure 3

Culture Encounter Model

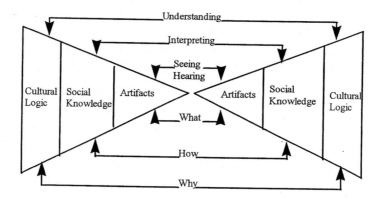

journalistic "why" about underlying group assumptions of people, human nature, human relations, and our relationship to the environment, by itself it will not give much information for day-to-day respectful and knowledgeable interaction. Elements of social knowledge, on the other hand, are subject to continual reinterpretation and change; this is why they are not easily obtained through consulting cultural "cookbooks" of behavior, no matter how popular these have become. While cultural logic usually changes less quickly, no specific actions flow from it. Its normative values orientations are ideological and treated as absolute.

Field Sketch: Cultural Learning Heuristics for Business in Japan

The importance of learning culture by interrelating artifacts, social knowledge, and cultural logic became evident early in the efforts of an American-based multinational pharmaceutical company, Pharmco, to renew previous acquaintances and increase business activity in Japan in the early 1980s. For the business goal, Reeves-Ellington, then a regional vice president for that area, was asked to provide an analysis of the basic values orientations known for Japan—that is, its cultural logic. In Pharmco, as in most other large Western organizations in the early 1980s, relatively little was known of day-to-day, insiders' social knowledge for doing business with Japanese partners, and none had been previously sought in any systematic way. Initially, Pharmco's senior management only requested the Japanese side of the cultural differences.

Reeves-Ellington's region undertook an academic research review project as their first approach for gathering the requested information. The result was a basic cultural logic description of Japan. This material is summarized in Table 1. As just stated, published information was virtually nonexistent at the time (well before the American fascination with Japanese business and the associated quality movement crested in American management literature) for how specific artifacts and social knowledge were enacted in Japan in general and how these were used in Japanese business organizations in particular. This would be the critical information for Pharmco employees working with potential Japanese joint-venture partners. In short, Pharmco Africa/Asia (A/A) people needed to become more culturally competent in their business encounters with the Japanese.

Pharmco A/A's initial experiences in attempts to renew and develop some of their earlier business contacts in Japan demonstrate how badly things can go when there exists cultural logic and world view knowledge in the abstract, but no database for arriving at successful behaviors and appropriate judgments in actual cross-cultural encounters—a lack of social knowledge. Tables 2–4 provide social information that was lacking at the time of the initial adventures. That Pharmco's cultural missteps were so successfully addressed later shows not only the effectiveness of this three-part cultural learning approach, but also how gracious Japanese company employees will be when a foreign company's employees are

TABLE 1. Japanese Cultural Logic Description

Environmental relationships
Japanese, as well as other Asians, view the physical and human environments as intertwined and not in opposition, as do most Western Christians (Campbell 1960, 1989; Pelzel, 1974). As exemplified in the Japanese garden, humans control and shape the environment in ways that suit the artistic feeling of people. The garden connotes the desire for environmental harmony and orderliness.

Nature of human activities
Human activities are determined by situations and social contexts, in which people find themselves (Hall and Hall, 1987; Lebra, 1976). In a social group, only the insiders determine what is true and real. The accuracy of this determination is based on the degree of harmony and orderliness obtained within the insider group. Activity is focused on working toward ideals of harmonious relationships and involves an orientation toward human interdependency (Doi, 1990a; Hayashi, 1988; Lebra, 1976). Activity is necessarily done in groups and by groups.

Nature of human nature
Humans are driven by emotion and not by logic (Doi, 1990b). Mutuality of love and obligation (within the context of the concept of obligation) ties in closely with that of hate (Ishida, 1974). This mutuality in human relations forces the concepts of consensus into human social organization. Since human nature is not believed to be inherently "bad," it is assumed this behavior is caused by ignorance and not evil intent.

Use of time
Time is polychronic (Hall and Hall, 1987). The time system is characterized by the simultaneous occurrence of many things and by a deep involvement with people. There is more emphasis on completing transactions than holding to a schedule. A person confronted with too many subjects to be covered in too short a time chooses to expand the time available to complete the tasks rather than reduce the number of tasks.

---

trying to learn. They understand that the foreigners will never get it "right" because they are always working from a stereotype that is "somewhat right," yet also it is much better than being "really wrong." There are always new and more subtle nuances to learn.

Business Card (Meishi)

During the initial meeting with the Japanese, the first item of business is introductions. The role of the *meishi*, or business card, in this context, is instructive regarding how artifacts interact with social knowledge and cultural logic. How the Japanese use the meishi helped Pharmco staff to understand its importance. Japanese companies value a high degree of consistency with those with whom they work and in the handling of personnel in a company. Failure to demonstrate consistency toward internal employees indicates a probable inconsistency in relationships outside the company. Some Pharmco employees learned this painful lesson at one meeting with a senior Japanese executive. After the Pharmco team explained the purpose of their visit, the executive took a number of meishi from his desk.

TABLE 2. Introductions at Business Meetings

Artifacts	Social Knowledge	Cultural Logic
Technology • Meishi. Visual behavior • Presentations of meishi by presenting card facing the recipient. • Senior people present meishi first. • Guest presents first, giving name, company affiliation, and bowing. • Host presents meishi in same sequence.	• Once given, meishi is kept. • Meishi are not exchanged a second time unless there is a position change. • Before next meeting between parties, meishi is reviewed to familiarize with people attending the meeting. • The meishi provides status for the owner.	Human relations • Meishi provide understanding of appropriate interpersonal relations. • Private interpersonal relations. • Meishi take uncertainty out of relationships. Environment • Meishi establish insider/outsider environment. • Meishi help establish possible obligations to environment. Human activity • Meishi help to establish human activities.

As he turned each of them up, he asked, "I see that I met with Mr. Young of your company 10 years ago, where is he now?" Then came the next card, "I see I met with Mr. Phipps of your company 8 years ago, where is he now?" The questioning continued through eight separate meishi. The Pharmco team leader had to respond each time that the person was no longer with the company. At the end, the Japanese executive said, "People are not well treated in your company. In our company, people do not leave until retirement." The meeting ended on this unsuccessful note.

The Meeting

When introductions are complete in a Japanese business meeting, both sides join in the conference at the conference table. Seating is ritualistic and stylized. The power position is flanked by advisors; next come suppliers of data and information; finally, interest parties are seated at the extremities of the table. Understanding this and the communications program at the table was essential for success in Japan (see Table 3).

Not understanding the analysis of culture again caused Pharmco problems early in their relationship. Pharmco organization members did not understand that the power seat was not always taken by the senior person, but rather might be taken by the person designated to be the most informed contact for a specific meeting. Pharmco members wanted the person who was competent for the business at hand to sit in the power seat. At a meeting called to handle a technical matter, but one at which senior people were present, Pharmco's senior person took

TABLE 3. Conference Seating Arrangements

Artifacts	Social Knowledge	Cultural Logic
Technology • Rectangular table. Visual behavior • Hosts sit on one side of the table and guests on the other.	• Set seating allows all parties social/business understanding. • Person responsible for success has the authority. • Guests are treated as customers.	Human relations • Seating allows an established order and power structure function between people. Relation to environment • Responsibility and authority are combined. • Inside/outside environment maintained.

the power seat. Japanese body language indicated something was wrong. The Japanese at the other side of the table, a toxicologist, was of the wrong status to sit across from a vice president. He could not discuss the matter at the meeting. His colleagues did not know what to do when such a breach in manners occurred. The meeting was a disaster. Only later, over drinks in a bar, did a Japanese manager explain the problem and why it occurred.

Dinner

Being a guest at a Japanese dinner is a simple task. All that is necessary is responding to what the host suggests. The intricacies of organizing a dinner are the responsibility of the hosts. Pharmco personnel, by making mistakes, learned to host dinners and thereby gained substantial "insidership." Being able to host required understanding what to do, how to do it, and why it is done (see Table 4).

At one point, Pharmco headquarters decided that the cost of entertaining in Tokyo was too high and dictated that cheaper places be found. The edict was followed and, at the next business dinner with a Japanese company middle manager, disaster resulted. When the guest arrived, his first comment was that one of his subordinates often brought suppliers to the restaurant. Pharmco had clearly insulted him in the choice of eating establishments, causing Pharmco managers to spend the rest of the night apologizing. Trying to rectify the situation, the next time this manager was hosted, Pharmco took him to a very exclusive place. The first comment was, "The president of our company likes this restaurant but I have never been here." This time, Pharmco had embarrassed their Japanese guest by

TABLE 4. Going to Dinner

Artifacts	Social Knowledge	Cultural Logic
Physical • Guests • Restaurant • Meals Visual • Hosting • Guesting	• Relationship building is the purpose of eating. • Status is honored by correct dinners. • Dinner group has some "insider" attributes.	Use of time • Effectiveness with people. Relationships • Identifies how two companies' people are positioned in hierarchy. • Confirms status matching between guests.

taking him to a location beyond his status, causing him to have to explain to his colleagues the next day why he had been there.

Pharmco's cultural performance greatly improved when Reeves-Ellington applied the three-part cultural heuristic model shown in Figure 3 to Pharmco's field practice. He worked out a program of general interest to all Pharmco personnel who would be doing business with the Japanese—how to get through a Japanese business day. The most intensive part of this information, always subject to practice and feedback in the field, was social knowledge. The business day included how to do introductions, meetings, leavings, dinner, and drinking with Japanese in Japan in the early 1980s. That the success of this orientation, for each practitioner, depended on iterations of fieldwork, data collection, sharing, and feedback should be clear. We return to the processes for doing this in more detail in Chapter 4 in regard to the organizational roles and information systems aspects of socially responsible business.

Expanded Moral Community and the Threat of Relativity

Can issues of social responsibility then be summarized as the learning by the practitioner of various folk models, each a different and equally valid rendition of moral community? Isn't this really a kind of cultural relativism or situation ethics, which may be learned equally well either through culture-specific training programs or through simple trial and error in the field? No. If these had been adequate solutions for social responsibility, there would not be the issues of personal disempowerment and ethical crisis that we see widely lamented in today's corporate world. The biggest error in most of social science is trying to make an idea do more than it is capable of doing. Social responsibility in business, like full adulthood, requires both danger and trust: This involves criticism, doubt, empathy, and, often, risky leaps of intuition.

This too, a concerned practitioner might rejoin, is all very well and good, from the point of view of moving toward mutually acceptable and respected customs of interaction, in the partner's cultural setting. But, what has this to do with my own cultural, not to say moral, integrity? Will not my own values orientations get lost, putting me and my company on the slide toward a more extreme cultural relativism?

This depends on what it is you regard about your image of yourself and your company that is subject to change. Learning about another's cultural logic and even aligning with it to enable interaction to occur successfully, provide opportunities for insight into the home cultural logic, social knowledge, and artifacts that were not previously visible. Change is then subject to more knowledgeable, responsible choice. As two North Americans with a particular intellectual and cultural heritage, the authors prefer to see the making of this choice as an individual's decision, part of responsibility to the self—but even the notion of selfhood could be and has been responsibly adapted by and for those business persons and organizations from different cultural traditions.

Clearly, such conscious change does have practical limits within a given context, although exactly where these lie is the subject of much debate in anthropology and other social sciences, as we have tried to indicate, in our thumbnail sketch above, of positions and models of human action. Microeconomic self-interest and political economy models of human nature surely assume different things about the limits of consciously directed change and the location of its agency. They even disagree regarding the extent to which individuals' choices can have any impact at all. Some might argue that conscious change is impractical or impossible for individuals or that their self-selected changes are inherently ill-advised or are canceled out by the larger power arrangements in which they find themselves.

Our own outlooks are more optimistic about peoples' choices in a social context. At the same time, we do not see cultural self-appraisal and reflexive practice necessarily as constituting moral or cultural relativism. In responsible cross-cultural business relationships are built by people who may come from two diverse, relatively monocultural orientations, but they move, through dialogue, toward new common ground. Neither highly collectivist-oriented Japanese businesspeople nor highly individualistic American businesspeople will be expected to change their deepest world views on the basis of a single encounter or even a single relationship. Each can discover and respond to those features of the other's social knowledge, which gives cultural affirmation—each understanding it with reference to the logic of his or her own tradition. To be responsible, each has to see the other in a common moral plane, in some sense as part of a common moral community.

In the broadest sense, the issue of relativism and social responsibility resembles certain aspects of the tension between rational scientific method and epistemological relativism. The late Ernest Gellner (1992), a staunch defender of the rational scientific approach to social phenomena, has distinguished the basic alternatives. He says fundamentalism claims to possess knowledge of a unique and absolute truth, and that rationalism, a modern descendent of fundamentalism, also claims that unique truth exists, but that we do not or cannot possess all of it definitively. Further, we can only begin to approximate it through adherence to certain procedural rules. Relativism denies any absolute truth and sees only multiple truths, each of which may be ephemeral, yet each alternate version can be treated in practice as equally valid (pp. vii–viii).

> The relativists' . . . insights apply to the decorative rather than the real structural and functional aspects of our life. When they try to apply their insights too far, they constitute . . . a travesty of the real role of serious knowledge in our lives, and even . . . of the actual practice of social science. Societies are systems of real constraints . . . and must be understood as such, and not simply as systems of meaning. (p. 95)

Learning the more decorative aspects of Japanese meetings and dinners, for example, leads the American practitioner toward a more acceptable approximation and implied acknowledgment of the different world view behind it. Social knowledge of respectful participants may indeed look fairly relativistic, even unimportant, on the surface. Willingness and effort to learn these aspects signals something more important. In a responsible commitment, it serves as metacommunication of the intent to begin establishing a deeper relationship—especially important in Japan, where people's relationships can be seen, at least from the heuristic stereotype of a Western learner's point of view, as immersed to a great degree in their participation in group life. The implications and worth of such decorative competencies then begin to widen *as long as the relationship is maintained.* As the relationship wears on, greater approximations to the common truths of divergent world views can emerge.

As we will emphasize again and again throughout this book, it is the attention to the ongoingness of these relationships, not a set of a priori structures or rules, that creates the primary context for social responsibility at the level of personal agency. And this, for us, is the cornerstone for integrating organizations into their wider societies.

We believe, then, that in pointing out the limits of modern Western cultural constructions of human nature, responsibility, and power, we are not being relativists about our increasing knowledge of human social life in all its cross-cultural variations. These are observable as patterned sets with their own coherence or logic, and they interface in a complex environment of power, economic, and social exchanges. Indeed, we advocate the use of knowledge-creating procedures and heuristic models that require repeated observation and the testing of ideas against field experience. This enables practitioners to understand better the basis for their own orientations and to make choices to align their behavior according to their growing knowledge, as is fitting for other cultural settings. This creates opportunities for practitioners to begin to approximate what the truth is for these contexts. It may be only partly knowable under the circumstances, yet it is amenable to learning and thoughtful ordering, so that others may learn more rapidly, systematically, and rationally.

Ritual and motif are the artifacts that signal access to the beginnings of cultural meaning. Responsible relationships may grow along the paths begun in early encounters. To strive for meaning in the longer term is to reach for a common moral plane with the partners across the desk, on the dock, or at the border crossing. For this, the arid agendas of political strife and unified rational science provide only part of the information practitioners need. There must also be a rich engagement of motivation and affect, an engagement that, in the frequent absence of all the answers, calls for creativity and intuition.

Our approach regards as uniquely true the discoverable parameters for action and adaptation that all humans share. We support a rational procedural approach to cultural learning, toward more adaptive relations at a pan-human level. And, we seek, amid the appearance of relativity in day-to-day practice, to understand better the full range and constraints of cultural possibilities for conducting responsible business practice.

A prepared and sophisticated approach to social responsibility requires knowledge and acceptance of the practitioner's home perspective and an informing set of moral priorities expressed through a world view. There must also be a commitment to pluralism and purposeful, continuous, and interactive discovery with attention to the fitting response for the world. This is the view of expanding moral community. Over time, the process of learning is less a matter of education than of self-learning. Ultimately, social responsibility has no gurus. Practitioners will need continuous efforts to meet the unfamiliar with new and different vocabularies of behavior and thought.

Notes

1. These principles were first developed intensively by Frederick Taylor and adopted in the Fordist manufacturing paradigm (see Nelson, 1980). They came later to inform the American adaptation of total quality management (TQM), and statistical process control as its primary technique, in reaction to the American-perceived need to answer Japanese market and manufacturing competition (e.g., Womack, Jones, and Roos, 1990).

2. We certainly do not hold Wilk answerable for the characteristics of much of Western thought, which we feel he has correctly identified. What we suggest is that a more radical and complex pluralism is needed for practitioners, and there is a need for an empirical skepticism for viewing the subdivisions he has synthesized so nicely.

3. This does not require that all cultures be internally in the modern western European scientific sense, only that they "make sense" to their users in ordering their experience. This sensible quality, and its basis in a world view, can be recognized and learned by both the infants and children the insiders raise to become adults within that culture and, to a lesser extent, by outsiders who want to learn more so as to interact with the insiders more effectively.

4. Dr. Kim was clearly less interested in looking for difference in the nature of things desired: Hunts for such "difference" have historically been associated with some severely erroneous assumptions and antisocial, ethnocentric policies and behaviors, rather than for the much more variable and interesting differences in how particular social and cultural milieus influence the way that primary human objectives are socially regarded and pursued in different places. Kim's own work (e.g., 1996) shows how individualism and collectivism can be

differently construed with respect to different social role relations (e.g., intrafamily relationships) within a cultural setting.

5. Hofstede points out that leaders seldom give as accurate a picture of their behavior regarding power differences as their subordinates do (1991, p. 28).

2
Through a Cultural Lens

We have said that in times of organizational and institutional uncertainty, social responsibility is best effected by the full range of practitioners located throughout the structures of profit-making organizations. If business relationships are responsible, the chain of meaningful and fitting exchange extends beyond the borders of the organization to include those linked partners and customers who anchor an industry in its local market settings within the wider society. Practitioners can integrate their organizations at multiple levels. They can define and follow personal frameworks that are culturally significant to them. They can identify responsible and ethical action through a morally coherent cultural lens rather than rely on the artifacts filtered and imposed by formal authority. At the cultural level, responsibility can positively occur even as people cope with unstable or incommensurate social institutions.

Heuristic cultural elements we have identified—cultural logic, social knowledge, and the artifacts of outward expression—help businesspeople sort, analyze, and experiment with their own responses and perceptions. This leads to increasingly fitting response and increases the capacity for personal responsibility and effectiveness as a practitioner. Applying these conceptual tools critically also presupposes the existence of a home base. It calls for the ability to locate a self or other moral center consciously within an identified, originating normative context. Learning other cultural frameworks and accommodating them mutually and responsively are not, as we have argued, a matter of relativity. Whether the home base is the traditional culture of a social region, as applies for most people, or whether it is something consciously adopted is unimportant. What is important is that it furnishes a philosophy of meaning about relationships with people and the world and orientation priorities regarding right dealings with others. Normative traditions can emerge at both formal-institutional and informal-cultural levels, but in complicated business environments the informal-cultural realm becomes indispensable. Without such a social compass, there is no basis for responsible discernment and choice.

At the same time, cultural learning presupposes a capacity for flexibility, allowances, options, choice, and revision. Increased exposure to and experience with other cultural traditions almost always results in some revisions of the compass itself. This is the chief point of reflexive learning, and it is also how a culture-based expansion of moral communities occurs.

How do practitioners identify the nature and location of their social compass? Strong discouragement and disorientation are presented by communication technology, media, proliferating sets of procedures and regulations, and saturation by increased encounters among strangers and strange ways of doing things. Not to be overwhelmed and discouraged requires a leap of faith and an active moral imagination. If the first step toward personal agency in social responsibility is being aware that we see things differently and from particular cultural points of view, then the second is engaging in a far more sophisticated use of moral imagination than ever before. Western business ethics offers mainly cautions and cautionary case examples. The practitioner's vision cannot be limited to these.

Approaches of Western Business Ethics

The way social responsibility is widely viewed now, in Western business ethics[1] practice and education, differs little in many respects from its more naively optimistic Enlightenment forebears. It generally still assumes normative uniformity and for the most part only replaces the obviously parochial specifics with more vague, but still parochial, generalities. It is dominated by a utilitarian concern with the prediction and control of outcomes and particularly the avoidance of liability. To accomplish this control, managers and leaders usually resort to the imposition of procedures that attempt to appear universal but originate in culturally particular settings. In DeGeorge's conception of moral imagination, for example (1993, pp. 108–109); he invites practitioners to construct scenarios imagining newspaper headlines, the course of action an admired role model would choose, and the probable reactions of various stakeholders.

Constructing these scenarios resembles certain features of the activity of strategic planning: They are very useful exercises in stable times, but laden with data and assumptions to which future social conditions may no longer apply. Alternately, the people to whom they should apply may not receive them as the strategic manager intended, in new and unfamiliar circumstances. Practitioners need something more flexible and will not find it by staying wholly within their own culturally specific social knowledge.

In some cases, outcome-control scenarios may still be useful, but they are largely limited to those people whose positions afford them discretion over many resources and people. These persons are generally senior managers and corporate leaders of large companies. The much larger group of people they direct must make the actual encounters in a diverse array of localities. In times of great change and uncertainty, even top leaders often find that they have very limited rational suasion over the wider society's responses to their actions. Their influence may have begun to wane among their own workforce. These conditions are on the increase in the contemporary globalizing and multicultural business environment.

This calls for a different sort of moral imagination, and this imagination will be in great demand at operating positions below top management. It requires practitioners to envision and begin to create a persistently engaged and gradually widening moral community, but not just as a theory or an abstract ideal. Through this envisioning, practitioners increase their power to extend a business organization and reintegrate with the wider community. They do this as commercial actors in order to develop unforseen mutual benefits.

Reeves-Ellington has observed that this kind of community resembles in certain respects the consciously emphasized identities of ethnic communities inside complex and multicultural settings (1995a). In far-flung businesses, this kind of community cannot rely on physical proximity and the formal institutional or legal arrangements of the corporation. Ethnic identification is based on shared views and common attitudes toward experience—the cultural logic—which in turn influences social knowledge of expected behavior. In organizations with great physical separations, the external artifacts may well be vastly variable on the surface.

The creation and maintenance of an ethnic quality within moral identity is a process wholly different from strategic imaging or the corporate-culture building that is generated from a head office. These head office scenarios are a variant of agenda, are usually artifact driven (as those who have witnessed the dissemination of quality pins, company styles, and other logos or emblems will recognize), and control the social knowledge to be expressed in proper behavior.

The creation of an ethnic type of moral identity proceeds in the opposite direction from transcultural alignment and learning in the field. It differs from the situation in which outsider businesspeople respectfully align their artifacts on the outside and work toward the cultural core, to arrive at greater interpretive understanding of the cultural logic of their new partners. It is also unlike rank-and-file employees aligning their artifacts with those displayed by the head office to improve their social acceptability for employment survival and possible promotion. Ethnic identification is indicated by shared interpretations, whereas ethnic exclusion tends to be indicated and maintained by a difference in artifacts.

The moral imagination by which people arrive at a more inclusive ethnic identity, an expanding moral community, combines bold guesses in initial interactions with a readiness to correct earlier perceptions continually. The practitioner does not legislate and disseminate, but always predicts, always expects to be surprised, and always uses findings to adjust what Argyris and Schoen (1978) call theories-in-use. The general procedural skills of readiness to learn persistently and respectfully, making mistakes along the way, call for continued and practiced attention to guided and serendipitous discoveries alike. This approach places the major emphasis on adequate response to discovery.

If business practitioners can realize socially responsible practice only in dialogue with other people, then to create new effective dialogues they must thoroughly understand the basis of their originating language of responsibility. A culturally informed approach to ethics involves understanding how to bridge a person's own sense of rightness of action with the prescriptive guidelines that the practitioner's partners and customers bring from other contexts. No inclusive interaction at a personal level remains multicultural for very long. Continuing dialogue always moves the language of exchange in a monocultural direction. The responsibility of both partners is the continuous effort to make their accommodation as mutual and bidirectional as possible.

The evidently self-taught process of all responsible cultural learning will benefit greatly from a careful consideration of the cultural roots of a home perspective. For the authors, this home perspective was located within the western European tradition. However, because it relies on experiential learning and focuses on expansion and inclusion, responsible practice also has the potential to be adapted and reframed based on the normative premises of other home traditions. How might business practitioners view responsibility, from the perspective of its Western origins, through a widening cultural lens? Using an approach common to anthropologists, we can begin by observing its correspondences with and divergences from similar interpretations in other cultural settings, times, and contexts.

Enlarging on Responsibility

Michael Harmon (1995), in his strong philosophical criticism of rational approaches to responsibility in public administration, develops his argument entirely within the Western cultural framework, but his analysis of responsibility's meaning in this context lays a solid conceptual groundwork for enlarging the concept usefully, in transcultural business settings. Bringing an anthropological perspective to bear on responsibility allows a clearer view of how this concept mirrors prevalent Western cultural interpretations and agendas. As that region has expanded militarily, politically, and economically over 500 years, its agents too often assumed they could as easily export a formalized ethical form, rooted in an earlier cultural logic, as they could people, services, finished goods, and finance systems.

People, artifacts, and behavior rules can be imposed so long as they are backed by political and economic force. Cultural logic originates differently and takes much longer to adapt. It is not quickly and easily assembled and packaged for export. Still, we can align our home cultural usages with those of other times and places. In a larger comparative frame, we can view the primary forms in which responsibility is recognized in the West. Using combined approaches of philosophy, historical interpretation, and current observation, Harmon (1995) revisits three distinctive Western meanings for responsibility—agency, accountability, and obligation. Seeing them in a comparative context of other traditions is instructive.

Agency

Harmon's first sense of responsibility, agency, is the one most neglected in the personal and professional development of modern practitioners. Agency evokes the capability, both effective and moral, of persons for causing and being answerable for their own actions to other members of their communities (1995, pp. 19–20). Harmon explains this using Niebuhr's (1963) emphasis on self-knowledge as a basis for guidance in one's choice and commitments (cf. Harmon, 1995, p. 12). Ironically, the prevalent discourse in social responsibility maintains a sharp focus on individual *interests*, but too easily loses sight of personal agency. Harmon associates personal agency with Sartres' (1956) sense of inalienable authorship, a term that had been reserved, in earlier times, for the proprietary use of sovereigns. Personal agency and authorship have comprised the modern cornerstones for the development of responsibility. The authors' own roots in this tradition are reflected in the way we give the focus on agency and authorship a central place in all the field examples we examine.

Accountability

The second sense of responsibility Harmon recognizes, accountability, more directly implies liability; that is, the individual actor is subject to enforceable sanctions, as a result of having performed or not, according to some authoritative rule (1995, pp. 25–26). In late modern times, this has become the most highly developed and emphasized aspect of responsibility. It is also the sense most closely associated with reliance on agenda and on formal institutions. Exclusive reliance on accountability and its associated agendas tends to discourage, limit, and, ultimately, morally stunt the development of social responsibility in times of rapid institutional and social change.

Obligation

A third sense of responsibility that Harmon identifies is obligation. This implies a more forward-looking sense of responsibility, such as the duty to discharge a moral requirement (1995, p. 26). Because it relies least on explicit specification of particular individual-authority roles and relationships, obligation is probably the oldest cultural gloss that corresponds to any modern notion of responsibility. Among the three meanings, it is probably the form, from a Western observer's point of view, that would be perceived as most widely distributed throughout the world. Obligation evokes the moral basis of an action and immediately refers to the existence of a moral community. Differing interpretations of obligation and its importance are especially visible to Western business practitioners when they encounter it in other societies, such as Japan, that have traditionally had less individualistic values orientations to human nature and human relationships.

Trustworthiness

To Harmon's three-part collection, above, the authors could add a fourth dictionary sense of responsibility: trustworthiness ("dependable, reliable" (McKechnie, 1983, p. 1964). This implies a normatively positive or culturally inclusive evaluation of a person, who may be expected or predicted to fulfill one of the other three senses of responsibility. This face of responsibility is a frequent concern among practitioners when they appraise or deal with new business partners or employees. Its reflection in personal agency—the trust that one's partner in trade will act in good faith and rightness, as is fitting—is readily apparent.

Building this kind of responsibility is also critically important in sustaining ongoing relationships of business. But, depending on the context, trustworthiness can be anything but straightforward. One aspect relates specifically to subtle obligations of deference that come with insider status in the organizational culture of many American corporations. Jackall (1988) reports this, citing his long and difficult search to gain admittance as a researcher and to observe corporate life from the inside. Managers inside the competitive hierarchy are constantly gauging whether they feel "comfortable" with particular people, whether indeed these potential colleagues are morally fit for inclusion in managerial life (p. 13).

This constant assessment of fitness reflects corporate rituals of power and can extend to great lengths. Reeves-Ellington can recall the rituals and artifacts of such corporate fitness testing for potential high-ranking management candidates in one multinational company. All job candidates had to play cards with the chief executive officer (CEO). The successful candidate had to prove worthiness as an opponent. It was also necessary that the CEO win.

Cultural Variability of Obligation

For a view of the variability of personal agency and responsiveness, obligation furnishes many good illustrations of the cultural lens through which responsibility passes. Obligation can be formal and subject to regulation, even be part of a social institution and agenda, for example, in one's obligation to serve in the army of a sovereign state. At the same time, it may also be informal, customary, and serve on other occasions as a resistance to outside and formal attempts at control. This often happens if it is part of a long-established and vital cultural tradition that bridges public and private contexts or connects people to positions in different organizational and institutional contexts.

Kinship or ethnic ties in business and positions in organizations that are based on belonging to a family, a class, or an association membership that links people across different formal organization roles are all areas in which obligation may operate in different ways. For example, the *habatsu*, or university clique that operates in some large Japanese corporations, links newcomers and lower level managers in close group life with senior officers in what is otherwise a formal, power-distant, and hierarchical organization setting (Whitehill, 1991).

Through obligation, social ties may crosscut or become part of business activity, but obligation also works at the customary level to regularize even the more purely economic trade relationships. In Middle America, obligation can be seen in the institution of *compadrazgo*, a relatively elaborate set of godparent customs. Relatively well-to-do owners of cattle and land that Ellington (1966) observed in a village in the Mexican state of Veracruz in the 1960s gained new market entry and price information, giving their businesses a profit edge, by establishing ritual ties with compadres from among both kin and non-kin merchants and traders who lived in villages outside their own. The absence of local lending institutions at the time also made compadres the only systemwide source for borrowing cash (p. 52).

In Indonesia in the early 1980s, the Javanese cloth traders (*bakul*) that Alexander (1987) observed in interaction with their ethnic Chinese wholesalers observed a different form of obligation. The long-term creditor, the bakul's *langganan tetep*, or regular customer, would have no desire to initiate any extra social ties. Unlike Mexican compadres, these were not patron-client relations (p. 129). Yet, these regular customers counted on reliability in their dealings; they operated on predictable (nonbargained) credit prices, with ongoing business obligations institutionalized at the level of custom. These customs assured a regular flow of goods and cash—the primary reason for using credit to begin with (pp. 129, 152).

By contrast, Alexander (1987) observes that the short-term credit partners (*ngalap-nyaur*) were often itinerant traders. These suppliers had to work to build up trust into longer term relationships with their partners. Their relationships with the bakul depended more on demonstrating personal trust "so the supplier seeks every possible means to extend social ties, offering and reciprocating invitations to weddings . . . visiting traders when they are ill. Small sums of money or other gifts . . . cement the relationships further" (p. 130). These, too, however, were business relationships and not socially embedded patron-client relations. In them, the voluntary gestures were designed to incur a feeling of future obligation. Layered atop such varied customs were additional ones, such as the mandatory debt repayments required of either kind of business partner at *Labaran* (*Idul Fitri*, the annual high Muslim holiday).

Obligations are not simple, monolithic, or all-encompassing. In settings outside the modern West, it is a culturally constructed judgment or interpretation to draw immediate conclusions regarding the way in which behaviors may be seen as fair or unfair, selfish or altruistic. Actions between commercial actors often do occur to cement and maintain regular relations, assuring unbroken rice bowls (that is, livelihoods) under uncertain and shifting conditions. Hence the futility of reaching for immediate moral or ethical interpretation, or of assuming control of beneficent outcomes, until more is known about the particular cultural and institutional context in which actions occur. In Western business across such borders, field and operations personnel frequently find that local conditions are incommensurate with head office expectations and guidelines. These are among the most sensitive and critically important situations in which to apply interpretive and cultural learning approaches responsibly.

Accountability and Power

Many Europeans and Americans are relatively confident of accountability; they expect it to be understandable and predictable: They should be wary of such expectations. Accountability is probably the most culturally specific and Western of responsibility's meanings in late modern times. It focuses on the individual but also extends to surrogates, such as the legal fictive persons embodied by corporations. The late modern legalistic interpretations of accountability have provided as much suffering as relief. They tend to strip people of moral agency without providing a positive substitute. Under the felt control and surveillance of large and impersonal organizations, people often perceive themselves as struggling in what James Coleman has described as the asymmetric society (1982). When they seek redress from felt wrongs or intrusions from these fictive persons, they cannot make the formal entities accountable to them in the way that they themselves have been made accountable. This marks a conflict point, both institutional and cultural, in the relationship between responsibility and power.

Interpretations of Power

If we return for a moment to the Western industrial cog-and-wheel metaphor for the human condition, we find a clear symbolic artifact of institutionalized Western beliefs about power and, with it, the ambivalence this interpretation creates. Are not all people in modern settings relatively powerless in relation to top executives and officers? This popular cultural construction of power combines with assumptions about rule following, shaping legalistic behavior and thought and often hindering personal agency in public places. With either undue faith or undue fear, legalisms can stultify responsibility. Sometimes, the felt disempowerment ends in a struggle with existing authority, either through disobedience or by counterorganizing.

While struggle at the political level is widespread, businesspeople's work is not primarily involved with civil society politics, no matter what various social agenda companies may tell us, as we also argue at greater length in Chapter 4. For the most part, the accountability they experience is to their superiors in the organization. On occasion, as organization representatives, people may also address the organization's accountability to other legal authorities.

Western cultural constructions of power have been complicated by their extensive theorization, which spans disciplines and centuries. In his synthesis of power theory, Clegg (1989) delineates the two early and significant frameworks for viewing power and its uses. The first, associated with the writings of Thomas Hobbes, has shaped most mainstream power concepts of personal agency—that it is lodged in the person of the sovereign—and episodic power, in which a sovereign is entitled to periodic extractions, traditionally, for example, through rent (i.e., annual taxation of subjects; Clegg, p. xvi). Hobbes's (1972) practical concern was "to provide a theory that will persuade people to obey the law" (p. 9). In this regard, says Hobbes, "The greatest power is that which is compounded of the powers of men, united by consent in one person, natural or civil, that has the use of all their powers depending on his will" (p. 12).

Later, Hobbes clarifies the authority of the sovereign, either natural or legal:

> They that are subjects to a monarch, cannot without his leave cast [him] off . . . nor transfer their person from him . . . for they are bound and he reputed author of all, that he that already is their sovereign, shall do, and judge fit to be done: so that any one man dissenting, all the rest should break their covenant made to that man, which is injustice. (Hobbes, 1972, p. 160)

Finally, Hobbes protects the sovereign from liability by lodging accountability only with the subject population: "He that doth anything by authority, doth therein no injury to him by whose authority he acteth" (1972, p. 163).

A very different view is offered by the second major source of Western historical political philosophy on power, Niccolo Machiavelli, whose concerns were quite distinct from those of Hobbes. To Machiavelli, power was imprecise, contingent, strategic, and organizational (Clegg, 1989, p. 4). While Hobbes endlessly legislated on what power was and on its consequences, Machiavelli and his successors interpreted what power did. Rather than write from a position in the employ of a king whose power he would legitimize, as did Hobbes, Machiavelli's environment was one of uncertainty and change for everyone, including his prince (Machiavelli, 1990, p. xiii). Machiavelli, therefore, viewed power more pluralistically (see Clegg, 1989, pp. 5–6), with less certainty about justice. In *The Prince*, he explains,

> It seemed more suitable to me to search after the effectual truth of the matter rather than its imagined one . . . for there is such a gap between how one lives and how one ought to live that anyone who abandons what is done for what ought to be done learns his ruin rather than his preservation. (Machiavelli, 1990, p. 52)

Power interpreted pluralistically is morally ambiguous and context dependent. Its players may negotiate or deceive each other, but together they determine the specific nature of their power relationships. By contrast, in the sovereign agency model of Hobbes, there is a single predetermined power identification. Hobbesian power is causal, legitimate, culturally uniform, and orderly. It is necessary to constrain an inherently selfish, disorderly, and strife-riven human nature (Clegg, 1989, p. 34). An enduring cultural preference for this view of human nature has supported the demonization of so-called Machiavellian behavior, in which strategic power and ambiguous authority are associated with evil and amorality—and Machiavelli's vividly amoral examples from 16th century Florence did nothing to discourage this impression.

At the same time, Machiavelli was speaking in the stance of a neutral, pragmatic, and empirical observer. Quite apart from his examples of abuse or amoral use of power, there are certain benefits for personal responsibility in a more contingent view, in marked contrast to Hobbes's moralistic and prohibitive version. A responsible use of strategic power would clearly require the existence of a moral community and people who were both responsive and responsible to that community. However, as long as the Hobbesian assumption of amoral self-interest defines basic human nature, Machiavellian power will more likely be seen as manipulative, subversive, and illegitimate.[2]

Building on the more recent work of Bauman (1987) and Foucault (1977), Clegg (1989) delineates a third framework for viewing power. This is the subtler means of influence brought by tutelage, discipline, and scientific surveillance methods—in short, the growth of rational discipline as a means of governance and control (Clegg, 1989, pp. 35–36). Inheritors of this framework, in late modern times, include those who emphasize management development over management training and who employ increasingly rationalized approaches to quality as the continuous improvement of uniformity and control of products and services. This is epitomized in the American total quality management (TQM) movement (Anderson, A., 1993).

With the emergence of more thorough disciplinary approaches to regulating human activity, there have also been renewed attempts to recapture the spirit of individual responsibility through a cultural lens. This has occurred through an appeal to moral community with the rhetoric of employee empowerment slogans. Yet, most of the methods of surveillance as realized in TQM's American versions end by subtracting discretion from, rather than adding it to, the workforce. They continue to reflect Hobbesian assumptions about power: Trust, but verify!

So, despite rhetorical emphasis on development and discipline, most of the writing about social responsibility in business, and most American management writing in general, still begins and ends with a Hobbesian view of both power and human nature. Formal agendas, seen in slogans, principles, credos, and ethics statements, stipulate the proper roles and authority relationships of the corporation, the state, labor, the press, the public, management, and stockholders.

The Hobbesian promise of control by agenda continues to elude the would-be sovereigns: Both strategic and Hobbesian power continue to coexist in late modern organizations and, as we illustrate in the next chapter, continue to compete for application. As Jackall (1988) has reported extensively, for middle managerial ranks in highly bureaucratized American work environments especially, there is often a relative paucity of trust between supervisors and subordinates. In the managerial ranks, alternate interpretations of Hobbesian principles are made in far more Machiavellian ways in day-to-day practice than the written artifacts suggest. Unfortunately, for social responsibility, this occurs all too often in a relative moral vacuum.

That accountability is closely tied to cultural interpretations of power is clear. Competition for sovereignty between pretenders to positions of authority brings their agendas to the fore. Hobbesian and organizational power circuitry remain the chief avenues through which agenda is pursued in business. Programs of legitimation or reform can be advanced in a variety of ways, at a variety of levels, but because of their construction as agendas, they are usually hotly contested.

In agenda-dominated business thinking, both individuals and organizations are held accountable, but overwhelmingly in day-to-day practice it is individuals who are called to account first and foremost to the officers of their employing organization. The competitive business aims of corporate authority are placed at the top of their decision-making priorities, whereas the business organization itself is more often thought of as accountable to its owners and only more remotely to the wider society. In this context, the suspended interpretation of conventional morality can become severe. As Jackall's (1988) managerial informant told him, "What's right in the corporation is what the guy above you wants from you. That's morality in the corporation" (p. 6).

Alternate views of corporate accountability have theorized different corporate social models. Business ethics books often concentrate on case illustrations of specific corporations in the midst of controversy. These are useful, to an extent, to assess the alternate models. Yet, these rival corporate perspectives share certain limitations owing to their near-exclusive reliance on agenda interpretations of accountability. Uzl (1992) provides a good summary for framing our examination of these limitations.

Accountability and Theories of the Corporation

The social permission theory of corporations, which Uzl associates with Ralph Nader and with the ethicist Keith Davis (1990), is that corporations, as creatures of the state, have been trusted with large amounts of resources, thus incurring the obligation of responsible stewardship (Uzl, 1992, p. 139). The idea of social permission has general merit and is not unlike some other conceptions of obligation; it offers the abstract ideal of an imagined wider community, of which business should be a part. Davis then goes on to propose an agenda of the five propositions of this position: (1) social responsibility arises from social power; (2) business shall operate as a two-way, open system receiving inputs from society and disclosing its operations to the public; (3) business should calculate the social costs, as well as benefits, of a business activity; (4) a price should be established in social costs so that a user pays for the effects of the user's consumption on society; and (5) businesses have social responsibilities in the areas of their competence and of social need (1990, pp. 166–169).

Thus, Davis (1990) follows Western preferences for agenda promulgation and would legislate a general agenda that spans specific social contexts. While his general ideas are appealing, the most neglected avenue for improving social responsibility has not been addressed. The cultural aspect of context lies *beyond* agenda—that is, beyond a primary resort to the legal rules and remedies that the social permission theory heavily favors. For this reason, the guidelines alone, like many before them, are unlikely to improve corporate social responsibility substantially.

An amoral, ecological version of this same type of theory is more popular in mainstream business circles. This variation states that those corporations that do not use their economic power in ways society considers responsible will tend to lose it (Uzl, 1992, p. 142; see also DeGeorge, 1993, p. 196). Below, in our discussion of Nestlé, and in the main illustrative case in Chapter 4, we suggest that this is not necessarily a very accurate assumption. The grossly imperfect information about the details of a business that is realistically available to most suppliers, stockholders, customers, and even employees often does not allow them to recognize and respond in a timely manner to the bad social bargains they may be getting. Especially if customers, suppliers, and critics receive most of their information about a business through mediated or mass communications, they are not likely to receive operating information or to give direct feedback such as either staying loyal or buying or working elsewhere.

Under the amoral model, direct economic consequence would be expected to be commensurate with irresponsible performance of a corporation, as would be fitting to the situation. But, especially if the business is good at manipulating marketing communications and is aided by the overwhelming technological reach of mass media, it could effectively decouple irresponsible business behavior from its assumed natural consequences, at least in the short term.

A prominent third theory consists of what we here call the pure-business school. Its proponents are led by Milton Friedman, who holds, based on the primacy of the business aim and on the contract as its sacrosanct instrument, that corporations are responsible only to their stockholders (Uzl, 1992, p. 141). There are also functional, institution-based proponents who approach this same theory from a separation of functions' perspective; the chief example is Theodore Levitt, who views social responsibility as properly the government's job (Uzl, p. 143). The pure-business position rests in general on a functional view of outcomes for the greater social good, yet this greater good has not been demonstrated in the views of many of the Western public nor has it convinced those Third World critics who can observe the widening global gap in wealth.

Uzl's conclusion, that an individual approach is best within the institution of business as it exists today (1992, p. 144), is correct, but neither he nor any other source inside business institutions today have offered the resources, methods, or approaches for its development at the cultural level. For most practitioners, certainly, accountability alone is surely not the answer. Accountability is useful, and indeed necessary, to reduce uncertainty within well-known situations by identifying outside limits of what is fitting, but it can do little more in a positive direction. By contrast, the internal power and authority of a business organization leaves little space for doubt about where *economic* sanctioning and directive authority lie.

In the current institutional environment, attempts to impose accountability from outside the corporation may make significant inroads, but these will take time. For business practitioners caught now in the midst of new situations, competing political and legalistic frameworks only raise competing agendas in situations that have become increasingly less well defined. Accountability and agenda are necessary, but by themselves are insufficient to support moral life in a turbulent business world.

Agenda Interpretations: The Nestlé Controversy

A main trouble with relying on clashes of corporate sovereignty against external accountability and agendas is that it provides no basis for a positive integration between business organizations and the wider society. The well-known Nestlé infant formula controversy, which extended from the 1970s through the 1980s, gives ample illustration of this. European and American activist groups held Nestlé, the multinational consumer products company, responsible for the noted marked increase in Third World infant deaths due to the misuse of infant formulas that the firm aggressively marketed in maternity health care settings.

These formulas had replaced breast feeding in a number of developing country locales, and among the charges were that consumers could not read instructions that were in English; that they did not have sanitary drinking water to add to the formula; that they lacked economic resources, which caused them to water down the formula; and that they were unduly influenced to adopt it by marketing pictures of middle-class formula users and the presence of salespeople who appeared to resemble health facility personnel.

In his book-length study of the controversy, Sethi (1994) traces the intricate strategy, flanking maneuvers, and artful publicity in which both the firm and its antagonists engaged over a period of 10 years. Eventually, the American Methodist Church became involved and there was a nationwide boycott of Nestlé. This had little impact on the firm's revenue (p. 219). The firm counterorganized, forming an American public relations subsidiary designed to "broaden corporate social responsibility . . . not in terms of how the company's management has traditionally seen it, but how its many external constituencies perceive it" (p. 227).

Sethi assesses this public relations subsidiary, a lighting rod to draw controversy away from the firm's U.S. operations, as having "negligible" long-term impact (1994, p. 238). In other words, the company sought to insulate its business purpose from the social purposes thrust on it by critical spokespersons for a wider community.

The affair culminated in the reluctant involvement of the intergovernmental World Health Organization (WHO) and the voluntary adoption of a special code for the marketing of infant formulas. This code was later ignored by a number of countries and firms, and Sethi reports that WHO, acting mostly as an informational conduit, had no responsibility for monitoring it. In the end, there were no neutral parties for oversight. Sethi concludes that the impact of the entire experience on Nestlé was very modest. He notes Nestlé's published company history version of the boycott was aimed for the benefit of institutional memory and demonstrated the power of the establishment in the organization (Sethi, 1994, p. 240).

While Sethi clearly interprets this case as an instance of assumed sovereignty by a powerful multinational company, we can also see in it a lack of orientation to the cultural characteristics of the wider society and to the local contexts of the overseas business. Those actors and organizations who were appalled by the infant deaths sought accountability almost exclusively through sanctions against the company. They did this chiefly by adversarial legal and economic actions, and the company responded with defensiveness and counterorganizing: No dialogue was flowing in either direction. The first public shot was fired with the 1974 publication, through a London publisher named War on Want, of Mike Muller's book, titled (in translation) *The Baby Killer* (cited in Sethi, 1994, p. 45).

Of further dismay within the consumer products and pharmaceutical industries at the time, Reeves-Ellington can recall the dismay within the pharmaceutical products industry over the fact that, when firms had complied and pulled their own marketing staffs out of the designated less-developed countries, the company people were simply replaced in locales such as Nigeria by salespeople who had neither been trained in the product's requirements nor provided any customer information at all. The formulas remained for sale in these locales. Pro-boycott and anticorporate critics later responded to queries on this, in ways suggesting they were more interested in punishing Nestlé than in developing better local social integration and communication for a responsible market relationship: The logic of such a view is plainly that the only good relationship is no relationship. The prime agenda was the war with Nestlé's agenda people, that is, the Nestlé public relations arm in the United States, rather than for either side to direct its attention to achieving greater social responsiveness to needs in the field localities. It is clear that no moral community, no common grounds in outlook, existed on either side.[3]

A recent development of concern in the rhetoric on social responsibility is the strategy many businesses have taken in trying to predict what the public's opinion will be regarding the firm's social commitments. Just how dubious the amoral theory of economic consequences is, especially as regards the conditions and mechanisms for the predicted failure of an irresponsible firm, is not lost on practitioners. Many now focus substantial efforts on presenting an ethical public relations face. This activity may take the form of advertising a firm's environmental support, as does Mobil, or in even more programmatic green marketing efforts (Ottman, 1993, for example, published a book full of advice on how to turn one's environmentally and socially friendly activities into a marketing strategy). These public relations campaigns are strategic interpretations of power use, but they are directed unilaterally to the mass market, not worked out throughout the business chain within the businesses' operating contexts. Whether the same firms establish a dialogue with mutually intelligible cultural connections between the senders and the communities in which they do business remains an open question.

The aspects of power most amenable to variable individual interpretation are indeed these more strategic, relational aspects. If practitioners have learned to view power in a more relational and strategic way, they can be potentially more effective as socially responsible practitioners. This requires close-in communications of exchange and knowledge of the specific social situations and immediate effects of firm activities. Advertising is good relational power use, but it does not produce the fitting response. The danger of relational and strategic power use, when using the power of media communications, is that it can allow businesspeople to lose sight of more local, socially integrative connections. If practitioners learn to see their social responsibility in dialogue, through a cultural lens, rather than simply receive it or broadcast it as instructions from an organization or program, they will have approached it in a way that goes beyond agendas.

Reification and the Loss of Personal Agency

Personal agency, the most adaptable source of responsibility for businesspeople in the field, finds its chief threat for practice in the reification of power, institutions, and roles. Responsibility most often becomes dislocated from responsive agency when power is viewed and used as a concrete, limited entity. People can use and view power as a scarce commodity in an economy or as an abundant, yet potentially renewable, resource. Strategic, or relational power, the power that is inherent in relationships between people and in creative interpretation of the situation, is less fixed, more easily invented, and more easily dispersed throughout networks of relationships. It is therefore potentially widely available to people wherever they are located in an organization. Power reified is a scarce good, subject to being grabbed in a zero-sum contest, less freely accessed, and harder to change in social life.

To understand better what we mean by reification of responsibility, Harmon's (1996) description of personal responsibility is useful:

> Personal responsibility derives its moral nature from the actor's [inherent] status as agent of his or her actions, for which responsibility cannot ultimately be lodged externally in, for example, a higher authority or learned principles. (p. 86)

Harmon notes the lack of such a self-reflexive understanding of responsibility invites the unreflective reification of principles that underpin actions. This abrogation reduces morality to "petrified legalisms" that simply justify rather than become the self-reflexive symbols informing a relevant context for responsible choices (Whitmont, 1982, p. 90, in Harmon, 1995, p. 86).

A similar tendency to reify in institutions and their associated roles, Berger and Luckman point out, bestows on them "an ontological status independent of human activity. . . . Through reification, the world of institutions appears to merge with the world of nature. . . . The paradigmatic formula for (role) . . . reification is the statement 'I have no choice in the matter'" (1967, pp. 90–91).

Accepting this constricted space for personal agency dooms many well-intentioned people to give up on being responsible any time they perceive their roles or institutions as being too rigid, specific, or ill suited to be adequately responsible to the situation. It is not the presence of the rules and laws themselves that necessarily creates or encourages rigidity or avoidance, unless they are particularly poorly constructed or culturally ill-suited (e.g., through rapid imposition of social and political environmental changes). Such problems can obtain, in emerging or changing political states, as our Bulgarian example illustrates below. It is when people rely slavishly and unreflectively only on rules or authority; when they react at the opposite extreme, throwing off response to authority in the absence of perceived good authority; or when they rigidly cling to one particular authoritative interpretation in the midst of turbulent social change, that the real doom of social responsibility occurs.

Field Sketch: The Cultural Logic of Blame in Bulgaria

A good example of constricted space for personal agency can be seen in Bulgaria after the cold war. Despite much public discourse about the American tendency to blame, in recent years of change and anxiety about our economic and social future, American attitudes toward responsibility still stand in vivid contrast with those of the Bulgarian university students and staff with whom Reeves-

Ellington did ethnographic and survey research from 1993 to 1995 (Reeves-Ellington, 1996b). The American faculty at this jointly established, post–cold war American university had come more or less anticipating a full replication of their home models of academic freedom, along with the characteristic American optimism about self-reliance, with collegial give-and-take, while teaching abroad. By and large, these professors were upset to find that the Bulgarian university professional staff and the Bulgarian students, who made up the vast majority of those they taught, operated by a far different cultural logic.

By survey instrument responses, as well as by behavior and their own folk explanations, university Bulgarians reflected a value orientation of distrust toward human nature—both others' and their own. While the American faculty reflected a generally optimistic, "trust until proven untrustworthy" attitude, Bulgarian respondents reported that, from their point of view, it was all right to cheat until or unless caught, and, indeed, that one could not trust oneself *not* to cheat. If some Americans are aghast at this bit of Bulgarian social knowledge, they might consider that the rest of the cultural context, and its related values orientations, supported this behavioral expectation within a coherent cultural logic.

In this cultural logic was a specific Bulgarian view of history as deterministic—in their memory, a history filled with capricious and unjust oppression, impervious to any attempt at individual understanding or intervention, either political and economic. Furthermore, this oppression was always thrust on them by cultural outsiders. These received experiences presented a cultural challenge in their attempts to integrate with the globalizing West: Theirs had become a blame society; they tended to orient themselves to an unchangeable present, which they defined as being determined by past events.

The Bulgarians with whom Reeves-Ellington worked thus experienced themselves as dependent on an untrustworthy and "illegal" social and physical environment; accordingly, in cheating they were only adapting a pragmatic orientation to the oppressive present. Such a cultural logic restricts the space for optimism, risk taking, or the kind of personal ownership and investment that the authors, as Westerners, would see as needed for a maximum sense of personal agency to invest in social responsibility. A self-perceived severe lack of personal independence further restricts one's willingness to become more interdependent. Offers of help are thus judged with suspicion; they are inherently intrusive and suspect: "After all, if you Americans want to be helpful and do help, I am under your obligation." Notice the decisive cutoff of further flow of the social stream of exchange in this statement, the emphatic rejection of I–Thou.

Bulgarians expressed an intense desire to be free of their oppressive environment and enacted this in the visible artifacts of small rebellions against rules. At the same time, without all those rules, they could not trust human nature enough to feel safe, and they became anxious. Thus, in comparison to Americans, they had a relatively emotionally intense response to rules and laws. As one student told Reeves-Ellington,

> The Turks and then the Communists have taken each of us into its grasp and fashioned us. They were the supreme power. Both covered us with small complicated rules, minute and uniform, in ways none of us could penetrate. We learned not to act but avoid public actions. So we rebelled against these illegal controls in small and petty ways. We thumbed our noses at the state.

That the target of small antisocial acts was specifically authority, and not necessarily all other people, was evident in the Bulgarians' willingness, at the same time, to help one another through hard economic times. It should also be noted that Reeves-Ellington later saw many Bulgarian students successfully move on to enter a number of highly sought-after graduate slots in American management graduate schools in the United States. Many were motivated to increase their personal agency, and some became increasingly successful in doing so. In their eagerness to Westernize, some Bulgarian students voiced their intent to throw off the cultural "contamination" or "baggage" of their heritage—a choice that can, of course, create for them further problems of credibility and integrity if pursued in too antisocial ways.

It is easy to see how such culturally constructed scripts, with their assumptions of reified power and moral/immoral dichotomies, can preclude the thoughtful extension of practitioners' social responsibility as persons. Extreme cynicism about power and authority can actually encourage the further socialization of business practitioners to an attitude that assumes the hostile social environment requires mainly skills of offensive and defensive public relations and marketing strategies and cleverness at devising legal protection and justifications. From the point of view of social responsibility, these are pathological organization-environment relationships. Their associated strategies, especially in American companies, indicate a moral bankruptcy and acceptance of the cultural myth of reified power. If companies assume they can and should be able to control everything, without need for a socially integrative dialogue, then power will be treated as if it were a thing immutable in itself and in the minds of practitioners and critics; there will be only one soul-constricting set of alternatives for perceiving and interacting with it. In such morally impoverished circumstances, both business and its critics begin to behave and predict one another's behavior accordingly—thus both are part of the problem.

Power reification, combined with exclusive focus on outcome control at a large and programmatic scale, allows organization members to shed responsibility so long as they can dodge or shed accountability for any mishaps. This becomes an amoral Machiavellian strategy that then alternates with its dominant Hobbesian counterpart, resulting in the attempt to regain innocence by locating and fixing blame elsewhere. The blame-shedding, blame-fixing contest can be seen in the endless legalistic working out of calculations of obligation and accountability, for example, obliging Exxon and Union Carbide to spend more time and resources on precision pinpointing the precise locus and quantity of blame for an oil spill or disastrous foreign plant explosion. Focusing on these calculations concentrates attention on efforts to contain cost, when efforts to heal, to understand the situation that created the accident, and to reconnect with the affected communities are of primary importance.

Legalities are not in themselves the source of what is, at base, a culturally interpretive problem: It is just that, as power and rationality have come to dominate most discussions of ethics and business responsibility, they do not by themselves provide answers. Their exercise without the presence of moral community only leads to further irresponsibility. As we also saw in the Nestlé controversy, reliance on focusing and fixing blame for bad outcomes, and the ensuing countercampaign in public relations, did little to ensure dialogue and responsible action or to see that conditions of communication and fitting response improved between the firms and the communities in which the problem emerged. The changes business needs lie in an awareness of cultural context and the sensitivity of dialogue and response. This must become a more integral part of the way people practice business in ongoing, live relationships. The alternative is that representatives of entities culturally construed as powerful or as victims will continue to maneuver with nonintegral public relations wars and to talk past one another.

There is great untapped potential for the expansion of business practice to include adequate cultural response to interpretive issues of communication. As agents of responsibility, people exercise their own authorship in the interpretation of the roles and institutions in which they participate. This is especially important in times of change, and the responsibilities and complications for interpretation grow more challenging with roles of increasing organizational authority. In the following chapter, we attempt to illustrate this further with a culturally interpretive view of social responsibility in leadership.

Notes

1. The basic division is often made, in Western discussions of ethics, between analyzing judgments and recommending actions (cf. Runes, 1960). Because we focus on practice and begin from the perspective of individuals working in organizations, our chief focus is the action-and-guidance aspect, rather than the more broadly philosophic judgment-of-value aspect, of ethics. The occasional exception to this occurs when a judgment interpretation arises out of direct necessity to aid in a rudimentary gloss or "translation" of unfamiliar cultural examples.

2. When a source of authority proves very imperfect, there is the impulse, to which long-noted American cultural yearnings for individualism and perfectability are particularly susceptible, to give up completely on either the model or the person in charge of it, or both. If you can't be perfect, why try? We Americans especially have a tendency, therefore, to believe in and demand accountability for others, to fear and even avoid it ourselves in our day-to-day work and yet to harbor a distrust of its sources of authority.

3. For those who believe this split simply reflected the activist 1970s, this was challenged by Anderson's own recent experience as a visitor touring the Nestlé head office with American business students in 1996. In presentations and discussions with Nestlé, the two traditional sides to this now-legendary corporate story again took shape. American audience partici-

pants in the Nestlé lecture auditorium were neatly divided between some who categorically defended Nestlé's savvy response to its critics and others who, with equal passion, called on their hosts to defend their position. At least in the minds of those Americans in business higher education, blame and not dialogue still held priority.

3
Altered States of Consciousness
Leadership for Socially Responsible Organizations

As Hanna (1988) has aptly observed, "Every organization is perfectly designed to get the results it gets" (p. 34). The nature and self-defined missions of most modern business organizations, and the roles of the people who run them, discourage a holistic integration between economic activity and the mores and desires of the rest of society—an integration that could advance social responsibility. This chapter is about the different ways that leadership can facilitate cultural and moral community to enter and inhabit modern organizations or to be barred from them.

Most traditional business ethics books discuss the social responsibility of business organizations as a whole, either singly or in aggregate. Occasionally, they mention the responsibility of the top officers, usually as limit defining: "National or international businesses can be no more ethical than the persons who run the firms" (DeGeorge, 1993, p. 194) is a typical statement. Thus, agendas largely define these specialized ethics. Rules and prohibitions, if convincingly modeled by the chief executive officer (CEO) and enforced in the breach, are supposed to take care of the rest. At the same time, textbooks and practitioners repeatedly emphasize the necessity for all businesspeople to personally develop appropriate judgment capacities for particular situations.

We certainly agree that the need for greater responsibility of individual businesspeople exists whether or not they occupy positions of public prominence or personal influence in their organizational roles and functions. But, there are times when leadership must exceed the boundaries of the Hobbesian role model. In the case in Chapter 5, we address organization systems issues through a detailed description of how role linkage and information flow can achieve responsible relationships across an organization, not only through traditional chains of command, but also through customer chains that span a multinational company's formal boundaries. Through an entire workforce, the extended organizational community can be awakened to greater social responsiveness. How can leadership roles in organizations limit or facilitate this process?

This chapter describes how socially integrative organization leadership works. This includes (1) how a paradigm of socially charged commerce, rather than rationalized pure business, promotes greater social responsibility; (2) how different types of leaders can be expected to facilitate socially responsible outcomes; and (3) how organizational uses of power underpin leader-member relations and affect practitioners' opportunities for social responsibility. Toward the end of the chapter, we offer a comparison of meanings through alternate metaphors of power as they relate to leadership activities.

Pure Business and Its Commercial Alternative

The interpretive cultural logic of for-profit organizations retains many of the motifs of the historical era of early modern western European expansion. The American public imagination is competitively ambivalent about large and affluent organizations and expresses, and institutional supports, aggressive and rugged individualism (e.g., as Brown, 1991, illustrates). We expect large organizations to respond aggressively to threat and to differentiate themselves from wider communal mores. Adam Smith's enlightenment view of economic activity as a pure product of competition among individuals, while regarded as a philosophy of a perfect marketplace, has nonetheless persisted in popular business myths that have extended from the social Darwinist era to late modern media arenas populated by larger-than-life CEOs. The linked Weberian themes of capitalism, Protestantism, and individualism live on as a pervasive cultural and ideological motif in most large American businesses.

The values orientation question of social responsibility, whether these Western corporations put primary emphasis on their human connection to those who buy and use their products, and a related institutional question, whether economic gain is or should be the first and overriding consideration of business, continue as sites of modern public and private contention. This in turn has led to popular myths of amoral business and discussions of its moral neutrality in an enlightened pursuit of progress (Chesher's discussion, 1992, is one of the best on this issue).

The mainstream institutional position in business is the classical liberal view that holds that business should be pursued as a purely economic activity. In this case, social responsibility in business can be attained only to the extent and in the manner that exchanging businesspeople can individually and mutually make cultural sense of their behavior. That is, they must be able to reconcile their actions with their respective sets of social mores. The definition of these larger social mores, in the traditional view, is left to the authority of the church or, in immediate breaches with significant social harm, to the state's courts.

A consciousness of public dissatisfaction betrays the inadequacy of this view. Again and again, management ethics theorists have looked inward to the core of their own institution for answers. Kanungo and Mendonca (1996) note that not much progress has been made toward greater social responsibility within business. Ohmann (1989) asks, "Can it be that our god of production has feet of clay? Does industry need a new religion?" The critics of business agenda would also change this religion by overriding it and imposing a different set of rules from alternate institutions of law and religion.

It is not new religion business needs, but altered states of consciousness: Social responsibility requires the increased awareness and ability of businesspeople to integrate the social and cultural with the economic, creating avenues conducive to commerce in a broader sense. This integration shifts attention away from pure business as the pursuit of rational efficiency to include a more socially laden conception of economic activity as commerce (Reeves-Ellington, 1995b, p. 250).

Commerce

In contrast to purer conceptions of business, the idea of commerce is older. It predates the rise of Western capitalism. It is bundled with additional meanings because it had been merged institutionally and embedded in earlier social forms and contexts of exchange. Commerce's meanings still linger in its contemporary connotations. It can never be morally neutral because of the active presence of persons who are continually responding with interpretations and decisions. More than just economic exchange takes place in commerce. It is closer to the ground, involving not only goods, currencies, and instruments, but also contextual and tangential information and all kinds of social contact. It is social traffic in things valued and cannot long exist without an I and a Thou.

When responsible business interactions occur in practice, most often they involve commercial actors situated marginally to the centers of authority in either business or state institutions. This is because these marginal actors are operating closer to the other institutional centers of the immediate social and physical environments. In exchanges between organized systems of different size, complexity, and resources, the circumstances are asymmetric, and socially responsible business is always organizationally compromised. What responsibility can be exercised rests on the cultural relationships that the local parties can improvise with one another.

What is general about specific exchange relations? Commercial actors occupy themselves with opportunities, not problems. They interact continuously and pragmatically in the present, always with an eye to maximizing future choices and benefits. They necessarily mediate and interpret between systemic levels and often must resist, avoid, work out, or reinterpret mandates and limitations imposed by governing and outlying systems. This occurs especially when they perceive local relationships to be at risk as a result of poor fit with the larger entities' demands. If they cannot avoid imposed constraints, successful commercial actors creatively reinterpret and avoid overt dissonance with their larger systems.

Pure Business

Achieving the purest rational management to maximize overall business return means studiously avoiding the more ambiguous and compromising considerations of commerce. A pure-business paradigm, solidified in the mass-production era of industrialism, is one of producers and consumers, not customers and suppliers (Reeves-Ellington, 1995b). It relies on an I–It paradigm to avoid social entanglements. The drag of interdependency and responsibility is anathema in environments assumed to be hostile. We (the producers) provide goods for *them* (the consumers), whom we do not know personally except through scientific study. The producers furnish goods or services to people chiefly for the company to thrive. The exchange relationship is, to borrow a term from Sherry, McGrath, and Levy

(1995), a monadic one in which there is no external partner: The gift is given to the self. Thus, external customers exist to serve the interests and success of the producers and purveyors.

Joseph Campbell describes this modern type of organization: "an economic-political origination. Their ideas are . . . of the secular . . . in hard and unremitting competition for material supremacy and resources" (1973, p. 401). The most efficient producers tend to drive the social out as being irrational and inefficient.

This Western cultural logic of pure business can be seen in Calvin Coolidge's famous remark, "The business of America is business." Peter Drucker (1955) articulates it in the postwar era: "Business performance comes first—it is the aim of the enterprise and the reason for its existence" (p. 16). Levitt (1958) stipulates it more forcefully: "Altruism, self-denial, charity and similar values are vital in certain walks of life. But for the most part, those virtues are alien to economics. Further, the governing rule in industry should be that something is good only if it pays. Otherwise, it is alien and not permitted" (p. 48). Levitt looks on businesspeople who are concerned with social responsibility as dangerous. Socially oriented activity contaminates the aim and diverts attention from profit making and stock enhancement, business' ultimate and purest purpose.

Examples of business operating in ways divorced from the social have become commonplace.[1] Reeves-Ellington attended a meeting not long ago that was scheduled for Passover and Good Friday. When an invitee pointed this out to the account manger, he responded that business comes first. For another meeting, in a top five worldwide company, the organizer told prospective attendees, "The conference will start on Monday so people will not lose work time traveling." When someone asked about lost personal time, the organizer looked puzzled. After all, he responded, "Business takes priority."

This separate ethic of work and its effects have been thoroughly institutionalized under business organizations and professions. Intrusions from the wider society have become highly politicized issues. Tom Mahon comments on this separation: "We are the first generation to experience the full effects of the three-centuries-old decoupling of the physical landscape (as understood by science, manipulated by technology, and capitalized on by business) from the moral landscape (as taught by our religious institutions)" (January 7, 1996, p. A24). Pattee observes, "It is little wonder we are witnessing a global moral meltdown. The industrial revolution is dying with the severance of man from nature and spirit into a dismemberment more global and severe than at any period known to history" (1989, p. 151).

People working dissociated from their moral community and its traditions experience fears, anxieties (Heinze, 1991, p. 207), isolation and powerlessness, and limited access to information and energy beyond themselves (Klimo, 1988, p. 207). There has been a lack of cultural support for these new situations. It is not surprising that the pure-business paradigm draws negative reactions to business, equivalent to those accorded a loan shark or a tax-evasion schemer. The hostility toward business has constituted an ethics crisis. Increasingly, although they continue to consume the products and services, many of the public view all business, large or small, as occupying a profane moral status.

Heinze (1988) has called for a more holistic integration of the profane tasks of earning a living and people's cultural heritage of the spirit, which they view as sacred. Business could become more moral by being less focused on the purity of its economic drivers and the authority of its inward-looking social knowledge. Giving practitioners the support to be socially responsible as people could expand the morality of business as it becomes compromised with wider social entanglements. If social issues become an integral part of the considerations and advantages of commerce, socially responsible relationships can be realized even under the heavy pressure of globalizing, competitive systems.

TABLE 5. Operating Paradigms in Business and Commerce Organizations

Business	Commerce
"Pure"	Complicated and compromised
Amoral	Morally charged
Task completion—product	Ongoing social interaction—process
Efficiency in profit making	Relationship effectiveness
Well-defined boundaries	Diffuse boundaries

Kinds of Leaders and Their Organizational Contexts

A less-pure view of organizations in commerce bears directly on leadership for social responsibility. Leadership has been the traditional site of responsibility for the business-driven organizations. Stogdill (1974) underscores this as follows:

> It is by virtue of participating in group activities and demonstrating a capacity for expediting the work of the group that a person becomes endowed with leadership status. Leadership implies activity, movement, getting work done. The leader . . . occupies a position of responsibility in coordinating the activities of members of the group in their task of gaining a common goal. (p. 63)

Sinha (1955) concurs:

> The leader [has] a strong drive for responsibility and task completion, vigor and persistence in pursuit of goals, venturesomeness and originality in problem solving, . . . initiative, self-confidence and sense of personal identity, willingness to accept consequences of decision and action . . . absorb interpersonal stress . . . tolerate frustration and delay, [and to] . . . structure social interaction systems to the purpose at hand. (p. 17).

In this chapter, we will distinguish three kinds of leaders and their relationship to social responsibility. First, the role of manager is designed for success in task management; this leader's focus on people is primarily instrumental. Social exchange beyond the direct task focus mainly facilitates smoother task completion. There are two other kinds of leaders who have a wider social scope, and both can be regarded as inspirational specialists. These are transformational and transactional leaders (Bass, 1985; Bass and Avolio, 1994). But, when these inspirational types try to lead an organization toward the pure-business ideal, they do not substantially improve that organization's social responsibility. This is because they lack the outward-shifting view necessary to achieve wider social integration. Social responsibility in business requires the entry of a particular kind of transformational leader. This other type of specialist must be allowed to change the nature of the organization for an integration that spans beyond organizational borders. The shaman as healer is the best metaphor for this inspirational model.

Shaman-healers have not been traditional figures in modern business organizations, no matter how socially oriented they claim to be. In periods of stability and reasonable cultural alignment between an organization and the wider society, managerial and transactional leadership usually suffice for public satisfaction with business responsibility. There is little or no need for the metaphor of the shaman. As an ambiguous role, it is marginalized, if not driven entirely out of the organization. Until the past two decades, such stability characterized most large American businesses, and manufacturing was the model for the stable, efficient, large-scale ideal.

However, in the more recent years of globalization, change, and uncertainty, the institutional cultural logic and social knowledge have been challenged, even in the largest organizations. People need an inspirational specialist to help them reorient themselves. There is often a loss of trust in the more traditional business leaders and managers and their institutions. People need the skills of someone who can envision altered states of reality during stressful times of change.

Two close, yet contrasting, figures among late modern business leaders illustrate these differences well. John Sculley, the Pepsi warrior and bringer of order to Apple Computers in the mid-1980s, was a typical transactional leader with managerial roots. Until the late 1970s, it had been only the startup businesses in America that required more risky, shamanistic visions. Steve Jobs, in his earliest role as a cofounder of Apple, is an exemplar of the other type, the compromised, outward-looking, commercial shaman.

A popular belief is that change leading to improved social responsibility must always occur at the center of an organization's power structure. But, in contexts of rapid change, the leadership for wider integration, and with it opportunities for responsible social relations, take place at the margins, at some distance from the organizational center. Steve Jobs's early work at the margins of the computer industry illustrates how this transforming leadership works. His effectiveness at Apple remained only while he stayed marginal to both the larger industry and the central business operations of his own company. In Jobs's case, the core against which he consciously foregrounded his cultural vision was represented by big business as embodied in the computer giant IBM. Shamans similarly reside at the margins of existing belief and normative behavior, as the incarnation of wider societal norms and values orientations. From this position, Jobs gained the capacity to translate wider social knowledge in novel ways. But, particularly in large and highly rationalized organizations, the shaman must remain marginal; only at this juncture can the healing bond with society be effected.

To realize the creative urge for organizational transformation and move from a business-driven to a commercial organization, one that exists in dialogue with wider social knowledge, requires complementary roles of leadership. This was the kind of relationship assumed initially, sub rosa between Jobs and Sculley, when the corporate visionary first brought the Pepsi executive into Apple. Leaders can achieve and sustain this complementarity by focusing on what each type does, not relying on the superficial artifacts of their roles. The differences between these artifacts and the social knowledge and cultural knowledge underlying them are often subtle.

The complementary leader types must converse with each other at the social knowledge level. With Jobs and Sculley, this conversation did not continue as a dialogue once Sculley entered Apple. Sculley moved Jobs into a role resembling his own—a managerially oriented, transactional leader. The two then became competitors for a redundant niche within the organizational ecology. Business-driven leaders and their social visionary counterparts must translate one another's metaphors for a more socially integrated commercial organization. Each must be able to see this integration in his or her own terms.

A Tale of Two Apples

Apple Computer, Incorporated, founded by Steven Jobs and Steven Wozniak, had been a marriage of the technical and social climate of the mid-1970s (Garsten, 1994, p. 2). Umberto Eco captures the initial Apple spirit by metaphorically describing the company as "Catholic, with 'sumptuous icons' and the promise of offering everybody the chance to reach the Kingdom of Heaven by following a series of easy steps" (Marshall, 1997, p. 145). A computer prototype, designed in Jobs's bedroom and built in his garage, led to the sale of 25 machines to a local electronics shop. This led to the creation of Apple, named by Jobs and based on a happy summer spent in Oregon apple orchards (Halliday, 1993, p. 205). The first real computer, the Apple I, was marketed in 1976. Apple II soon followed and revolutionized the computer industry. During this time, Jobs brought needed technical personnel into the company. It was these people who helped Apple obtain adequate financing (D. Valentine and M. Markkula) and improved marketing (R. McKenna and N Bushnell). All of this was accomplished by the end of 1977 (Halliday, 1983, p. 206). Until 1981, sales skyrocketed. Then came two failures: Apple III and Lisa.

It was the Macintosh, launched in 1984 by an Apple with a less certain future, that really revolutionized the personal computer market. Both the machine and its introduction were unique. The print ads suggested that the Macintosh was the computer "for the rest of us" (Scott, 1991, p. 71). The rest of us were inclusively self-defined by themselves, with Jobs as visionary[2,3] leading the way. The artifacts, resonating with the American counterculture of the 1970s, playfully identified this contingent as outlaws and revolutionaries. The Macintosh building in Cupertino, California, flew the pirate flag as an apt symbol for the entire operation.

In 1984, John Sculley arrived as CEO and president of Apple. In the beginning, both Jobs and Sculley had belonged to a mutual admiration society, but soon the more socially oriented, eccentric, and rebellious Jobs was in conflict with the more traditionally charismatic, "modern generation" ex-Pepsi executive. Sculley wanted to control costs, reduce overhead, rationalize product lines, and, finally, generally to instill discipline (Gelman and Rogers, 1985, p. 46) Ultimately, Jobs was exiled. By late 1985, he had resigned from Apple and started NeXt, a new computer company.

From that time, Apple has been in a constant decline, launching unsuccessful products and generally losing profitability and market share. In 1996, Jobs was invited back to Apple through the purchase of NeXt.

During an interview with Terry Gross on Public Radio (February 23, 1996, WSKG), Steve Jobs clearly expressed the idea of the wider social integration of business in his comments about Apple during his tenure there as CEO. Jobs claimed that the business operated on the promise that Apple's duty was to provide customer services that people wanted, not that Apple wanted. He said that people at Apple did not work on a hierarchy of knowledge but rather on equality of knowledge. They hired people or invited people with knowledge into the company to tell them what to do. His job was to create an environment in which people could work and feel good about themselves. In other words, Jobs tried to integrate Apple into the lives of the company's customers and employees.

As Jobs learned, running or working in an emerging, integrative company has both organizational risks and personal risks for the visionary leader.[4] When people live in a business-paradigm organizational environment and attempt to create a commercial paradigm, integrate it, and live it, there is personal risk for all the members. However, many, like Jobs, believe the risk is worthwhile. Table 5 provides the interpretive contrasts necessary for understanding why there is such risk.

To make an interpretive change, morally responsible leaders must make a similar transformation. They must move from business-dominated assumptions to commerce-dominated ones.

John Sculley tells a very different story in his book, *Odyssey. Pepsi to Apple* (1987). Sculley's version clearly reflects Jobs's ideas of a commercial organization, but his account, and his actions in the Apple of the mid-1980s, show subtle cultural differences between the two Apples. Sculley clearly shows his mastery of the vocabulary and artifacts of business change when he says:

> Third-wave companies are the emerging form, not only for high-tech companies, but for all institutions. Simply put, the source of their strength lies in *change*—in the ability to transform their products and organization in response to changes in the economy, in social habits, in customer interests. By contrast, the source of strength in industrial-age companies is *stability*. Everything about them is geared to establishing stability—including their emphasis on title and rank rather than on making a difference, on structure over flexibility, on putting the institutions needs before the individual's. (pp. 92–93)

As a good manager (cf. Clegg, 1989; Jackall, 1988), Sculley has scanned the environment and clearly identified the direction individual commercial organizations are moving. However, the listener hears a different message from Jobs's transformation when Sculley delivers it. Jobs wanted to create change and expand information access to a broad range of people. Sculley's success had been in the control of markets for a stabilizing, modern company. Jobs inspired and transformed. Sculley managed and aligned. The difference strongly influenced the resulting organization, its concepts of personal involvement, its concept of power, and its usage. In the remainder of this chapter, the differing views of Apple of Ste-

ven Jobs and John Sculley serve time and again to demonstrate the alternate realities of Apple and its leadership during those early and middle years.

Managers and Those Who Inspire

Management researchers understand that management is task and resource oriented, and that leadership is people and society oriented. Both roles can work
within business-focused and commerce-focused contexts. The roles of managers
and inspirational leaders also contrast sharply within business-focused and commerce-focused organizations. Their actions of visioning and vision implementing
have differing effects on organization structures and outcomes.

Within either a business or a commerce-oriented organization, managers and
inspirational specialists both play a role. Their effects depend on the extent to
which business practices or, alternately, commercial activities of the organizational
culture are paramount. The context, its influence on the organization and leaders'
desire for change, and what type of change they desire further define the type of
inspirational specialists that will help the organization most.

Managers in Business-Focused Operations

We begin with manager definitions as they are the backbone of business-focused
organizations. *Webster's* (McKechnie, 1983, p. 1094) states that manager (in the
original) is one who can "train a horse in his pace, make docile in order to control;
one who conducts affairs with economy and frugality—good economist." The
major traditional skill set required for managers is controlling and directing others.
There is another dimension to managerial activities: "management is concerned
with goals and objectives; getting things done, in efficiency" (McKechnie, 1983, p.
1094). To the skills of controlling and directing, a manager must add efficient task
management. Wesson (1964, p. 403) agrees when he says, "Management denotes
the process of formulating and executing business or industrial policy through the
functional activities of planning, organizing, directing, coordinating, and controlling." Managers are above all rational and efficient, and their purpose is to produce
stable predictable controlled results.

Inspirational specialists, by contrast, are leaders who deal with organizational transformation and change effectiveness. This contrast reveals the underlying priorities of business-driven management—*that the tasks of business are immutable but culture is not*. From a management point of view, culture must "answer" to the aims of business. The reason given for "downsizing," "rightsizing," or "firing," for example, is to assure the successful completion of the business task—sufficient profits and other desirable business outcomes. All other managerial tasks revolve around the increased productivity (efficiency) of human and material resources (Drucker, 1955, p. 12).

John Sculley's assumption of the position of CEO at Apple Computers, driving Jobs and, ultimately, Wozniak out of the company, demonstrates a managerial focus. As reported by Garsten (1994, p. 9), these events marked a turning point in the organization. More business-related goals were added to its vision. There was a major transformation from an entrepreneurial phase to one of increasing bureaucratization and structure. The company was reorganized from an open learning environment to one of functional structure. In particular, a major downsizing effort, causing a loss of jobs for 25% of the Apple workforce, was done to improve the bottom line—which occurred. (Garsten, 1994, p. 11; Sculley, 1987, pp. 264–265).[5] Business managers and economists tell employees to become accustomed to frequent changes of jobs, not having ever-rising levels of income and previous levels of retirement benefits. With the assumption of Sculley to power, Apple employees learned this lesson (Garsten, 1994, p. 20).

Managers have roles to play in both business-focused and commerce-focused organizations. They are responsible for the success of the business-economic aspects of commerce. Managerial responsibilities are primarily task oriented. They define the business objectives, recommend resource needs (human and material), and must produce agreed economic results.

Managers in Commerce

Within the commercial organization, managers have an added responsibility: they must use organizational systems and knowledge in ways beneficial to those working in the organization. They effect personnel organizational change and integration. They actively design new work processes and participate in their validation.

Managing change *processes*, not just producing change for new stability, entails additional risk; so, their success depends on sufficient trust being established between them and their subordinates and coworkers (Reeves-Ellington, 1995b, p. 251). They build trust in the organization by assuring total organizational focus on agreed objectives, establishing clear loyalties that run in both directions, and having well-executed coordination (Reeves-Ellington, 1995b, p. 253). To operate in this context, managers need knowledge obtained from scientific methods. This knowledge is produced to assure maximum certainty, is considered necessary and sufficient for success, and therefore is superior to other forms of knowledge.

Inspirational Specialists

Inspirational specialists (Humphrey, 1997, p. 194) have been separated in the literature into two subtypes, transformational leaders and transactional leaders (Bass, 1985; Bass and Avolio, 1994). Inspiration is "concerned with vision, integrity, values, states of mind, energy, sense of community, acknowledgment" (McKechnie, 1983, pp. 1030, 1667). Contrary to managerial *efficiency*, these specialists relate to *effectiveness* (Kanungo and Mendonca, 1996; Sinha, 1990; Yukl, 1989).

Transactional Leadership

Transactional leadership is based on negotiations that are controlled by the leader. The negotiations are based on the personal agenda of the transactional leader (Bass and Avolio, 1994, pp. 12, 13). Transformational leaders, on the other hand, attract greater self-definition by having their own strongly internalized values and ideals. They are able and willing to forgo personal payoffs and, when necessary, to risk loss of respect and affection to pursue actions they are convinced are right. These leaders have a sense of self-worth that is self-determined, not in a self-serving way, but in a manner that allows them to make tough, unpopular decisions. They exhibit a strong sense of inner purpose and direction (Bass and Avolio, 1994, p. 18).

The traditional business literature makes little distinction between the kinds of leadership and management, we are suggesting. When such a distinction is made, it is not long maintained. Mintzberg (1973, 1979) believes all the roles, characteristics, and descriptions of business leaders are constructed on being first a manager, then a leader. Jackall's (1988) findings in American manufacturing companies support this view.

Kanungo and Mendonca illustrate this confusion: "Leaders are expected to provide direction, exercise control and generally execute such functions that are necessary to achieve the organization's objectives" (1996, p. 2). Rightsizing, flattening, hollowing out and use of devices such as market-focused divisions (Fatsis, 1992, 1993; Xerox Corporation, 1993) reflect an American management and leadership readiness to develop and implement visions that shed and change people and organization culture as necessary to increase penetration and control (see also Robbins, 1983, pp. 316–317). From Garsten's (1994) analysis of Sculley's activities at Apple, these descriptors very well describe him. The task before him was one of organizational change—a task that required the transformation of Apple—for this, the managerial role was insufficient, and a transformational leader was required. It was a task in which John Sculley failed, as measured by traditional business measures.

Transformational Leaders

Traditional roles of transformational leaders include being sense makers, whole makers, moral architects, value definers, stewards, servants, guides, optimists, and warriors (Campbell, 1973). They are more spiritually, as opposed to materially, oriented. They may be either charismatic (direct divine inspiration) or learner-teacher (conduits of the divine). Inspirational specialists either have followers (attendants or adherents), who take the inspirational specialists' guiding doctrines, opinions, or examples, or they may have disciples (pupils and adherents) (McKechnie, 1983, p. 1030).

Inspirational specialists, whether transformational or transactional, may take on four different kinds of role characteristics: (1) effectiveness, to have an effect and produce results; (2) transactional, to perform, complete, negotiate, manage; (3) transformational, to change an outward appearance, change the personality or character of someone's or something's rules of conduct (cf. Kanungo and Mendonca, 1996); and (4) self-empowering, to provide systems and processes through which organizational or societal members participate in defining a new vision of the social milieu. The first two characteristics are usually considered those of the transactional leader—the manager metaphor controls. Transactional leaders work within a framework of exchange, most often through paying followers for delivering a leader-developed mission (Bass, 1985). Characteristics 3 and 4 are usually considered those of the transformational leader—the shaman metaphor controls. The transformational leader works to integrate all associated with an organization in tasks and missions all agree to be important.

At the Center or the Periphery

The diverse orientations of inspirational specialists require them to inhabit different locations in the power structures of organizations and societies. All of them must work in relationship to a hierarchy because none is inherently antihierarchical. However, each operates under a different sense of hierarchy. Leaders working as managers need control, so they operate from an organizational center at the top of a hierarchy. As we discuss below, this is where the formal modes of organization power usually reside. Leaders, working within a managerial paradigm, believe the most important hierarchy is the business-focused organization in which they operate. Transformational leaders may think of hierarchy in terms of a wider society. They work from the margins of their self-defined organization and societies. These margins are where different forms of organization tangentially touch one another.[6]

Transactional leaders, through occupying positions of power, are necessarily central to the business organization. They may occupy an official model or "icon" position to emulate and have power, prestige, and authority. From this position, charismatic leaders provide a motivating context and focus on the business at hand, generating profits, consolidating a centralizing hierarchy, and protecting the organization from intrusion from the external environment. Traditionally, this role in Western business organizations, as elsewhere (Thomas and Humphrey, 1994, p. 21), embodies the normative cultural values of the social region. In periods of stability and reasonable alignment between organizations and society, there is little or no challenge to the transactional "icon" leader. Transformational-type leaders embodying the ambiguous shamanistic metaphor are marginalized, if not driven entirely out of the organization.

In a commercial context, shamans occupy themselves with options and opportunities; they interact with and focus on the integration of their company into a wider social environment. They therefore must mediate and interpret between systemic levels. They often must resist, avoid, work out, or reinterpret mandates and limitations imposed by governing and outlying business and social systems. If imposed constraints cannot be avoided, successful commercial shamans creatively open the organization to reinterpret its dissonances with the larger systems in which they operate. Once open to these dissonances, which are usually expressed as ambiguity, the shaman, as a commercial actor, offers interpretations by which other organization members can integrate the ambiguity while they maintain their drive toward the business objectives.

Transactional Leaders and Business-Focused Organizations

The transactional business-focused leader, then, is responsible for making an organization vision and gaining others' alignment to it. To do this, transactional leaders use charisma to develop followers, define organizational values, generate optimism, and gain others' alignment to desired outcomes. Such leaders change people's attitudes within the organization through the dissemination of their own visions.

In this context, Sinha says the business leader's responsibility is to establish a vision that "touches the very core of the followers' thoughts, feelings, and aspirations. The leader should communicate it in a manner that followers perceive to be genuinely natural" (1995, p. 41). Pfeffer (1981) and Smith and Peterson (1988) state the problematic slightly differently: leaders create shared meanings.[7]

The vision is the basic tool of ideation that transactional leaders control to create a sense of the organization's structure and boundaries. Within this context, leaders set visions and goals in terms of strategic visioning (House, Spangler, and Woycke, 1991). They focus on setting group goals and moving the group toward these goals by providing meaning to organizational ideologies and values. Transactional visionaries strive to achieve change by establishing their view of order within the organization—one that will replace the old. In this context, they also can become transformational leaders. For business-oriented leaders, the primary mission and goal are to mediate internal alignment for maximum uniformity and protect the organization from the external environmental pressures. The transactional leader appropriates charismatic power and uses it from the center of the organization (Thomas and Humphrey, 1994, p. 4). Bass (1985, p. 23) implies that the goal of transactional leaders is to get followers to reassess their values and visions. Transactional leaders must transform followers' goals and values in ways that will align them with the leader; they transmit their knowledge through and to an organizational elite (Hugh-Jones, 1994, p. 32).

The measurements of success for the business transactional leader are the same ones that appeal to business managers according to Yukl (1989, p. 6):

> The most commonly used measure of leader effectiveness is the extent to which the leader's group or organization performs its task successfully and attains its goals. . . . Objective measures of performance or goal attainment are available such as profit growth, profit margin, sales increases, market share, sales relative to targeted sales, return on investment, productivity, cost per unit output, costs in relation to budgeted expenditures and so on.

Sinha (1995, p. 33) would measure a leader's effectiveness as depending "on the extent to which the demands are met and the subordinates are motivated to realize shared goals." What transactional leaders are really interested in is organizational business *efficiency*. The transformational leader centers concerns on a social and business mixture—on *effectiveness* of an organization. The confusion of the use of efficiency and effectiveness when discussing management and leadership further blurs differences between business management and leadership (Sinha, 1995, p. 33).

Managers and transactional leaders are essential to meet the business goals of commercial organizations, but to be socially responsible, these organizations must also integrate with the wider societies in which they operate. In a paradigm of commerce, business aspects are subordinate to the social and are only gainfully and constructively exploited after social integration has begun. The commercial organization must understand and then integrate into the larger social whole while meeting its internal business goals. Such integration requires knowledge that is both scientific *and* artistic,[8] for art has an effect in reorganizing one's world and, therefore, deserves equal status to scientific knowledge (Goodman, 1978, pp. 102–106).

While managers' and transactional leaders' roles remain relatively constant across business-focused and commerce-focused organizations, the roles of spiritual specialists in commerce-driven organizations tend to diverge. A need for managerial and transactional skills remains necessary, but another inspirational specialist type—the learner-teacher (conduit for the divine), who is a sense maker of the whole, servant, and guide—is necessary for commerce. This is a transformational leader. This specialist has disciples who learn and not followers who obey. Two primary outcomes desired by learner-teachers are self-empowerment and self-healing, as well as democratic and flat work and personal relations (Hugh-Jones, 1994, p. 33). The transformational leader uses a shaman metaphor. Steve Jobs played this role in the early days of Apple. As reported by Sculley, "There was no sense of boundaries or barriers. I was amazed how open an environment it was. A picture on one wall showed the Mac team sitting lotus style on the floor, enraptured by a lecturing Steve Jobs, their leader" (Sculley, 1987, p. 86).

Transformational Leaders: Why Shamanism Is a Good Metaphor

The shamanistic metaphor functions as a guide to transformational leaders[9] (Hamayon, 1994, p. 75). Shamanism, by practicing self-empowerment and healing, is an appropriate inspirational specialist model for commerce-driven organizations. It is healing that humans need to reconcile the methods by which they earn their living and the social environment that they inhabit. Shamanism is "Humankind's earliest and longest-lasting healing, psychotherapeutic, and spiritual tradition" (Walsh, 1994, p. 7). While shamans have a keen awareness of differences and peculiarities (Krippner, 1988, p. 306), they alter the Cartesian paradigm of dichotomous thinking by drawing a sense of relatedness and continuums (Klimo, 1988, p. 396). They must satisfy the need of abolishing polarities (Eliade, 1964, p. 352). Harmon provides specific context in his discussion of social responsibility, agency, individualism, and organization under his section, "Avoidance of Individual Accountability as a 'Rational' Consequence of Social Responsibility." He says:

> The paradoxes of agency are produced by the splitting off of . . . the responsible self—that of maker, one who is responsible for the authorship of his

or her actions—from the second image of answered—one who is accountable to other members of a moral community. Because agency for and accountability to are complementary, the denial or neglect of one inevitably leads to the atrophy of the other . . . when agency is construed chiefly as entitlement, the atrophy or individual agency, or under-responsibility, predictably follows. (1995, p. 156)

Shaman agency is responsible *to* their communities *for* making the sacred available and thereby helping their community to discover shared belief and value systems. This role is crucial because shared belief and value systems are a vital part of effective relationships (Frank, 1985, p. 7; Walsh, 1994, p. 17). Shamans help commercial organizations recover their souls, according to Krippner (1988, p. 306), a compelling metaphor for understanding how the role works in an organization. The shaman is responsible for integrating the sacred (values and ethics) with the profane (the mundane) (Winkelman, 1992, p. 25). Again, Sculley reports this integration of the sacred and profane that Jobs attempted when trying to get Sculley to join Apple. He found the challenge to join Apple and the vision of changing the world to be a compelling call (Sculley, 1987, p. 9). They are transformational leaders who live out of fantasy and imagination, have an indulgence in humor, and have more profound philosophical interpretations than leaders. The shaman is a traditional cultural-driven model.

Determination of the acceptability of "shaman as empowered and healer" requires an in-depth look at shamanistic definitions, mission, personal attributes, activities, roles, and outcomes. Walsh describes shamanism as "a family of traditions whose practitioners focus on voluntarily entering altered states of consciousness in which they experience themselves or their spirit traveling to other realms at will and interacting with the entities to serve their community" (1994, p. 9). Eliade finds that the core of shamanism is "in interaction with the spirit world on behalf of the community, particularly in healing and protection" (1964, p. 5). "Shamans can be defined as men and women who deliberately alter their consciousness to obtain power and knowledge that can be used to help and heal members of their community" (Krippner, 1988, p. 294).

Steve Jobs's early days as a student and traveler reflect the shaman's altered consciousness and spiritual travel to other realms as a means to further social integration and responsibility of himself and those around him. His choice of Reed

College in Portland, Oregon, reflects his preoccupation with alternative lifestyles and religions, personal pursuits, inner voyages of discovery, and self-fulfillment (Young, 1988, pp. 51–53). His travels took him to India in a search for enlightenment. There and after his return, he turned to Zen for its emphasis on experience, intuition, and spontaneity. Elements of his involvement with Zen would later put an imprint on Apple and its employees (Young, 1988, p. 72).

Shamans achieve their mission of integration through catharsis from "disease" to wellness. "Being a shaman is not based on a diseased state but rather bein healed from disease" (Ackerknect, 1943, p. 46). In fact, shamanistic disturbances have been described as a positive disintegration, regenerative process, renewl and creative illness (Perry, 1986). As mediators, shamans work between the spiritual and human worlds. They suspend normative rules of social order, and they screen their encounters with the omnipotent spiritual world. On one hand, shamans protect the spiritual world from being polluted by human weaknesses and ignorance; on the other hand, they channel spiritual energy in a useful way so that it does not overtax the capacity of their contemporaries. Shamans' modes of mediation have included vision quests, impersonal power, and moral status (Winkelman, 1992, p. 31).

In their ambiguous roles, shamans actively empathize with both genders to heal individuals, families, and societies through actions as counselor, healer, prophet, spiritual guide, and more (Jeter, 1989, p. 318). The shaman's compassion for both sexes and harmony with all life is the basis of wisdom sought to provide insight to one's self, family, and community (Jeter, 1989, p. 319). "Shamans give this information to reduce stress and ameliorate the living conditions of members of their social group" (Krippner, 1988, p. 294). Shamans' healing arts and power are to synthesize a comprehensive world view. This is the root of human cultural processes that mediate spiritual, cosmic, and material forces.

Successful shamans learn theory, become mythologists, and are world-wise within the contexts in which they work. Shamans must learn the terrain of this multilayered, interconnected universe in which they will quest for knowledge and power for their community (Walsh, 1994, p. 16). They create altered terrain for those disciples who want to learn. Responsibility starts individually, with individual agents, and expands to the wider societal/communal context. Unlike charismatic leaders, shamans are not missionaries working with divine inspiration. They are not trying to save people and organizations that do not recognize their need to be saved. Rather, shamans are visionaries who transfix those capable of seeing a part of a holistic vision and are open to being healed (Pattee, 1989, p. 152).

Their clients gain the power to transmute elemental forces into spiritual dimensions directed toward self-healing and integration (Pattee, 1989, p. 137). The purpose of shamanistic creativity might be said to follow Sufi advice: "If you hear hoof beats, expect to see horses, but watch out for zebras" (Le Vie, 1988, p. 16).

When shamans support commercial activities, they attempt to identify and develop a unifying whole with the external environment. Their mission is that of world making. They must move beyond lateral, verbal, or mathematical denotations to take a holistic concern with the structure of several symbol systems: sciences, philosophy, arts, perception, and everyday discourse (Overling, 1990, p. 603). Shamans discern several constructs of their visions—those demonstrating unity and others demonstrating differences. Success in world making requires commercial shamans to increase their clients' (often charismatic leaders') ability to learn the external world for application in the organizational one.

Within this context, shamanism becomes a metaphor for spiritual possession (freely accepted and given) of self and others. The language expressing this ability is that of creation. As a creative human being, the shaman experiences empathy with all sentience and thus can enter into the spirit of other sentient beings. In this way, shamans and clients contribute to the maintenance and regeneration of human culture. Pattee (1989, p. 138) describes shamanistic creativity as "power to manifest spiritual directives close to the source for the benefit of sentient beings and their greater purpose." This creativity also transforms emotions, from fear and anger to love, joy, and compassion—all of which play a role in shamanistic healing practices (Walsh, 1990, pp. 153–154).

Shamans also must create the ability in leaders to share in the making and remaking of prospective worlds. The prospective worlds under consideration are international. They involve chosen ways that are considered socially acceptable and responsible to the commercial organization and to the society in which it is situated. Reeves-Ellington (1995a, 1995b) has described how one organization shaman developed methods that permitted a wide constituency to develop socially acceptable commercial practices. These were based on community shared values and ethics. The shaman attempted to integrate the sacred and the profane—to act as

healer between business and society. In commercial organizations, the most frequently used role and method for accomplishing shamanism is that of action research or action inquiry. The action researcher as described by Reeves-Ellington
(1995b, p. 251) acts as a type of transformational leader using the shamanistic
metaphor.

However, the prototype of creation is that of the shaman and not the leader.
Clearly, when the same word *leader* is applied to the different personalities, confusion results. If both roles have identical tasks in an organization, there is conflict,
for they work from entirely different viewpoints and assumptions. However, if they
can be viewed as complementary functions in a commerce-focused organization,
the dichotomy becomes unimportant, and their relationship becomes synergistic.
Again, Apple well illustrates the point. Sculley occupied the center of both the organization and the industry culture. He behaved in ways to ensure continuity of the
business, not people. Sculley constantly affected organizational change that moved
Apple away from integration with its original customer base to closer alignment
with pure-business outcomes. He accomplished this through the traditional business leader's transactional activities of status and power. In the beginning, however, both Jobs and Wozniak had worked as marginal outsiders. They came from a
hackers' club, worked with marginal technology and concepts, and felt more
closely related to civil society than to the formal institutions of industry. Even the
Macintosh was created on the margins of Apple, which was, in turn, still on the
margins of the computer industry. In case the point might be missed, the Mac research building flew a pirate flag (Garsten, 1994, pp. 2–10).

Early in his career, Jobs, inspirational specialist, wrote in *People's Computer
Company* (Levy, 1984, p. 172): "Computers are mostly used against people instead of for people, used to control people instead of to *free* them. Time to change
all that—we need a people's computer company" (italics added). When a special
team was assembled to create the Mac, "Jobs took pains to give his team the feeling that they were really making a difference, and that their new product would
significantly alter the way people related to technology" (Garsten, 1994, p. 9). The
members of the Mac team had a Ping-Pong table, video arcade games, a high-tech
stereo system, a Bosendorfer piano, and massage when needed. Sculley comments,
"Steve called them artists, not engineers. There was so much passion in their eyes"
(Sculley, 1987, p. 158). In Sculley's eyes as a transactional leader, passions are

also valued, but here they had been created under a transformational paradigm. Both paradigms use the same words but inspire in totally different ways. Transactional leaders must first create their vision and then "see" it, then communicate and impose their visions on organizational structure and form through the process of alignment. Transformational leaders require an ability to envision alternate states of consciousness. They need to "live" in alternate potential realities. Shamans first "see," then create, and finally communicate alternate possibilities in which their organizations can work. It is up to others to adopt them or not.

The Metaphors of Leadership

Table 6 reflects the personal metaphors for managers, leaders, and shamans. Western managers and transactional leaders have much in common. They think in dichotomies of choice—either I am a businessperson or a do-gooder, I earn money or I give it away. The transformational leader, on the other hand, feels comfortable with Harmon's (1995) ideas of integration of communal and individual responsibility to cause socially responsible actions. The manager and transactional leader are comfortable in social spaces that call for social distance. This is expressed in terms of boss/subordinate, whereas the relationships between transformational leaders and managers are based on small to nonexistent social distances. In the first set, managers work *for* transactional leaders; in the second set, managers work *with* transformational leaders. When being task oriented, the manager consolidates, the transactional leader aligns others, and the trans-

TABLE 6. Personal Metaphors:
Manager, Transactional Leader, and Transformational Leader

	Manager	Transactional Leader	Transformational Leader
Thought	Dichotomous	Dichotomous	Holistic
Role	Boss	Teacher	Learner
Relations	Subordinate	Follower	Disciple
Activities	Consolidator	Transformer	Creator
Methods	Controller	Aligner	Liberator
Focus	Task	Organization	Community

formational leader creates. When working with people, managers control, transactional leaders align, and transformational leaders liberate. Within the task and human interaction contexts, managers and transactional leaders are far more comfortable with structure and constancy, whereas the transformational leader prefers less structure and greater ambiguity. These differences rely on differing power and power use paradigms.

The Metaphors of Communication

As Weedon states:

> If language is the site where meaningful experience is constituted, then language also determines how we perceive possibilities of change. Further if experience is based in cultural contexts of cultural logic, prescriptive ethics and cultural artifacts, language is at least partially shaped by these. (1987, pp. 86–87).

Business and commercial language communicate the attitudes, behaviors, and linguistic contexts of managers, transactional leaders, and transformational leaders. Different language offers different versions of meanings and their effects on the individual (Weedon, 1987, p. 86). Communication includes all methods of delivering messages: orally with words, by body language, or by a form of media.

Business-focused language and communication as a discursive form focused on the author or speaker and directed toward others is used predominantly by managers and transactional leaders. It is the prevalent language of "pure" business-focused organizations. We are using "discursive" in the philosophical sense of moving from premises to conclusions in a series of logical steps. In other words, managers use the language of control and action. Transactional leaders similarly use a language of control and alignment. Action and alignment logically assume control through the manipulation of organizational premises. Business discourse is legislated by managers and transactional leaders. It excludes others from premise formation and thereby permits denigration and control of others in ways that assure self-gain for those controlling the discourse. Managers and transactional leaders using business discourse want to control it and legislate its meaning to others.

To them, discourse is a method of possessing power over everything with which it comes into contact. It is a possession of force over others. Business discourse is discourse of monologue as expressed by transactional leaders and disseminated by managers.

Commercial-focused organizations still rely on discursive language for communication of pure business, but require dialogue when dealing with social and societal issues. Through dialogue, transformational leaders use a language of inclusion and relationships. Here, we use dialogue in the sense of interchange and discussion of ideas that are open and frank and lead to understanding and harmony. Transformational leadership dialogue emphasizes celebrating inclusion and humor and is supportive of the group. The expected result of the dialogue is the creation of heroes. Table 7 presents the various communications metaphors.

Business Language

The sole language of business is discourse controlled by centralized narrative. Within the business context, discourse might be defined as the act of telling or communicating the results of a study or thought process in a logical and organized manner. Arguably, within business-focused organizations, leaders (Hobbesian legislators) control discourse centrally by grounding it in their personally inspired needs, as we saw above with John Sculley and his discourse to others in Apple about his personal mission for Apple. Managers and transactional leaders engage in organizational discourse in order to maintain focus, direction, and outcomes of business activities.

Business language is designed for purely business matters. It is the language

TABLE 7. Communications Metaphors

	Managers and Transactional Leaders: Discourse	Transformational Leaders: Dialogue
Reasoning	Calculating	Rapture
Process	Excluding	Integrating
Methods	Controlling	Liberating
Results	Vilification	Celebration

to create static situations, not change. Its architects are managers and leaders. Business language is structured for discourse on efficiency of delivering profits, sales, and other key business measures. It is designed to drive out ambiguity. As a manager[10] of one of the authors once offered as advice: "There are only three reasons for communicating in this company: to inform management, to recommend to management, or to ask management for help on an issue of interest to them. In communications, there should be only business facts and each communication will start with a position of why the communication will drive business forward." This keeps businesspeople focused on business and away from social responsibility issues that might deflect attention from profits.

Kanungo and Mendonca (1996, p. 2) support this point: "When morality [socially responsible actions] intrudes into the using organization, it has the potential of directing business leader from the organization's primary objectives, and as a result, causing it to be inefficient and to deprive stockholders of their due returns." The underlying assumption is that the two are at odds. Transactional leaders, managers, and followers use language to focus on achieving efficiency of business. As Sculley took over Apple, the language shifted from "a genuine passion to want to change the world" (Rose, 1989, p. 4) to "growing up," "more than technology," and "follow-through accountability" (Rose, 1989, p. 4). When Steve Jobs said, "a computer on every desk," it meant something different to people than when John Sculley said the same thing. From Sculley, it meant profits, sales, and volume increases. From Jobs, it meant inclusion and knowledge for all.

Transactional leaders' visionary language focuses aligning organizational members and then aligning outsiders to the leaders' goals for the organization. Within transactional leaders' activities and language, Sinha (1995) says that it identifies the transactional vision in language that touches the very core of the followers' thoughts, feelings, and aspirations. However, the formulation and articulation of the vision are those of the leader. This is discourse controlled by the leader, driven down the organization by managerial focus and logic. Management and leadership in today's enacted business environment both reinforce and rationalize, through the use of language, the marginalization of inputs from organizational extremities. Language describes power and its flow. It follows power flows as depicted in Figure 4. Each arrow in the three captions illustrate both power and language flow. Marginalization of outside influences and considerations protects business from the text of social responsibility. Business language, developed internally, provides a purely economic rationale for business actions. Both business language and business action free managers and leaders from what they see as the drag of interdependency and responsibility.

The exclusionary drive of business action language is shown in Leo Burnett's organization vision: "to create superior advertising." As reported in *Bulletpoint* for the informed leader: "Leaders imprint the organization with actions not words" (1996, p. 2). The language of the vision of the leaders' actions is all important, but the advertising that earns its income does not refer to words (written or otherwise). In fact, for the manager and transactional leader, words are only necessary to reflect directed and focused actions in directive ways. When discussing the imprint in more detail, as expressed through visions, one leader reports, "Visions that are action oriented, innovative and responsive to competition provide employees with the sense of purpose and direction they need in times of rapid personal change" (*Bulletpoint*, 1996). One wonders if the employees were asked about that.

When touting their publication, the editors boast that, "Our research and writing team is made up of current and former executives. Leaders writing for leaders, not journalist or others writing of the world at large." "Our aim is to improve the quality of management information for managers" (*Bulletpoint*, 1996, p. 1–2). In discussion about outside reading, a *Bulletpoint* editorial suggests that readers ignore authors from academia or consulting backgrounds because they "(1) have no real management experience to clutter ideas (2) suffer from spiritual zeal; and (3) publish their books globally" (1996, p. 5).

- Managers and leaders villainize those who interfere with their needs and desires—those who do not support the organization. Workers and outsiders villainize managers and leaders for not sharing benefits and rewards created by business. Or, returning to Apple, as Jobs was driven out of Apple, Sculley, through Apple, brought a lawsuit against Jobs. The suit claimed that Jobs had violated his fiduciary duty by scheming to lure away key Apple employees for a competing venture. It also claimed that Jobs was planning to use Apple's trade secrets in his product (Rose, 1989, p. 329). Both counts are a form of demonization of Jobs.

Today, business discourse prevents commercial dialogue in many parts of the world. Bill Gates's pressures on the U.S. Trade Department to stop U.S. trade with China in order to stop patent infringements against Microsoft is one example.

With its urge to control, based on legislative power, business thrusts its discourse into society. By doing so, it impoverishes social language and, eventually, social organization. People have no way to hold self-empowering dialogue. Two business language examples are "Our people are our most important resource," and "We empower our people." Such slogans are often found in human resources departments and signed by the CEO. "We" and "our" drive the words *empower* and *people*—yet another example of the creation of passivity, not agency.

Dialogue: The Language of Commerce

Discourse is the form of business language in commercially focused organizations, but it is an internal form. The external and interactional language of commerce occurs as dialogue (e.g., exchanges of ideas and thoughts). This reflects the traditional dialogue of society: healing and integration. However, both languages must be used—dialogue, to effect healing and integration of the organization with its wider environments, and discourse concerning business subjects to assure focus and direction. Understanding when to use discourse or dialogue requires knowing who is involved; this is the problem at hand for the shaman and action researcher.

Shamanism also takes place in transformational leaders' dialogue, in this context, dialogue between the internal commercial organization and its wider social environment. Shamanistic dialogue makes social processes more transparent; it expresses relationships between the sacred and profane so others can understand and use them as opportunities that their relationships can offer. In this way, shamanistic dialogue provides the language of helper and healer to those wanting to integrate. Although expressing empathy, the shaman does not take sides in this dialogue. Instead of confrontation, the shaman makes available healing powers to bridge differences or disharmony. The actual healing starts within the client organization and moves outward just as healing power starts with the shaman and moves toward the client. The power of clarifying and synthesizing is the power of the shaman. The power of outcomes is the prerogative of the client. The shaman, through dialogue, makes it possible for others to see things more transparently.

The mode of communication used by shamans, as creators of a state of interaction between the material and the spiritual, requires them to adopt an ecstatic role that permits them to inhabit altered states of consciousness and reality (Siikala, 1978, p. 28–29).[11]

Shamanistic language is that of wholeness, wellness, and integration. Shamanistic dialogue is the dialogue of androgyny. The outcome of transcending the pairs of opposites, it attains equilibrium among polarized forces in a relationship of dynamic tension, the unification of planes of beings, the intuitive and the rational, the visionary and the ordinary (Halifax, 1978, p. 28). The Apple logo provides a vivid example of an icon setting an entire organization's dialogue and discourse. It is a rainbow-colored apple with one bite gone. The shape of the apple holds a sensory attraction suggestive of excitement and temptation. The bite speaks to the urgent and eternal quest for knowledge. The colors of the rainbow point to the spectrum of varied but related people and ideas (Garsten, 1994).

Paradigms of Leadership Power

Power use is intrinsic to managers and inspirational specialists—no matter the type. However, how power is legitimized and how people use it varies substantially in the context of manager, leader, and shaman. Also, the location of power within an organization dictates its use: the organizational center wants to rationalize what exits; the margins want to change.

As depicted in Figure 4, managers use power entirely within the organization to resolve specific tasks and interact with colleagues for self-gain (Griffin, 1991; Jackall, 1988) The primary interaction, however, is with other managers. In this framework, power is messy and diffuse. Context drives power use, not centralized authority. The transactional leader, by contrast (Figure 5), assumes control of power and legislates downward and outward. While power use is focused primarily internal to the organization, the transactional leader uses power outwardly to influence the surrounding environment in ways that will enhance or protect the leader's organization. The political action committee (PAC) is a favorite tool of transactional leaders for gaining political influence in exchange for case and personal support.

As indicated in Figure 5, there are two lines of defense used, one at senior levels of influences (arguably with PACs, lobbies, and personal influence). The other imposes barriers oriented toward the bottom of the organizational hierarchy to prevent outside entry into the organization. In this context, power is central and logical. However, the locus of power for both managers and transactional leaders is centered inside the organization.

The shamanistic transformational leader (Figure 6) views power as diffuse, interactional, and at the points of contact between the organization's members and whatever outside contacts are necessary. As with managers, power is less unilaterally controlled and therefore messy, but in contrast to managers, shamanistic power is to be shared—a primary responsibility of the transformational leader. As reflected in Figure 6, shamanistic power intersects, interacts, and overlaps with power from other societal sources. Power is diffuse, shared, and shifting according to contexts in which it is used.

There are two significant foundations for each of the power sets described above: those of Hobbes and Machiavelli. Hobbes is responsible for Western mainstream power concepts of agency and the episodic notion of power. Power investigations seek precision and are cast in individualistic terms (Clegg, 1989, p. xvi).

Managers and transactional leaders, in their various Western corporate uses of power, practice "I win—you lose" propositions (Griffin, 1991, p. 1; Jackall, 1988).[12] John Sculley was uncomfortable with a competitive "vision" source in Apple and worked diligently to rid Apple of Jobs. As Rose reports (1989, p. 1):

Figure 4

Manager Power Strategies

Reinventing the corporation: That's what John Sculley had been doing these past few months. . . . Now with the man who'd lured him there [to Apple] expelled from the company, the time had come to talk . . . his own vision. Sculley's job was . . . to promote the idea that the company's vision . . . had not merely survived the messy and unpleasant departure of Steven Jobs . . . but had in fact been transmuted into this new and improved vision that he, John Sculley, would now articulate.

In his reading of Machiavellian management, Griffin advises that "Managers [and leaders] will always resist attempts to change their behavior and assumptions that reality is building kingdoms, controlling empires, playing politics, taking power plays, kicking someone out of the organization, and being number one" (1991, pp. 2–3). This is exactly what Sculley did to Jobs. Further, he saw that Apple had to change, not John Sculley. "As a package-goods guy, as the marketing man behind the 'Pepsi Generation' he knew . . . what he had to do to . . . make the leap from intangible benefit to intangible product" (Rose, 1989, p. 1).

Transactional leaders use organizational culture as a control over other organizational members and, by extension, to other organizations with which they come in contact (Gregory, 1983, p. 361; Wilkins and Ouchi, 1986, p. 464). By contrast,

Figure 5

Leader Power Flow

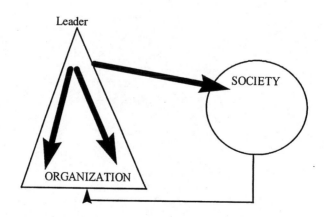

Figure 6

Shaman Power Strategies

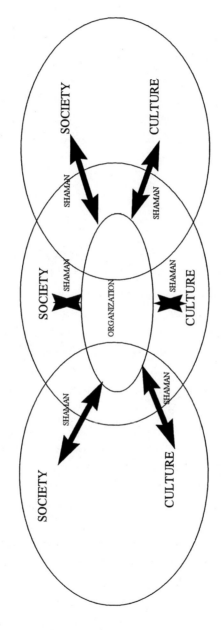

shamanistic power is channeled from society, social context, and knowledge, which is then transmitted to those seeking help and healing. In this sense, it reflects context rather than originating from one individual (Hamayon, 1994, p. 81; Winkelman, 1992, p. 9). Transformational leaders as shamans recognize that cultural knowledge provides reflected power; that is, power comes from others, through recognition of their specific expertise. To understand these differences requires that we revisit Machiavelli and Hobbes for their different contributions of sources and uses of modern power, Machiavelli for understanding strategic power and Hobbes for understanding reified power.

The Manager's Power Strategies

Within the modern business organization, there is a dialectic of power—that of the leader and that of the manager (Lukes, 1974). Managers are interested in what power does and how to use it strategically for self-gain (Clegg, 1989, p. 5; Griffin, 1991, pp. 3–10; Jackall, 1988, p. 8). Most managerial power causes a sense of push and pull; of desire, fear, or anger; of manipulation and control in those manifesting power with selfish motives. Like a manager's world, Machiavelli's world was dissonant and difficult to play, characterized by disunity within and strategic maneuvers made in contingent circumstances (Clegg, 1989, p. 22). Machiavelli wrote to interpret the strategies of power rather than to fix and serve power (1990, p. 55). This is exactly the environment of organizational managers who perceive themselves as powerless and marginal within their organizations. Strategic power becomes an important concept for these managers because they must interpret the extant games rather than legislating their own form. Machiavelli (quoted in Griffin, 1991, p. 13) says: "Men who are to [accomplish] any thing are first to learn which way it is to be done [to play power games] that they may afterwards be the more able [to put in into operation when the occasion arises]."

Managers without sovereign power must discover the rules of the game through systematically analyzed processes of experience[13] in order to find the gaps in structure and rules. For the manager, power is generated by relationships, and these are established in the context of work processes set within policy discourse.

The modern manager is always competing for a sovereign position—the main chance as Jackall (1988) puts it.

The ultimate purpose of this relational power, for a manager, is that it provides self-gain. Sinha's (1995, p. 212) advice clearly makes this point:

> A manager is open to . . . ideas and influence. But nevertheless, the manager must be ready to stoop low and fight back if his power base is being deliberately eroded. He would be justified in forming alliances, being aggressive, manipulative, and coercive to those who are openly challenging his power.

For the manager, then, there are two basic challenges: gaining control of the organization and then keeping it.

The first challenge requires a manager-strategist who applies interpretive skills to a world of movement (Wolin, 1960, p. 213). Managerial-run organizations provide individuals with opportunities for personal wealth and power. However, for the system to work, there must also be agencies of discipline (Law, 1986, p. 16). Transactional leaders, like Hobbes's sovereign, may achieve this by using power through legislation.

The Transactional Leader's Power

A transactional leader has become top "manager" by first using the manager's relational power strategies. Once managers become leaders, they attempt to deny these strategic power games. They seek to reify power from the leader's office so power will then radiate outward and downward. This power reification and radiation occur in the following sequence. First, followers (those who supported the new leader's climb to that position) are aligned with the leader based on their identification with the leader on issues of key interest and the leader's stated values and idealized vision. The implication is "I will attend to your personal growth and competence but you must be loyal to me" (Kanungo and Mendonca, 1996, p. 69).

McClelland (1961), following the classical liberal model of individual competition, argues that leaders still engage in personalized power (managerial power strategies), but that this power is masked by the appearance of organizational power. Thus, power is expressed in organizational (legislated structure) terms, but it is ultimately used for self-aggrandizement. Through consolidation of organizationally sanctioned power, leaders want this power used on their own behalf, as discipline in order to gain obedience (Etzioni, 1961; Mintzberg, 1983).

These are the same purposes for which Hobbes originally developed his power theories. The agency or source for this power is the sovereign or leader. Within the organizational context, reified power lies in and works with a specific structure. The juxtaposition of the two—sovereign agency and its enabling structural circuits—drives modern Western business organizations (see Clegg, 1989). Transactional and charismatic leaders hold sway by using myths, after they create them through personal inspiration.[14] The myths are "shared" downward only selectively, and this process leads to marginalization and alienation of many organizational members. The result is hierarchical power—with a transactional leader at the apex of each nested hierarchy (Sinha, 1995, 15).

At Apple, it was Sculley taught who Jobs this skill during the time the two of them worked there together. Rather than Jobs teaching Sculley the art of transformational leadership, from Sculley Jobs learned the logic of transactional leadership.

The Transformational Leader's Power

Transformational leaders, like managers, follow the precepts of Machiavellian power—they use it strategically in specific contexts and for specific purposes. This is also the shaman's use of power, a master of moral or spiritual power.[15] As purveyors of this power, shamans for an organization tie business-focused activities to the cultural logic and prescriptive values of the societies in which their activities take place. All successful transformational leaders must use power in this way.

The shaman's power comes from uniting clients with all the sources of the operating universe. This makes shamanistic success more opaque and take longer to realize, but a basic measure has been suggested by Heinze (1991, p. 216): "Power usage is intimately related and instrumental to solving vital problems of the community." Shamans' measures of success are the self-empowerment of others and the alignment of their clients with societal cultural logic and prescriptive values.

Transformational leaders who use the shaman's power create the opportunity for clients to re-create themselves, their organizations, and their societies (Pattee, 1989, p. 14). The power to act on the shaman's guidelines, however, remains with the shaman's clients.

A shaman's social function is providing greater social understanding as supported by shared communal myths. Shamans interpret an image and understanding of the cosmos and of humankind's roles and responsibility in it. Unlike either Hobbes's and Machiavelli's classical and modern managers and leaders, shamans act for altruistic reasons, not as defined by themselves, but rather as defined by the community (Kanungo and Mendonca, 1996, pp. 36–37). Shamans, therefore, must put the benefit of others before their own needs (Heinze, 1991, p. 117). When power is used in a relational mode from communal and spiritual directions, a person's motivations are less likely to be questioned. Use of this power leads to the well-being of the whole, rather than the aggrandizement of a separate or particular part. Communal power creates greater motivation in others.

Shamanistic power comes from individual creativity, the crux of the culture-making process (Pattee, 1989, p. 138). The shaman presents an idealized vision of the sacred, but that vision can be interpreted by clients and adapted to fit within more ambiguous parameters. The resultant shared vision touches the cultural logic and prescriptive values of the shaman and clients' thoughts, feelings, and aspirations.

After using power strategically to define what their social contexts are, shamans and their apostles use shared power to integrate themselves into these contexts. Their guidance relies on the community as legislator. They, as individuals and as members of organizations, perceive themselves voluntarily as subordinate to their community and receive their power through its agency. Power comes from the community and only by reflection from inside the organization. The early Apple and Macintosh startup operations reflected this kind of power. Once agreed by all participants, this moral community creates a voluntary and self-monitored discipline.

Power depends on shared communal myths. Campbell states: "The role of the myth is to develop, socialize, and provide a meaningful cosmos and provide spirituality" (1968, p. 23). Power comes from the myth and not the purveyor of it (Walsh, 1994, p. 16). This is why shamans, and not leaders, are better suited to be trust agents who facilitate new power flows and understanding between the spirit of communities and the business of organizations. Thus do shamans channel spiritual power from the cosmos to those in need.

At the turning point of the early Apple organization, a shamanistic interpretive power informed the company's first commercial. As reported by Garsten:

> The team wanted to make a major event out of the introduction of the Macintosh. At its introduction in January 1984, Apple Computer ran a one minute television spot commercial called "1984" during the broadcast of a superbowl game in San Francisco. The ad was meant to be comprehended in recognition of the year's Orwellian association, showing the face of big brother glowering down from a monumental television screen, onto a mass of uninformed marionettes. Suddenly a rebellious spirit, in the shape of a young athletic woman, emerges, rushes forward and disrupts the rally by swinging a Thor-sized hammer at the screen. It shatters, and the enslaved millions are free. (1994, p. 10)

Power in the Organization

There is no organizational power in the absence of context and agency. In both business- and commerce-driven organizations, managers and leaders use power both relationally and causally. Managers use power in relation to other managers, and within their authority as agents, to accomplish specific tasks. Transactional leaders use power in relation to deals made with their subordinates and as agents to craft visions that concentrate power (the organizational political myths that consolidate power). Transformational leaders use power in relation to a wide range of other individuals, inside and outside the organization, to bond with society and community.

Managerial and transactional power use is never equal and inherently unsatisfying, while transformational power is self-empowering and rewarding. Power use by managers and transactional leaders is often disruptive to the individual (creating villainization), but its use by transformational leaders causes power to be integrative, generative, self-powered, and creative.

Within the pure-business context, power lacks moral suasion; the goals of its use are ultimately amoral. In a pure-business context, therefore, causal power agency lies reified within the structures of the organization. Power is used day to day in a Machiavellian sense, but only intermittently or episodically in a Hobbesian sense (Clegg, 1989). Episodic power emerges when the need to reshape organization structure occurs, with the concomitant need to restructure the consciousness, interests, and ideology of organizational members. These are the interests and ideologies of pure business—profit, gain, control. Power is also a disciplinary apparatus. In business power games, social and cultural dynamics are enjoined only when they can be predicted and controlled to some other end. For this reason, business-focused organizations continue to fragment and alienate themselves from society at large.

In the commerce-oriented organization, power is gained from and continually integrated with a wider social context. Power is distributive and derived from communal spirit, the values of the wider social community. Table 8 outlines agency metaphors of power for managers, transactional leaders, and transformational leaders. The leftmost column provides the key contexts for each and how each is defined by, interacts with, or is the source of each of the column descriptors.

Managers and transactional leaders both use power in ways that Machiavelli would approve—strategically. However, power has the effects of self-aggrandizement for managers and altruism for the transformational leader. Since managers define power dialectically (in relation to leaders, who base their power and its use on legitimacy of position) and they expect rewards for its acceptable use, they are at risk of organizational sanctions if their leaders perceive power to be used inappropriately.

The risk of inappropriate use of power by transformational leaders is social

TABLE 8. Metaphors of Power's Agency

	Manager	Transactional Leader	Transformational Leader
Source of	Business myths	Political myths	Social myths
Defined by	Dialectic power	Reified power	Communal power
Purpose of	Monopoly of reward	Legitimacy of position	Distribution of authority
Agent of	Monopolizer of context	Legislator of context	Interpreter of contexts
Method for	Personal strategy	Absolute causality	Contextual strategy
Nature of	Contingency	Prime mover	Pragmatic
Descriptor	Military	Mechanistic	Relational
Effect of	Self-aggrandizement	Institutionalization	Communion
Risk from	Organization	Society	Cosmic

sanctions—either brought by the organization or by community. Soon after the arrival of John Sculley at Apple, he believed Jobs to be working against him and set to work to isolate him through various social and political sanctions. Creative activities are the greatest risk to transformational leaders—risk from either other organizational members or society members at large. The context of the manager is one of contingency: dependency on superiors that causes uncertainty of conditions and occurrences. Transactional leaders attempt to remain in contexts in which they can legislate. Transformational leaders work pragmatically and simultaneously within multiple contexts and within others' perceptions. This is why, although many times the words are the same, the metaphors they represent are substantially different.

Education and the Organization[16]

"Every organization is perfectly designed to get the results it gets" (Hanna, 1988, p. 34).[17] This is true of both purely business-driven and commerce-driven organizations. In both cases, the primary designers—transactional leaders in the case of business-driven organizations and transformational leaders in the case of commerce-driven organizations—have the organizations they want, with the purposes they want and the outcomes they want, using the educational methods they find comfortable. In either type of organization, managers play the role of implementor and executor of organizational missions and visions. However, in the case of commercial organizations, managers also have a say in the formation of the organization. In the case of the purely business organization, they largely do not.

Pure-business organizations' purposes are to create environments that are stable for them, ones conducive to organizational gain. The gain is distributed unevenly, starting at the top with the key transactional leader. Commerce-driven organizations' purpose is to "do business with" other people in ways they all find acceptable. The context for this is largely ambivalent and subject to constant change.

The purely business-driven organization defines success as efficiency: task completion, working within the law, and internal recognition of its leaders and managers. It does not concern itself with social morality unless defined and enforced by law. Leaders and managers define themselves as moral when they meet the efficiency and profit goals they set for themselves.

Commerce-driven organizations consider as socially responsible actions that satisfy them as people while generating acceptable profits as the primary organizational goal. They include measures such as how they meet the cultural logic and prescriptive ethics of the people with whom they work. Each of these organization types also needs different primary education paradigms to be successful.

The purely business-driven organization primarily educates itself through instruction by experts, on the assumption that any expert can give instruction.[18] Experts include consultants and technicians, but primarily the organization's leaders in terms of organizational development and organizational morality. Instruction is preferred for several reasons. It is delivered in controlled ways and in controlled places. Those delivering instruction usually provide highly structured materials that transfer information from the instructor to the student. Instruction takes place in hierarchical settings. The higher up the hierarchy the more "instructors" there are until there is the "high instructor"—the CEO or chief transactional leader. Instruction requires stable organizational structures for activities and processes to occur. The basic instructional metaphor is a "storehouse" of learning.

Commerce-driven organizations are primarily learning organizations that work through shared day-to-day governance.[19] They produce learning through the creation of powerful learning environments. These environments may require constantly changing structures (realities) in which to work. Learning is a holistic experience, with all organizational members having the opportunity both to learn and to teach. Knowledge is constructed, created, and shared. Learning is a constant, but the time required to learn is a variable.[20] Within the learning organization, transformational leaders will be the designers of environments and contexts, not of the material. Learning occurs in a nesting and interacting set of frameworks. The metaphor for commerce-driven learning is that of learning to ride a bike.

The leaders of an organization primarily determine the nature and type of organization they head. As we have seen, early in the history of Apple Computers, Steve Jobs, acting out a shamanistic metaphor, created a learning organization that was attempting to integrate itself into a particular cultural logic and prescriptive ethical set. The organization was generally viewed as being socially responsible. John Sculley, a trained transactional leader from Pepsi, moved the organization back to the instructional paradigm, back toward a purely business focus. In this context, with Job's recent return to Apple in the 1990s can be read as a yearning for the return of the pirate flag.

Notes

1. The two following examples include people who are nameless as they represent companies with which one of the authors works. Neither would want their names associated with the examples stated.

2. Jobs was not the first visionary in the computer industry, however. Robert Taylor, who ran Xerox Park in the early 1970s, was arguably the first visionary. He, like Jobs, kept the technicians focused and challenged them to achieve constant improvement (Cringeley, 1992, p. 86).

3. Cringeley (1992, p. 148) identifies the job of the visionary in the early computer days as the person who sees "neat stuff and recognizes its potential." He continues that these people "are listened to by others and, because they are listened to by others, all the real technical people who want the world to know about the neat stuff they are working on seek out these visionaries and give them demonstrations." The visionaries are then to pass the neat stuff to the general public.

4. Cringeley (1992, p. 191) argues that the true visionary is one who has a vision and is willing to "put everything on the line, including his or her career, to further that vision." On this basis, he sees Jobs as a true visionary.

5. As reported in the Saturday, March 15, 1997, of the *TimesFax*, the tradition is alive and well at Apple. In a recent restructuring move, management has agreed to eliminate 4100 jobs.

6. There are times that a transformational leader might occupy a center seat. This usually occurs when such a seat spans two organizations that are both undergoing major change. New social movement leaders and merger leaders come to mind.

7. Schein supports this position by saying "a unique function of 'leadership' . . . is the creation and management of culture" (1987, p. 171). He sees organizational culture as bounded as existing apart from its external environment (1987, p. 51).

8. By art, we mean the metaphorical in describing organizations, their affect and effect, their purpose in society, and their social expression.

9. For the remainder of this section, shaman is used rather than transformational leader or shamanistic metaphor. This is done for emphasis of the shaman role, skill, and position.

10. This person is not identified as he requested that his name be withheld.

11. This provides a powerful metaphor for change. Examples that come to mind are Martin Luther King and Gandhi. They both preached love and inclusion for their disciples and for those opposing them. Both discussed the value of an effective, inclusive society. On the other hand, those like Pat Buchanan and, earlier, Lyndon Johnson practiced the discourse

of exclusion. There are underlying differences between these two sets. King and Gandhi spoke for the need for dialogue involving love and unity. Buchanan and Johnson used narrative discourse of differences and war—war on poverty, war against the rich, war against foreigners. Hence, the discourse changed from joining to taking, from unity to class differences.

12. Jackall (1988) demonstrates I win—you lose at the middle managerial level. At more senior levels, newspaper articles discussing senior power positions at Time Warner, Disney, Turner Broadcasting, and others reflect the same phenomenon.

13. A discussion of these techniques is outside the scope of this chapter; see Reeves-Ellington, 1995b, for an explanation of ethnographic process as it is used above. For a broader view, books by J. Van Willigen are useful.

14. Arguably, the shaman has been replaced by the priest in terms of leader actions (Hugh-Jones, 1994, p. 33).

15. Here, we are using "spiritual" in a moral sense as opposed to "corporal." As spiritual masters, transformational leaders use their intellect in addressing societal issues of morality and social responsibility. Strategically, transformational leaders integrate the sacred and profane and normative values and social responsibility in the form of commercial activity in order to transact business activities.

16. Education, according to Bauman (1987), was designed in the Age of Reason and stood for the right and the duty of the state to form its citizens and guide their conduct. It stood for the concept, and the practice, of a managed society (p. 69). Education was the methodology by which legislators in the absolutist state could gain easy compliance.

17. We have already cited this but believe it is important to repeat here.

18. Learning takes place within a business organization, but it is not encouraged.

19. They will make use of instruction, but in highly specific cases and in episodic ways.

20. This contrasts with teaching organizations that fix time, but have what is learned as a variable.

4

Social Responsibility on the Face of It:
Complications of an Agenda Company

We have said that ethical behavior takes different shapes within the cultural contexts of a given society. Cultural interpretation and social institutions furnish precedents and suggestions for who is responsible and what kind of behavior is viewed as ethical, but when power and responsibility are reified, peoples' ethical responses and interpretations are more limited and directed.

Agenda always involves some reification of power, roles, and moral assumptions. Whether it is agenda of power consolidated in the person of a chief executive officer, an organizational agenda of market domination, or the agenda for realizing a utopian vision, once they adopt it, people usually proceed with decreased attention to opportunities to reflect and revise their approach. They make certain limiting assumptions about the relationship of standard procedures to desired outcomes, and by doing this, they narrow the scope of interactions with their environment, either physical or social. These interactions could have been the source of new and useful patterns of interpretation. In changing and unfamiliar business contexts, the social knowledge that could emerge with a more provisional working out of people's visions, in dialogues of commerce, is too often precluded. Agenda thinking too often raises the hope of large, programmatic, and simplified solutions for conditions to which a single solution may be inappropriate.

In America and in some quarters of Europe, variations in social values orientations toward power have combined with unique histories of class and occupation, giving rise to negative public images of business as an institution. Particularly in America, but to some extent elsewhere also, the greatest distrust is reserved for the large multinational firms. Notorious domestic quality and safety controversies involving big companies, of which Ford's Pintos and Firestone's 500 series belted radial tires are two examples, have received much space in the mass press and in contemporary business ethics textbooks. On the other hand, when the large firms behave responsibly regarding safety threats (e.g., by removing products from the market, as did Johnson & Johnson with Tylenol and Proctor and Gamble with Rely Tampons), they may find their way into ethics casebooks, but they receive much less public fanfare.

Vernon (1986) suggests that public distrust of large businesses is amplified by the firms' high visibility, perceived size, exclusivity, their prominent physical presence, and a feeling that no single state government can fully control their economic power. There have also been certain enduring historical symbols that, as artifacts, mark and help to maintain this attitude of exclusion and distrust.

Chesher (1992) historically traces the cultural myth of business as immoral to the Church's reaction to its loss of power in Europe (with the rise of capitalism and the state) during the period from the end of feudalism in the 15th century to the advent of modern science in the 17th century. Contrasting "the knight" with "the man in the grey flannel suit" (p. 48), he argues that an antibusiness romantic spirit has persisted into the 20th century and is reflected in the consumerism and environmental movements. He says these movements echo the romanticism of earlier thinkers such as Thoreau in America and Goethe in Germany: "In general we see in both the Green movement and in Romanticism a suspicion of reason and logic and an emphasis on intuition and emotion" (p. 50).

The public persona of Anita Roddick (1991), cofounder of the politically green and socially activist British cosmetics company, The Body Shop, illustrates just this kind of popular moral division between a pure-business rationality and a romantic, antibusiness morality that relies on intuition and spirit. Her business autobiography, *Body and Soul* (1991), includes a cartoon drawing of Roddick, identifiable by the pen-and-ink rendering of her long, curly hair, as a knight in shining armor astride a horse. In both visual artifacts and statements, Roddick would contrast her own intuitive approach with "those soulless and faceless multinational giants" (p. 226). She proclaims the antirationality public stance of The Body Shop, saying, "the business aspect, the science of finance, doesn't grab me" (p. 236). The same thing is reflected in other artifacts, such as the Disney-like, fantasy architecture at the Littlehampton offices (the main building is a giant pagoda), the pop-art statues on the grounds, and the headquarters "Trading Post," which is physically isolated and stocked with pricey products—as most historical trading posts were. There is also (for paying visitors) an entertaining plant tour especially designed to appeal to young children. Roddick's autobiography describes her on opening her first shop, as "so innocent I didn't even know what hype was" (1991, p. 20).

On the face of it, The Body Shop's institutional position in the early years did seem to resemble the counterculture of Steven Jobs—located at the romantic margins of business' institutional power and oriented to the wider society. The likeness was in surface artifacts only. Even in the firm's early years, when it was not generating annual sales in the hundreds of millions of dollars and operating in 46 countries, there were important underlying differences in its sources of ethical orientation and in the basis for its social knowledge of how to do business.

These differences existed at the level of cultural interpretation. Apple Computers, Incorporated, never promulgated an antibusiness ideology. It always promoted the designing, making, and selling of personal computers as an opportunity to make money, and in its early years it connected young people in its organization and the wider society market through a vision they all saw as empowering—greater access to and power in the use of information, hence a new and affirming kind of personal power that personal computers might facilitate.

The emergent cultural logic associated with Apple's premise involved liberation from dependence on bigness, egalitarianism, and promotion of experimentation and entrepreneurial spirit. The social knowledge of freewheeling invention, sourcing of different aspects of product development and marketing, and even Apple's early and widely noted business mistake, failing to license its operating system, reflected its underlying themes of autonomy, uniqueness, authenticity, and small scale—orientations shared by the company's relatively well-educated peers in the generation of Americans who grew up after the end of World War II. Partly for these reasons also, certain of Apple's small, elegant, and high-quality features would find appeal in the Japanese market. It is interesting that even though Jobs now says (G. Wolf, 1996) that he no longer cares about revolutionizing society or that technology could solve its most important problems, he maintains his primary interest in democratization and direct commercial interaction, which he expresses as "giving customers what they want" (p. 5).

These had never been the primary themes within The Body Shop. Despite its rhetoric of humanism, until the major changes that took place between 1995 and 1996, The Body Shop's primary emphasis was not on asking shop employees or customers what they wanted, but rather, on instruction—on telling the public the right ethical way in which to behave and view the world.

The Body Shop, which opened in England in 1976, has always based its identity on a quite different premise, even though Anita Roddick, in the firm's 1996 annual report (The Body Shop, 1996, May), still calls it a counterculture company. This global franchise in natural cosmetics has occupied the self-contradictory position of advancing a social agenda of protest against big and affluent business while becoming large and affluent itself. Through the 1980s, it achieved high profitability and financial growth, offered public stock, and became the most widely globally franchised cosmetics firm in the world. It marketed its cosmetics by denouncing, along with various social injustices associated with large and powerful institutions, the greed, mendacity, and frivolity of its largest competitors.

In the year or two just prior to this writing, there was evidence of a retreat from some of The Body Shop's earlier social agenda message topics, offering a sharp contrast with some of the most colorful, dramatic, and confrontational of its earlier rhetoric and artifacts. There has also been a change in the language of its leaders, with a new priority on purely business aspects of the company. This chapter reviews the events that led to this retreat and to the reorientation of the Body Shop leadership's focus.

With its structure and processes now more closely resembling mainstream business management, the company's core cultural logic, which has always reflected the Western traditions of managerial and legislative power, has at length also emerged in its public message content. We offer a cultural interpretation of why The Body Shop, perhaps the most extreme agenda organization within socially responsible business circles of the 1980s and 1990s, was so visibly nonintegral and what its most recent turn means in social responsibility terms.

Nonintegral Social Agenda

At The Body Shop, efforts to make a wider and responsible social impact took place from the company's inception through a language of exclusion and differentiating marketing messages. This communication depended on restricted circuits of power in which a founding family maintained tight control of all product-market relations, including the appearance of its stores and virtually the entire content of its franchise owners' and employees' interactions with customers. The organization was led principally by alternating between a managerial paradigm of manipulating relational market power, through the firm leaders' association with celebrities and popular social images, while legislating internal and external communications and assuming an adversarial environment.[1]

The firm's leadership assumptions remained Hobbesian, and its communication flow was basically unidirectional. The early Body Shop relied principally on legalistic and adversarial modes in its encounters with what it had clearly defined as the hostile, external business environment. At certain critical junctures, it resorted to adversarial public relations campaigns in which competitors or challengers were portrayed as villains and the company as their victim. These cultural interpretations and communication methods created a context precluding the company from responding sensitively and appropriately in some of its transcultural trade situations, and for some time also led it, in the new culturally interpretive contexts of different markets, to miss the point of social responsibility.

The firm has stayed in the business of producing and selling environmentally harmless cosmetic products, yet for almost all of its first 20 years, it has gone far beyond its first commercial mission and publicly advocated an agenda of social, environmental and political action. This second set of activities has sometimes led it to distort its public self-representations. The Body Shop has campaigned for political causes that draw on some of the noblest of pan-human adaptive themes. Yet, its rhetoric has often made an ideological enemy of the very kind of organization it is. Its social agenda has included what could broadly be termed public education and political promotion in the areas of animal rights, environmentalism, human rights, poverty amelioration, and indigenous cultural preservation. Until recently, The Body Shop's statements were usually aimed to stir controversy by naming other businesses, particular governments, or industries as being at fault.

This was how its leadership created a unique market identity—by using a rhetoric of adversity, exclusion, and confrontation.

Its political slogans and campaigns, as often dramatic and appealing as they were shrill, were used as marketing messages for the firm's products; as result, the public and some of its business partners were very likely misled, or at least under-informed.[2] Most important, many of The Body Shop's messages lacked an integral connection to the company's business activity.

Ambiguity and lack of integral relationships in marketing communications are neither new nor unusual. In the case of The Body Shop, they were bound to raise questions eventually, since the firm's market identity was based on a general attack of its competitors' and other institutions' integrity and the contrast that its own good works were supposed to present. Clearly, it is not necessarily socially or ethically dislocating for businesses to urge their employees and franchisees to personally volunteer, or indeed for a firm to canvass its own employees, especially in America, for example, to give to charities and donate time to civic projects. It is also not uncommon for particular companies (in the United States, social minority companies especially) to push civic participation and activism in an area of immediate and compelling interest to the customers of the business, donating time, space, or resources to civic projects and public education. Neither is it unknown for company leaders to proselytize their particular social or political stances and to "educate" their associates and employees to particular issues of social concern to the leader.

The Body Shop did all of these things and was pioneering in some, particularly in the cultural context of an English business in the 1970s. But, the agenda of this company neither began with nor ended with personal responsibility, discretion, and local interpretation of choices for how to be socially responsible. The agenda of at least one Body Shop leader was to make the business seem or become something more than it could be, as a growing and competitive globalizing business, while simultaneously keeping its operations and processes from becoming as locally fitting as they could have been.

The Body Shop's market differentiation strategy of accusing the established beauty industry of "lying," "exploiting," and producing "frivolous and useless products" (Roddick, 1991, p. 9) garnered a great deal of attention. During the 1980s particularly, the firm created a favorable public market for its cosmetics among a relatively well-educated and affluent contingent in Britain and Europe. Later, it did the same thing to a lesser extent in America—especially among people who shared the founders' historical experience of idealistic political activism as students and youth in the late 1960s and 1970s. The firm's sociopolitical agendas were a kind of normative litmus test for recruitment and identification of its customers and franchisees. They are still defined, in the words of one Body Shop staff member, as people who have "the right sort of values,"[3] and they often include those whose attitudes are critical or questioning of the morality of business in general.

The principal weakness in the approach of an agenda company like The Body Shop, and in the self-identified socially responsible business movement generally, has not been that they express social concerns per se or that these concerns have market appeal. Rather, the main weakness, especially for a few who have dabbled in promoting their Third World product sourcing, has been the absence of a concretely worked out theory for relating the realities of their business activity to creation of desired change in the institutions and conditions they would criticize or ameliorate. Their lack of integration resides in the way these firms either have to demonstrate outstanding records of charity, for example, if they advocate for wealth redistribution, or else show definitively that the business activities themselves have had tangible results, such as the greater distribution of wealth for those whom they claim to help. The alternative is to misrepresent their activities and possibly even the substance of their business.

In 1994 and 1995, a controversy over the ethics of The Body Shop raised just such questions of existence or magnitude of effect on social problems as the firm had implicitly advertised, and, with its credibility challenged on these issues, there was created a further opening to scrutinize a number of other aspects of the company's business and ethical practices. The company's ideological style, its methods of social adversity and dramatic claims led it, in a new and unfamiliar American market context of less brand loyalty, a more aggressive press, and more permissive legal and speech traditions, to become the target of exposé.

Such a challenge has been less of a problem for other businesses in the movement. Many, such as the American company Ben and Jerry's Ice Cream, would not make as dramatic claims or engage in ideological conflict as directly as The Body Shop. If no one looks too closely at the match between a company's rhetoric and results, general good intentions and the absence of major negative incidents will often carry a business in the public's estimation. The Body Shop's willingness to go further and assume a critical stance opened its practices and the core of its business to much closer—and unfriendly—scrutiny. The Body Shop's vocal animosity to its industry and to other entities that it identified by name; its adoption of controversial positions; its early, dramatic claims of social impact; its attempt at unilateral control of its communications; and the ferocity of its adversarial legal approaches to public critique and business competition eventually drew investigative attention.

This scrutiny, whether fair or not,[4] suggested The Body Shop's inability to demonstrate that it was as dramatic an exception in its business practice as it was in its ideological agenda and artifacts. It also cast light on existing problems related to traditional expectations of the firm as a publicly traded business, an additional circumstance which had an impact on both the company and its leadership. That The Body Shop undoubtedly was a positive, if modest, exception in several areas of progressive social and environmental concern received less attention than did the way the leadership used inflammatory and extreme rhetoric and legislated social responsibility in the firm. Particularly problematic for social change professionals and other observers was the way it appropriated sensitive social and political material for its most dramatic claims.

Mixed Purposes and Unclear Methods

The self-identified socially responsible business movement, including such business organizations as Business for Social Responsibility and the Social Venture Network and, in the past, some nongovernmental organizations (NGOs) such as Cultural Survival, has labored under a set of complications that arise with the mixing of missions and aims of competitive business organizations with purposes that had formerly been an organizing specialty for the not-for-profit charities, governments, and, to some extent, intergovernmental and nongovernmental bodies. Within the socially responsible business movement, these more inclusive aims tended to take the form not of concrete and extended work in particular places, but rather of politically correct positions on ideological questions and dramatic public relations events. The methods for reaching the desired conditions were not rigorously specified, nor was the way in which they might be measured.

In the view of many scholars and most of mainstream business as an institution, an agenda company's social change impact on world problems would be of little importance unless it was economically measurable, a requirement related to the pure-business paradigm and assumptions of an economic bottom line. Economic effectiveness, in the pure-business terms of economists, businesspeople, and many economic development scholars and professionals, is the demonstration of sustained business and market growth and the making of a profit.

For positive social change interventions through business activity, this basic economic benchmark is usually accompanied by the requirement, among social impact analysts, that localities of operation see direct or indirect measurable economic benefit and that the intervention or development creates a minimum of adverse impacts, whether social, cultural, or environmental. If the further object of agenda is to redress social and environmental inequities (such as increases in unequal distribution of wealth; the reversal of destruction of habitats, lives, and life ways; or the general amelioration of poverty), then there are additional requirements to demonstrate results in a particular problem locality.

The evaluation of these results and the nature of these requirements have been a challenging and absorbing object of study and planning for decades among governments, intergovernmental bodies, some NGOs, and academics. Various schools of political, social, and economic thought have clashed over their interpretation and solution. Because of the enormous complexity of these problems, and the consequent burgeoning of specialties and expertise developed to address them, issues of social justice and development are often viewed as larger, transsectoral issues, distinct from questions of business ethics per se. The separation between business ethics and programs of economic or social change also exists in part simply because business ethics has acquired, as we indicated earlier, its own detailed and specialized domain of authority and expertise, developed for its own specific contexts of operation.

Business ethics, even when agenda driven, is still patterned on the forms, if not the culturally integral logic, of a social knowledge about how to conduct business without exacerbating a practitioner's or an organization's moral problems while still making a profit. Not until the more youthful and experimental social responsibility movement of the 1980s, of which The Body Shop is the extreme case, did business ethical questions begin to turn to issues that had previously resided in the area of institutional reform—on a search for strategies to make one or more particular kinds of business activity profitable, for example, while also benefiting various identified social causes, whether of environmental or animal rights concerns or the betterment of economic and quality of life for disadvantaged people in particular places.

It has only been later, in the 1990s, that environmental and social change causes have been widely appropriated into the public relations vocabulary of businesses. Earlier, social activists for change had protested against business from the outside, for destroying environments, creating unequal wealth distribution, and generally increasing human misery. With the evolution, mainly during the late 1970s and through the 1980s, of the socially responsible business movement, a closer affinity was established among some young entrepreneurs, NGO scholars, and activists.

It was at this point that business ethics issues and social and economic development issues became blurred as the vaguely but idealistically related parts of a new proposed agenda for packaging prosperity with social responsibility. Business participants identified with this movement, such as Ben and Jerry's Ice Cream, Patagonia clothing, Rhino Records, and The Body Shop, have often included social messages in their choice of packaging and other highly visible elements of their products. Many of these businesspeople, including the Roddicks, have aligned with scholars and with representatives of NGOs such as Greenpeace, Amnesty International, Cultural Survival, and Survival International by witnessing or participating in conferences or political activity (Entine, 1995; Roddick, 1991; Turner, 1995).

In the eyes of the participating entrepreneurs themselves, social responsibility in business probably was fairly culturally integral. Many were young, liberal, and newly affluent; they had traveled widely; and, like the international elites of earlier years, they could see firsthand the unequal distribution of wealth and human misery. Unlike their affluent forebears, they shared exposure to the idealistic views and social agenda rhetoric of the activist 1960s. They could agree, based on these common experiences, on a desire to make positive social impacts. So, there was clearly the basis for a new community of moral opinion, but idealism and agenda, rather than reflective pursuit of social knowledge, drove the activities and methods that were adopted, and rhetoric and artifacts became divorced from evidence about results.

A reified agenda of the sort pursued by the socially responsible business movement lacks details of social knowledge worked out in dialogue at the cultural level. Most likely, a lack of experience with business, knowledge of economic conditions, and sophistication about other cultural and economic settings for this group, despite the leaders' travels and business success at home, also contributed to their inability to foresee that their assumptions would bring complications and, ultimately, the demand for proof of results. The movement's participants could relate enthusiastically to other entrepreneurs and activists about the adventure of untried strategies, but the larger problem they would not be able to solve would be how to proceed from desire to social knowledge, to integrate it and live it, in conversation with the wider community. For this task, the agenda of the social responsibility movement could not replace the cultural acquisition of social knowledge for a working context. The artifacts and rhetoric became disconnected from a holistic awareness of the operating requirements specific to understanding the cultural milieu of business.

During the late 1970s and early 1980s, the agenda of mainstream large Western businesses remained turned mostly inward on structure, profit, and growth, and, later in the 1970s and early 1980s, on concern with foreign competition in manufacturing. Newly successful businesspeople in the 1980s would have had a much different environment, with wide latitude for experimentation in the new social agenda thinking. Most had not yet encountered the problems attending the maintenance and growth of a larger company, such as public stock offerings and professional management. Financial risks that were acceptable and even necessary early in the creation of a business would no longer be so once the founders began to depend on financing from investors.

At some point beyond public offering, the socially integrative potential of a growing company has to move downward and outward through the organization. With larger numbers of people between the leadership and the customers, responsibility for a wider social integration often finds its best hope in the practices and beliefs that involve the discretionary and culturally interpretive activities of personnel spread throughout field operations and at all the critical junctures of internal, subsidiary, and partner relationships.

This kind of responsibility takes time to develop in the complex world of late modern business and cannot operate solely under the imposed agenda of even an inspired transactional leader. In most cases, the entrepreneurs of these companies have been described as personally compelling, as certainly Anita Roddick has, but none had the support of a long-established organization, and Roddick had no extensive organizational experience other than teaching and running a small business (1991; The Body Shop, 1996, May). The level of sophistication required for transcultural learning in business, as would come into play in global markets and supplier relations, requires extensive practitioner support and preparation and the further support of stable processes and practices in the organization itself. These issues will not be solved by the agenda of sovereign authors who blame institutions and attempt to legislate control of social responsibility.

Fast-growing entrepreneurial organizations of the 1980s would have found that sophistication of organization communications and preparation of personnel were among their most difficult challenges during rapid company growth. Sophistication and responsible discretion would be even more difficult to achieve if pursued as political and social agenda campaigns that the leaders could only tangentially relate to their business purpose. Also, there was the cultural response issue of a uniform, global store with social campaign choices legislated almost exclusively by the chairman and CEO of the group, as Roddick (1991) has reported she did: If the managers, franchise owners, and employees of a far-flung company cannot be trusted to work out, interpret, and respond to local impacts, it becomes nearly impossible to make substantial social or business impacts fitting all the locales of the operation. This collection of problems is exactly what confronted The Body Shop.

"Against Animal Testing"

Most regular readers of the business press throughout the early 1990s have heard of The Body Shop. Its cofounders, Anita and Gordon Roddick, saw rapid growth and profitability from the small retail bath shop that they opened in Sussex, England, in 1976. Their expansion with franchise shops began in 1977, and they reached public stock flotation in 1984. By the mid-1980s, the firm had a highly favorable profile in the British and international business media. The first U.S. Body

Shop opened in 1988 in New York City, with similarly successful press coverage. From the early 1990s, the company has been the parent corporation of a group producing and marketing over 400 naturally based personal care and cosmetics products (Kepos, 1995, p. 40). This had been done largely through franchises, which comprised roughly 89% of the business in 1994 (Siler, 1994).

By early 1995, the firm operated in 46 countries (Utne, 1995, p. 101). As of 1996, there were 1373 stores and 3670 employees, with an annual turnover of £256 million (Moody's, 1996, p. 10,145). The Body Shop owns production and distribution plants in Scotland; in Littlehampton, England; and in Raleigh, North Carolina in the United States. The firm's total stock value in mid-1994 exceeded $700 million in U.S. dollars (Utne, 1995, p. 101). In recent years, increased competition in the United States and problems of public relations and management have contributed to a drop in the firm's growth rate and in its share price, which went from $6.55 in 1992 to $2.29 in 1996 (Wallace and Brown, 1996).

Throughout the startup and early expansion period of the business, The Body Shop based its marketing almost entirely on social agenda messages, through these identifying itself as a socially responsible business. The message content, promulgated usually in public statements made by cofounder Anita Roddick, included saving endangered whales from illegal commercial depletion; donating to and joining in public education campaigns and demonstrations against domestic violence and homelessness; posting animal rights messages in the firm's shops, media, and literature (the slogan "against animal testing" has been the shop's enduring identifier, appearing on its product labels and annual reports); and participating with social activist groups. Throughout the 1980s, the Roddicks achieved dual celebrity for their financial success and their controversial pronouncements. They have reported throughout their company literature over the years that franchisees and employees volunteer and participate actively in a variety of these causes.

The marketing messages and campaign activity have been carried out in a variety of media, but mainly in forms of media and space that are owned and controlled by The Body Shop or in free advertising space and public forums. The media used vary from World Wide Web advertorials and broadsheets to political statements painted on the company's distribution lorries. The company's social agenda statements have also appeared in dramatic and colorful posters, displayed in shop windows and waved about at televised public demonstrations. The Body

Shop strategically times its participation for maximum publicity coverage. In late June 1996, for example, ABC News televised a Washington, D.C., rally on the AIDS/animal rights research controversy. In it, demonstrators could be seen using animal rights placards that had been supplied by The Body Shop: This was evident because the company's name and logo were visible on camera in large letters— except in some cases, in which demonstrators had visibly torn off the tops of the signs.[5]

Green Activities Within the Business

The Body Shop's agenda of social responsibility has included a mixture of in-house environmental and quality-of-life improvement projects, charitable and public relations activities, and a set of much smaller projects (viewed in terms of either dollars or personnel) of buying from socially exotic and economically marginal communities. The Body Shop's promotional publications have consistently emphasized the firm's activity and efforts to achieve environmentally nondestructive operations, animal protection, and humane treatment of the firm's workforce. These programs were established, but some have received criticism regarding performance. These have become a more prominently identified focus in the recent two years' corporate communications. Environmental auditing systems and activities exploring ways for the firm to reduce and treat waste and reduce or replace energy have been ongoing (Roderick, 1993; Wheeler, 1992, 1993). The impact has been modest, for example, a system that reportedly involved only 5% of the firm's effluent by 1993 (Roderick, 1993). The company's child care creche is reported in Anita Roddick's book (1991) to be the first of its kind known to The Body Shop, and throughout company publications the firm emphasizes in-house efforts to promote efficient and nonwasteful energy and materials practices.

Organizational Forms of The Body Shop Social Agenda

The Body Shop's involvement in social causes has taken three main organizational forms through the years of its greatest expansion. First, Anita Roddick formed short-term, social campaign partnerships with philanthropy and political organizations, mainly through establishing personal networks. These have included, at one time or another, public relations projects with Greenpeace, Amnesty International, and Cultural Survival, which linkage in part resulted in the firm's highly publicized Kayapo source for Brazil nut oil. The Body Shop supported financing for the "Millennium" television series on tribal people, for which purpose, in part, they raised several million dollars by selling roughly 2% of their company equity in mid-1994 (*New York Times*, 1994, July 11; Springette, 1994).

The Body Shop's second organizational strategy was to set up or contribute to various small but highly publicized (by the Body Shop) local charities, mostly in economically marginal supplier communities. In 1989, they registered a charity foundation to raise donations, initially to gather money from their own shop employees and franchisees. They subsequently expanded its functions to raise funds from outside sources also (The Body Shop, 1994, *Values*, p. 20). They publicized these charitable activities, including corporate donations to community organizations, projects such as their sponsorship of a newspaper for the homeless, and their supplier community charities through corporate and retail marketing materials.

A third organizational strategy involved the formation of their own separate communication entities. These are wholly controlled by The Body Shop founders. This approach allowed the founders to control and disseminate more effectively the Body Shop's name along with social agenda content of an ideological nature. One of these entities is Anita Roddick's New Academy of Business. The academy announced its opening to the British press and on the Internet in February 1996 as a college in the United Kingdom. Its purpose, as described to Anderson by its Littlehampton planning staff in 1995, was to teach socially responsible business practices. The New Academy planned to offer workshops, seminars, and courses in global management training, bringing in international management and social experts.

Roddick campaigned within the academic community for the academy's acceptance as a legitimate authority in social responsibility and international business. She frequently mentioned the academy, for example, in speeches at a May 1995 Academy of Management conference, "Human Dimensions of Global Change," to which she had been invited as plenary speaker.

Their marketing methods of protest and a high-profile, countercultural personal image brought Anita Roddick, as the shop's spokesperson, celebrity in the international and American business presses: Her unique public relations strategy was cited as the key ingredient in the firm's growth and profitability (e.g., in Burlingham, 1990–1991, p. 34, and in Jacob, 1992).

The Body Shop grew rapidly through the early 1990s, expanding into new international markets, especially in the United States, where it departed from its franchise strategy to increase direct ownership through the U.S. subsidiary. By 1996, it owned 113 of 272 U.S. stores.[6] Especially after its American market entry, The Body Shop began to find it necessary to defend vigorously its image and existing markets through legal activity, particularly in the form of threatened or actual suits. It sued a large U.S. competitor, The Limited, in 1990 for copying its image and settled this suit out of court. (Kepos, 1995, p. 41). In England, the firm had experienced one of the first attacks against its integrity when a television program, "Bodysearch," accused it of misleading statements regarding its policies against animal testing. The Body Shop sued the British program for libel in 1992 and won the suit (p. 41).

By the mid-1990s, The Body Shop had felt increased competition and regulatory pressures in the United States, and in 1994 the company's socially responsible image was publicly challenged by an exposé journalist, Jon Entine, who reported spending over a year investigating company practices and had conducted more than 150 interviews and personal observations of events, as well as secondary research, document reviews, and laboratory results (Entine, 1994, 1995).

The 1994 Controversy and Its Impact

There is little doubt that the company's righteous agenda claims and its combative communications, which had helped give its shops a high public profile, also made it more vulnerable to the negative publicity that was generated in advance of the Entine exposé, which appeared in the fall 1994 issue of *Business Ethics*.

The Roddicks again responded aggressively, trying but failing to block the article's publication. After threatening lawsuits against *Vanity Fair*, which did drop the piece, and against the smaller magazine that eventually published it, they mounted a letter campaign to the entire list of the magazine's subscribers, objecting to the article. Unfavorable press about this activity caused further adverse public reaction. At the same time, news emerged that the U.S. Federal Trade Commission was investigating the firm for the accuracy of its claims of helping developing nations. In further reaction, an agenda-oriented ethical investment company, Franklin, announced it was selling all its Body Shop stock (R. Davis, 1994; *New York Times*, 1994, September 23). This added blow caused The Body Shop's stock to drop 15% during the summer and fall of 1994, prior to the release of the Entine article (*Economist*, 1994, p. 56; Utne, 1995, p. 101).

The *Business Ethics* article (Entine, 1994) and a subsequent, more completely documented article Entine published in an academic source (1995) are unfortunate in several ways: Both present such exclusively negative material and interpretations that they raise the question whether the investigator was open to alternate materials or interpretations. Also, while these two articles taken together contain a comprehensive account of the difficulties encountered by socially responsible business companies, neither provides theoretical or philosophical light on the core problems of the movement or of The Body Shop as an agenda company. The impact of the exposé on The Body Shop was, however, substantial. It created pressures for the company to reevaluate many of its management practices, and the company responded by moving to a more traditionally prescribed business structures and processes. In doing so, it established a primarily management agenda of control and independent audit, with extensive reliance on outcomes measurements and quantitative survey methods. So, ironically, The Body Shop, to become more socially responsible, was forced to adopt the agenda of social knowledge established and approved by the codes and rules of traditional corporate business ethics.

The Entine exposé (1994) is a wide-ranging indictment of the company, contains a pastiche of materials and concerns, and mingles business ethics issues with social and economic observations and opinion. Entine's scrutiny extends from general company management and governance practices to issues of product quality control, financial management, and employee and franchisee treatment. There is included liberal reference to the personal characteristics of the cofounders (e.g., on pp. 23–24), which more likely hurts Entine's argument than helps it, because while it is only tangential to his arguments, it suggests the deliberate attempt to cast negative light on the character and competency of the principals of the company.

Entine's academic article (1995) provides a clearer historical tracing of the social responsibility in business leadership network. In this later account, he comments on a group of highly publicized rain forest projects (discussed in more detail below) and correctly points out that ideologies became separated from responsible operating methods in the socially responsible business movement.

Entine ends, however, by following in substantially the same path from which the social responsibility business movement itself had initially departed and to which The Body Shop was forced to return—a traditional management agenda of control by guidelines, peer review, and independent (scientific) audit. Although his second article's call for a "double bottom line" (1995, p. 267) only leads Entine to the same bits and pieces of unconvincing theory that we have already discussed under corporate ethics theories, he supports the adoption of the open model of audit and review, and his ultimate conclusion is that the agenda of control by ethical commandments wins.

Findings and Reactions

In the eyes of the traditional business community, The Body Shop's success as a business would overshadow any concerns that Entine's article raised, as long as it contained no news of major legal and ethical disasters. Indeed, despite all the negative advance publicity, when the article itself was published there was no evidence of legally actionable offenses to life, safety, or property damage. The mainstream business press accordingly responded as if Entine's article were little more than a collection of minor complaints. The British flagship magazine *The Economist* (1994) wrote off the controversy in a brief summary titled, "Storm in a Bubble Bath" (p. 56). Of The Body Shop's critics, *The Economist* said, "They have failed to prove that [Ms. Roddick] engages in mendacious profiteering" (p. 56). The Body Shop's stock subsequently stabilized (Utne, 1995, p. 101).

An irony of The Body Shop controversy is that, despite the thoroughness of Entine's 1994 investigation and the real doubts it raised about the firm's integrity, there is little evidence in it of a kind that would deeply trouble any firm's stock investors. What the article does recount are instances of poor product quality, a lack of integrity in The Body Shop's claims against animal testing, bullying of franchisees, and poor customer relations. Much farther along in the article, Entine (1994) offers testimonial material from observers in several economically stressed locales in the Third World. These sources say that The Body Shop has had no impact on the social or economic well-being of its Third World suppliers. Entine's interviewees for this exposé say that the firm does not pay its suppliers very well for their products. All his sources concurred that the volume of trade was too small to have any substantial local economic impact (p. 27).

Although The Body Shop's leaders met the initial controversy with adversarial tactics, and Anita Roddick vigorously defended the firm for some months after the Entine article's release, making public counterattacks on her critics (e.g., *Advertising Age*, 1994; Roddick, 1995), other changes over the ensuing months, including the firm's increasing U.S. competition and its discouraging profit picture, may have combined with the exposé as an impetus to reconsideration. For whatever combination of reasons, The Body Shop began reviewing its organization on a variety of fronts in 1995, at the same time altering the content of many of its public relations messages.

The Body Shop's *Annual Report and Accounts* for 1996 makes direct reference to some of these changes, such as Chairman Gordon Roddick's intent, after a year's delay, to comply with the Cadbury Report Code of Best Practices,[7] and to commission and respond to several independently verified audits that had documented needed improvements in The Body Shop's social, animal protection, and environmental performance areas.

With The Body Shop's management overhaul also came a noticeable change in the firm's published material about its Third World and indigenous activities. These changes are evident both in the 1996 annual report and in the firm's values summary (The Body Shop, 1996, January). The most noticeable area of reversal in the firm's communication themes is the near disappearance of indigenous and Third World suppliers' pictures in The Body Shop's promotional literature. These had included in particular a social and environmental marketing concept the firm had promoted, which it called "Trade Not Aid." Material from The Body Shop's own publications, from Entine's 1994 and 1995 articles, and, independently, from two works by the anthropologist Terence Turner (1992, 1995) during this same time period, cast some light on why this public relations content shift had occurred.

Reversing Social Inequities

The materials and evidence that inform the various opinions on The Body Shop's social development activities are very limited. However, the present authors have been convinced that the firm's Third World sourcing has had little economic impact on reversing social inequalities in wealth distribution, if only because the quantity of the activity is so small. Several of the firm's own documents give some insight to this issue. In financial year 1994, The Body Shop's *Values and Vision 94* report states the firm bought from suppliers in 10 countries: Nepal, India, Brazil, Mexico, Russia, Nicaragua, Bangladesh, Ghana, Zambia, and the United States (The Body Shop, 1994, *Values*, p. 12). The firm did not systematically report numbers of people employed at these sources, although a 1992 Body Shop publication, *The Green Book*, mentions direct and indirect impact on hundreds of persons in a few locations (p. 32).

Entine (1995), in his academic paper, states that The Body Shop employed 70 of 3500 Kayapo Indians in Brazil, who were paid, collectively, a total of U.S. $850 for the Brazil nut oil from a five-month harvesting season (p. 265). For this data, he cites a report document from the nongovernmental organization, Cultural Survival, compiled by Watson (1993). If accurate, this is, indeed, minimal business involvement. A Body Shop World Wide Web profile posted in early 1996 states the firm "provides direct and indirect employment for over 1,000 people" from "economically stressed communities, mostly in the majority world," (University of Bristol, 1996; similar material appears in The Body Shop, 1994, *Values*, p. 12). If the Kayapo situation is representative, then the figures would have to include part-time workers.

The firm reports its total direct sourcing from "stressed" areas at £1.2 million for the 1994 financial year (The Body Shop, 1994, *Values*, p. 12). The company's annual turnover the same year amounted to £195.4 million and its pretax profits were £29.7 million according to the *Company Profile* (1994, October, p. 3). The Body Shop's economically marginal suppliers represented a tiny fraction of total business activity, and this included industrialized areas such as the wholly owned Scotland soap factory, as well as the indigenous tribal sources. It was the exotic peoples, however, who had been disproportionately represented in The Body Shop's public relations media prior to 1996.

Participation in profitable business and the receipt of charity are two quite different mechanisms for wealth distribution, and the two methods have very different implications, but The Body Shop did not clearly separate these areas in its public relations communications. The Body Shop does report that its charitable donations were raised separately from the business-generated monies, and that these funds were voluntarily donated by franchisees, staff, and outsiders. The Body Shop Foundation, the group's not-for-profit entity, reported donations in amounts of tens of thousands of pounds each to several trust or organizational recipients, several of which were set up by The Body Shop in its economically stressed supplier locales (The Body Shop, 1994, *Values*).

One of the largest reported donated amounts reported for 1994 was based on locally generated after-tax profits. This was £106,000 dedicated to community projects near the company's Easterhouse soap factory, located in an economically depressed part of Glasgow (The Body Shop, 1994, *Values*, p. 19). The firm also says in promotional materials that it donated £230,000 in 1991 to the establishment of a newspaper for the homeless called *The Big Event* (The Body Shop, 1996, January; Kepos, 1995).

"Aid Not Trade": Turner's Critique

At about the same time as the Entine controversy, independent observations and analysis were presented and published by Turner (1995). His material was the first to address the theoretical strand that comprised one part of the social responsibility agenda, a set of related business projects the movement called the "rain forest harvest."

As is typical of competitive international firms, The Body Shop maintains tight proprietary control of access to its premises and information about its operations. Its supplier and operation sites in public and abroad were visible nonetheless to outside observers with an interest in social development. Perhaps the most heavily publicized and photographed part of The Body Shop's activities over the years, until 1995 and 1996, had been its self-styled "Trade Not Aid" program. This approach was sharply criticized by Turner under the rubric of "neoliberal ecopolitics." The Body Shop's founders promoted it as part of their green agenda: "We had to look for ways to make the rainforest economically viable" (Roddick, 1991, p. 203). Turner (1995) points out that this approach, which had been more fully articulated by Jason Clay, the ex-executive director of the NGO Cultural Survival, was never realized in the sustainable production of marketable forest commodities (p. 2).

Turner's sharpest criticism involves the way The Body Shop used and represented media images of the Kayapo Indians of Brazil to market Body Shop products. This marketing strategy had been characteristic of all the firm's more exotic supplier relations in the years between 1987 and 1994. The Body Shop's literature presented stories of doing a combination of charitable and investment work in the Third World, at the same time accusing competitors in the cosmetic industry of exploitation (e.g., Roddick, 1991, p. 9). The Body Shop used marginal peoples' local and biographical information for the promotion of the firm, especially video and photographic images of particular Third World individuals and communities. Disseminating these details impressed the upscale market audience and furthered The Body Shop's image of being legitimate, knowledgeable insiders in important sociopolitical causes.

The Body Shop's photographic and issue subjects included, in particular, political dissidents and protesters against rich and powerful state and business interests. The Kayapo of Brazil, and especially Payakan, one of their leaders, have been well-known examples. Payakan, noted for his role in successful indigenous opposition of a large World Bank dam project at Altamira, Brazil, in 1989 (Turner, 1990), suited well the firm's affinity with controversy and underdog heroes. In his 1995 article, Turner notes that The Body Shop marketed its cosmetics using images of the Kayapo without paying or disclosing the market value of these advertising images to the Kayapo. He describes The Body Shop's Trade Not Aid program as "Aid Not Trade," arguing that this unpaid advertising was free and unknowing aid from the Kayapo to The Body Shop, that the practice was exploitative, and that the consent that the firm obtained from the Kayapo was meaningless: "They cannot be said to have agreed to what they do not understand" (p. 121).

Turner (1995) had observed that (1) the quantity of product sourced was insufficient to be an alternative to government aid or to prevent the Kayapo from continuing to sign land concessions to miners and loggers to supplement their income; (2) there was no local market for the products; (3) The Body Shop's Kayapo suppliers were in a dependent, sole-buyer relationship with them; (4) prices were being dictated, colonial style, by The Body Shop; moreover, (5) the price paid, while market-commensurate for the product per se, did not reflect the huge unpaid advertising benefit to The Body Shop of using the Kayapo's visual images.

Ethics and Exploitation

The question of economic impact, whether through business or charity, may be interpreted as being of a different ethical order from the question of unethical practice. Turner's critique adds to the charge of lack of economic impact by pointing to a more active kind of exploitation, one that combines disproportionate economic benefit with a lack of full disclosure of market value and its implications to the suppliers. This raises a second issue, the firm's truthfulness; of this, Turner already had reason to be suspicious, as we will explain more fully below. The question of exploitation alone is one of great ambiguity.

Other examples of Body-Shop-mediated communication suggest similar possibilities of exploitation. The Body Shop's painted lorry messages and Internet postings invoke the names of political prisoners, for example. One strategically timed World Wide Web posting on November 24, 1995, begins: "Anita Roddick and a team from The Body Shop who have been campaigning on behalf of Ken Saro-Wiwa and the Ogoni people of Nigeria for more than two years" (The Body Shop, 1995, November 24). The firm also posted a dramatic, high-contrast photographic image of the executed dissident writer and activist.

Apart from the ethical questions of exploiting tribal peoples' images for free advertising that has a significant dollar value to the firm, or whether the social or public education value of using this material somehow makes up for their business advertising value, there remains a question of what is integral to the self-representation of a responsible company. For most people who see The Body Shop's messages, there is no direct evidence for the connection between the message and the firm's actions. The messages are untethered information—they may educate, they may indoctrinate, or they might even alienate, but their one predictable result is that they will raise the prominence of The Body Shop's name. This separation of apparent media content and the live activity behind it is well described by the business futurist and electronic frontier consultant Esther Dyson (Dreifus, 1996), who says, regarding the function of mediated messages as a business draw, "The free copies of content are going to be what you use to establish your fame. Then you go out and milk it" (p. 18).

Most mass print and media audiences have little time to reflect on the principal function of The Body Shop's messages. Some may conclude the firm had more first-hand involvement in the issues than simply attending rallies, doing postings, raising funds from franchisees, or taking brief trips for photo opportunities. In some cases, they might be correct, as, for example, in the case of Payakan, to whom The Body Shop furnished a light plane (Roddick, 1991; Turner, 1995). But, in most cases, the details for a thoughtful evaluation are not available. Some viewers may conclude that the firm is trying to appropriate the heroism or exoticism of the leaders and political martyrs whose pictures it uses. A good many others may conclude that this differs little from sellers of soda or cars who use pictures of affluent, attractive, and happy people with their products. In either case, the message is a matter of interpretation. Traditional business ethics might be considered breached when certain Western constructions, such as standards of truthfulness in advertising and fair play, are applied and found wanting in a firm. An instance of this situation is exemplified in a second, unpublished Turner report.

Turner's second paper (1992) documents events he witnessed during a London press conference of Survival International in 1992. His evidence strongly supports the conclusion that The Body Shop engaged in deceitful manipulation of the media, of several Kayapo representatives, and of their NGO colleagues. It documents the firm claiming public credit, in print, for sponsorship of an indigenous video project with which the firm was not associated.

Besides raising disturbing questions regarding the actual extent of socially responsible activities reported by the firm, Turner's account tends to corroborate the interviews in Entine's exposé in which former Body Shop associates reported untruthful representations in the firm's public relations. Anita Roddick further undermines the firm's credibility in her own account (1991) of her use of the press and media. To open her first shop in 1976, she describes herself as "pouring out a colourful story," telling local newspapers that she was being victimized by neighboring shopkeepers. "What I learned then," she adds, "was that there was no need, ever, to pay for advertising" (pp. 76–77).

As an academic, Turner probably had neither the time nor inclination to self-promote through the media, nor was he as likely to have become embroiled in a public relations battle as the journalist Entine was. Entine's 1995 article documents that he attended a conference at which Turner spoke on the nonsustainability and image appropriation involved in the Rainforest Harvest enterprise and on the continuation of the Kayapo's land concessions to mining and logging operations in Brazil, despite the presence of "Trade Not Aid." He also reports that the Rainforest Harvest partnership failed as a business (Entine, 1995). Whether these sources, the Federal Trade Commission pressure Entine reports in 1994 regarding its Third World activities, or other sources were responsible for the impact on The Body Shop is uncertain. But, within the following business year, notable changes were evident in the public relations artifacts and rhetoric used by The Body Shop. All the exotic pictures of people from disadvantaged supplier communities disappeared from the firm's newest public relations materials.

Controversy Aftermath

The public attention to The Body Shop and, by reflection, to its socially responsible movement colleagues, prompted extensive discussion and reevaluation of the meaning of social responsibility in business (e.g., Utne, 1995). The chief response within the company has been a move toward more conventional forms of management control, in particular, the use of independent customer and supplier surveys and of financial, governance, business process, social, and environmental audits.

At The Body Shop, a new emphasis on the core of the business was oriented to clearing up both internal concerns and public images of poor management and misunderstanding; in 1995, this included bringing in a professional managing director (the role Anita Roddick had previously occupied), restructuring the company, professionalizing the management team, and tightening process and inventory control (Wallace and Brown, 1996, p. 3). Another new content focus, the firm's pure-business aim, is now expressed in the firm's communications and artifacts. Instead of colorful images of indigenous suppliers, the firm emphasizes quantitative results of scientific surveys and multipoint agendas for program improvement, most often in bulleted or list form. After 1995, The Body Shop's public relations materials begin to look somewhat more like those of other large, established companies in the United States and United Kingdom.

Firm publications also contain more concrete information about the firm's social investments, however, and this material is presented in an unusually (for either The Body Shop or the industry) candid style. For the first time, the firm's values report summary for the year 1995 (The Body Shop, 1996, January) clearly states that the firm had just 12 Trade Not Aid supplier groups as of February 1995; also for the first time under a "Bad News" category, it adds that "Forecasting of future ordering volumes from Trade Not Aid suppliers has been problematic" and that "Some of the Trade Not Aid links are not commercially viable in the conventional sense and have a high level of dependency on orders from The Body Shop." Earlier, these observations would have been available only from unfriendly outsiders.

The Body Shop's 1996 annual report also underscores the impression of a reversal of the earlier years' public relations strategy of placing Anita Roddick in the most prominent position. While she is still present in the report and continues to use the artifacts and language of counterculture, it is Gordon Roddick, the company chair, whose report of financial and business performance, company management, and future plans dominates the document. The most absorbing new agenda for The Body Shop now appears to be its business' bottom line.

Bottom Line as Agenda

Other members of the original network for socially responsible businesses, for example, Ben and Jerry's, which has undertaken professional management and a larger salary range within the company, also appear to be moving on to a more traditional concept of business (*Business Ethics*, 1994; Entine, 1995). This direction might well have caused some second thoughts, if not nostalgia. In late 1995, the Roddicks had advanced a press release stating their intention to buy back shares and make the company private again. This was followed by an announcement in spring 1996 of abandonment of these plans. The reason they gave was that such a buyback would hinder the company's future growth (Cowe, 1995; *Wall Street Journal*, 1996). The second announcement resulted in an increase in the firm's stock price, which had sagged following the initial buyback announcement. The principals' and observers' comments on this buyback plan indicate primarily a concern for financial and business performance, but the plan itself may also have indicated a wish on the founders' parts to return to greater control over the management of the company and perhaps even to achieve a more satisfactory resolution of the contradictory aspects of running a business and aspiring to ideals of social change. The affluence the firm has gained, and its founders' acknowledgment of the imperative of future growth, have forced them to face the fact that a business is first a profit-making organization. Vander Weyer (1996), speaking entirely from a pure-business perspective, comments on the difficulty of entrepreneurial "tycoons" who try to privatize their publicly traded firms:

> A private company may be in some respects a more perfect model, because the interests of owners and managers are aligned without the interference of misleading stock-market signals. But privacy is a luxury which most ambitious companies cannot afford. And that, in the end, is why stock markets exist. (p. 9)

Public financing moves a business to manage purely economic outcomes with great finality, but Anita Roddick's early characterizations of The Body Shop's public flotation had attempted to dodge this self-evident fact. In 1991, she said, regarding her investors, "I have no obligations to these people at all" (p. 22). Later, after a decline in profits was reported for 1993, she again criticized the "speculators" for "greed" (Kepos, 1995, p. 4), even though she had been quite willing to sell them shares to underwrite the firm's growth. On the face of it, this is either disingenuous or a denial of business realities.

In any social institution, working at cross purposes at the same ecological level is like trying to defy gravity. The Body Shop does not defy gravity; its spokesperson only talked about defying it. A more integral strategy of social responsibility might be to acknowledge the business' creation and accumulation of wealth, but to exploit its other social benefits for society, while also seeking ways to decrease or compensate for negative effects. We have argued that the success of this is enhanced by finding, not legislating, bases of common understanding, and then through maximizing the agency and discretion of its people throughout the organization.

The rhetoric and largely public relations activities of an agenda company such as The Body Shop could be contrasted with the many projects that have been instituted from other sectors primarily for purposes of business and economic development to alleviate poverty in the Third World or to ensure the economic stability and competitiveness of a region. Two of the most well-known examples of independent business development illustrate the difficulty of trying to ensure a double bottom line for a particular activity in a particular area. The Grameen Bank of Bangladesh and the industrial Mondragón Cooperative in the Basque region of Spain have both been admired for balancing social considerations with wealth generation. Both have fundamentally involved social improvement equally with business for profit, but both have also depended on legal or financial buffers provided from other sectors to do this, from government and intergovernmental institutions.

As Wahid (1993, 1994) has reported in some detail, the Grameen Bank, although primarily development oriented, has never been competitively self-sustaining in global market terms. While at the time of his study its internal management was improving in efficiency and he viewed its future with optimism, Wahid reports that the bank still relied on highly concessional interest rates, arranged through the international development lending institutions. Likewise, the Mondragón Cooperative's socially engineered prosperity and industrial success since the 1950s, as described by Whyte (1991), has been buffeted in recent years by lowered tariff protections within its national setting with the coming of the European Union (Morris, 1995).

If these robust examples of social-equity-oriented businesses, with all their trans-sectoral support, face severe challenges amid an unprotected, globalizing business environment, how much more difficult it would be to imagine a highly niched specialty business bolstering fragile, marginalized supplier communities while competing across global labor and material markets. Even with the best of practices and multiple resources, this would be extraordinarily difficult. Both the other examples involved trans-sectoral activity from their inception. The Body Shop may indeed have been simply unaware of its Kayapo trading partners' alternate realities—including their survival hedge of making land concessions to miners and loggers. Given the firm's claims, irresponsibility would as surely describe the firm's ignorance as it would a willed inattentiveness.

Some companies attempt to redistribute some of their wealth or their customers' wealth through such schemes as matching point-of-purchase donations or through responsible credit card accounts. These techniques may indeed draw the market's attention to social need and motivate participation in charity. The results of this charitable donation brokerage could be measured, but it is only a convenient mechanism of disbursement and does not reverse the purposes of business. High-hype companies, even if they are not exploiting vulnerable mascots, could be argued to erode an affluent public's support, through competition for scarce time and attention, to those pet projects that primarily enhance the company's image, turning the market away from less sensational but more substantial and effective social projects. For the same reasons that ethics vary, despite the many rational schemes that have been devised to measure this in specific techniques or activities, there is not now, or is there likely soon to be, any blanket consensus on the identification of which such projects are best or most deserving.

Reflections

From a social change viewpoint, while social irresponsibility in business through misleading publicity about social activity should continue to be examined and publicly criticized, there is no decisive evidence of punishment for global firms for exploitation by association. The articulation of social responsibility praxis is more an issue for intellectuals and professional activists than for most customers and shareholders. The praise and awards that The Body Shop and its cofounders have received for ethical leadership, marketing, and raising public awareness of social issues well illustrate this.

The market does not punish a business because it depends heavily on the content of its mediated messages. To the contrary; the traditional business ethical mandate extends the conception of honesty as far as fair notice to consumers of risk or potential harm to them or, as is increasingly the case these days, of demonstrated risk of harm to the producers' employees and subcontractors.

Beyond a certain point, purity of product or of message content is an issue of market differentiation. It only becomes an issue if it is a company's chief means of product differentiation and if there is a good likelihood that competitors or critics can show that a meaningful discrepancy exists. There are many firms that possess the market knowledge, the communication, and the legal tools to countercampaign, stopping unfavorable publication in important markets, and which, on the strength of their success, may well receive the blessing of their financial stakeholders to do this. By the same token, in a globally mediated environment, those who

count on the single publicized exposé to achieve social correction or business solutions in a simple or direct way will be disappointed. Agenda drove Entine's exposé as surely as it did the ideological campaigns of The Body Shop.

For business, the core issues are defined by the values orientations of the
wider culture in which business is done. Viewed through an American business
cultural lens, with an emphasis on truthfulness, guilt about the frontier past, and
pluralistic competition, global companies cannot operate like frontier trading posts
and call themselves role models of social responsibility. Through a British business
cultural lens, which emphasizes loyalty to brand and particular meanings for fair
play, American exposé journalism probably seems a shockingly uncivil hatchet job,
a failure to be understanding of inevitable human shortfalls despite noble intentions. Thus, differences in the business cultures of the two market regions were
also part of the reason that The Body Shop found itself in a completely nonintegral
position, over cultural interpretations of ethics.

Over time, movements tend to become institutions, and the institutions that
survive have equipped themselves to respond to an ecology of thinking and relationships that is not necessarily integrated with, or responsive to, varying local
conditions. What began as an eclectic hodgepodge of good intentions may end in a
newly chastened socially responsible concept of business. The institutional merger
of unrelated and unproven bits and pieces of theory into a combined agenda, however, does nothing to guarantee against missing the point of responsible integration
again.

The consequences of capitalizing on the images and issues of agenda, while
forgetting to respond to the variation in practice and attitude, are further instances
of nonintegral business. The authors of this book have argued that there is an alternate, and complementary, way between the lines of battle or of standardization,
with greater attention to cultural interpretation.

It will always be inconvenient to deal with the basic moral neutrality of economic provisioning. Agenda attempts to legislate social knowledge—prescriptions
for how people should act—in the absence of direct access to, evaluation against,
and interpretation for an underlying cultural logic of the situation. It would be less
trouble initially to rely on categories of agenda or, alternately, to rationalize ethical
agendas into ever more secularized interpretations of their originating communal
spirit. Zealous companies and management control agendas alike take on unwitting

risks when they look no further than social responsibility on the face of it. Responsible practitioners find and occupy a common moral plane with their partners, their customers, and their public. This requires work at translation and understanding of relevant implications of the trade, tangible and intangible. To pretend that business is anything else misses the point.

Notes

1. Roddick's (1991) account describes the decision to make all shops uniform and to approve all social campaigns in the shops. *Advertising Age* (1994), Clark (1995), and R. Davis (1994) all give detailed reports of the Body Shop's combativeness and pressure campaigns to stop unfavorable publicity. Entine's (1994) exposé contains accounts of franchisees who said they were intimidated and not treated responsively.
2. It is not our intent to speculate whether or not any misleading as an effect of the company's activities was intentional.
3. This was a phrase also used in Anderson's conversation with New Academy of Business planners at the Body Shop headquarters in summer 1995.
4. A *Fortune* article (Wallace and Brown, 1996) reports that an unnamed research group characterized the Entine piece as "broadly unfair" (p. 6).
5. Later, the Body Shop amended and clarified its position, and supported the AIDs research movement (The Body Shop, 1996, May).
6. This was a strategy that was said to cause losses in the U.S. stores through the firm's unfamiliarity with this retail market (Wallace and Brown, 1996).
7. One of the Cadbury Code's stipulations is that a minimum of three non-executive directors be appointed to a public company of the size of The Body Shop (Kepos, 1995). Two non-executive directors were named in October 1994, just after the exposé was released (The Body Shop, 1996, May, pp. 3, 28).

5
Cooperative Action Inquiry and Culture:
An Ethnology of Information

In the last two chapters, we suggested alternative ways that the use and cultural interpretations of power, through leadership and facilitative roles, affect whether a business organization integrates for commerce with its social environments. The early history of Apple Computers, Incorporated, showed what happened to wider social integration when a shamanistic inspirer gave way to a pure-business transactional leader who placed priority on managerial control of the environment. The Body Shop case illustrated how the leaders of a business attempted to legislate a social agenda of the wider society, a mostly unilateral organization of reality, which they expressed mainly through controlled public relations and heavy reliance on manipulation of relational power through mediated communications.

Neither an ideology of institutional criticism nor a management control agenda by itself does much to guarantee organizational responsibility, which is the cultural integration of an organization by all the people within and across the organization's boundaries. This wider and immediate context of the firm is the community in which and to which practitioners must be responsible. This chapter points the way more specifically and technically, viewing an organization from the perspective of midlevel management within a multinational environment.

Specifying this perspective is important: Unlike the senior levels of management in the specially niched but global organizations such as Apple and The Body Shop, the midlevel manager in a large transcultural operation often has far more compelling opportunities to observe the seams and borders—organizational, national, and regional—across which locally varying operations must meet. Unlike chief officers, who have the greater luxury (and danger) of potential cultural self-isolation, the global middle manager must look both inward, toward the company core, and outward, on field and market, in a unique way. This person's job includes both personal responsibility in culturally interpretive work and responsibility for the more abstract work of a commercial system's orchestration and interpretation. Both of these aspects appear in our case discussion of this chapter. Through a practice illustration of the collaborative development of an organizational culture, we show how a conjoint process occurred between people's ethnological learning and an information system's learning, using guidance and feedback. For, while these are interdependent processes, they are not the same process. Socially responsible business, unlike a promulgated agenda of ethics or of ideological social responsibility, is not an organization *of* reality; rather, it connects people through enacted, shared meanings so they can organize themselves *for* reality.

Our qualitative case illustrates the methods of ethnology and organizational learning that were used to co-create an organization for maximum commerce with its wider and immediate environments. During a period of seven years in the early 1980s, one flagging multinational region of a large company became a transcultural learning organization. Its members researched, developed, and used cultural information for business results. We describe how the three basic heuristics for culture were deployed in a field ethnographic approach, using a variation on anthropology's principal methodology, participant observation. The process was guided through the development and expansion of an information system that transmitted business and cultural knowledge to all its members. In this process, the content of discovery itself played a role in the further development of information and its flow. The case illustrates the coexistence and interaction of multiple traditional and nontraditional research, leadership, and application roles.

Problematic Organizational Culture and Its Ethnic Alternative

To meaningfully begin what is largely a methodological story, we need to return to the concept of culture and its learning as a discovery process. In Chapter 1, we noted the usefulness of gathering field data about unfamiliar cultural settings and organizing them into three heuristic categories that roughly correspond to empirically observed dimensions of culture: *cultural logic*—the sense-making, conceptual "glue" that underpins and interrelates normative evaluations and is based on alternate world views; *social knowledge*—the "how to's" that comprise a culture's prescriptive ethics or behavioral expectations; and *artifacts*—those outward symbols, objects, and behaviors that are most noticeable to newcomers and that alert them to look for deeper interpretations and interrelationships.

The task of achieving a more holistic social integration relies on developing certain aspects of the cultural features of an organization. Yet, the current, copious literature on organizational culture presents a confusing picture. What is organizational culture, as distinct from one's culture by childhood socialization in a particular country or native social region? How do the three heuristic elements for interactive cultural learning fit with the concept of organizational cultureorganizational?

The cultural features of business organizations have been richly debated, theorized, and described in surveys and case examples within and across organizations. But, from an empirical standpoint, organizational cultureorganizational has, if anything, been more poorly understood than constructs such as national or regional culture. Organizations as cultural systems reflect the geographical and historical cultural patterns of their originators and leaders. These founder and leader effects occur to varying degrees, and the interplay of these with geographic cultural differences, in joint ventures and in multinational companies, has been observed to affect the success and direction of particular companies (see, for example, Brannen and Sanyal, 1993; Garsten, 1994; Hamada, 1991).

Hofstede (1980) has inferred patterned international distribution of underlying value preferences associated with different world-regional cultures, as determined from cross-national surveys, using empirical measurement of social psychological dimensions. Hofstede, Neuijev, Ohayv, and Sanders (1990) have tried to measure organizational culture in a somewhat similar methodology as used in Hofstede's earlier culture-by-countries study, although organizational culture has so far seen less corroboration or replication. The measures involved ideal or desired work goals, general work-related beliefs (normative values), and perceptions of workplace practices and expectations of work behavior (p. 295). The practices and patterns measures correspond roughly to our concept of social knowledge in the workplace.

This group of scholars found that clear variations existed in the normative values (most closely related to cultural logic and world view) within the subject organizations, reflecting the national cultures across which these organizations were spread (Netherlands and Denmark). In short, within organizations, there was a measurable influence on values orientations of the respective native social regions of the workers, exactly as we might expect. But, the differences between *organizations*, those that most people would view as organizational culture, came from the perceived practices questions—from social knowledge. Hofstede et al. argue that these, and not the normative values, are what constitute corporate culture (1990, p. 311). These social knowledge dimensions emerged as six factors, which Hofstede's group termed cultural orientations relevant to the workplace. The factors were (1) process orientation versus results orientation, (2) employee orientation versus job orientation, (3) parochial versus professional, (4) open versus closed system, (5) loose versus tight control, and (6) normative (i.e., principled) versus pragmatic. These six factors together explained 73% of the variance in organizational culture differences (Hofstede et al., 1990, p. 311).

Krackhardt and Kilduff (1990) derived a roughly comparable set of workplace-culture constructs in an American study of friendship networks and corporate culture. Notably similar were their dimensions of people versus task orientation, degree of relative flexibility, blunt versus diplomatic communications style, corner cutting versus formal rule abiding, and two dimensions that, taken together, resemble the Dutch group's informal-formal contrast; these were Krackhardt and Kilduff's easygoing versus competitive and their "letting things slide" versus efficient/organized (1990, p. 145).

A third study by Sackman (1992), done in a single American company, again comes up with several similar implicit dimensions. She calls social knowledge the employees' "directory knowledge," which she says is "knowledge about chains of events and about their cause and effect relationships . . . [and] delineates the 'how' of things and events" (p. 142). This is the part of culture that is distributed throughout the organization.

Taken together, the findings of these scholars cast doubt on a modern business management tendency to promulgate an agenda for responsibility through lists of "values" that they believe will regulate their employees' behavior, either ethical or economic. Krackhardt and Kilduff observe that much of social knowledge is cultural, that is, emergent from within the members' own experience and networks:

> To the extent that the culture of an organization is transmitted and transmuted by the friendship network, it is clearly outside the control of the formal organizational socialization and reward system. . . . Everyone in the organization may believe in the virtues of both honesty and initiative, but people may differ as to how specific behavior . . . should be interpreted. . . . Within any organizational culture the same set of cultural values can lead to discrepant attributions about the same people. (1990, p. 151)

The Hofstede group speculates about the formative historical and power relationship of the normative values orientations of a firm's leaders on the social knowledge of its workforce:

> The U.S. management literature rarely distinguishes between the values of founders . . . and the values of the bulk of the organization's members. . . . Founders and leaders' values become members' practices. (1990, p. 311)

Sackman (1992) describes her concept for leaders' values orientations, "axiomatic knowledge," as

> based on basic assumptions that cannot be further reduced. Lower-level employees acted on the leader's axiomatic knowledge (previously identified as the formative experiences for a firm's founders and top managers), but they were not cognizant of it, despite further probing by the researcher. (p. 153)

The implication of these findings and interpretations is interesting: An organization's culture boils down empirically to its social knowledge. This social knowledge is affected both by the organization workforce's cultural processes—as enacted in social networks of people who interpret it similarly—and by the historical influence of the leaders' values. But, the basis for these influences is not necessarily in the conscious awareness of the workforce. It will clearly be impossible to impose "culture" effectively from the top down through conscious adoption of an agenda based on the leader's "values" commandments because there is so much latitude for their interpretation in social knowledge. From the other side, it may be possible to legislate certain behavior, but then the attitudes—the social knowledge of its interpretation—still escape control. Why then bother to engage in a difficult process of learning how artifacts, social knowledge, and cultural logic form the whole of a culture?

From a holistic perspective, we must conclude that "organizational culture," if interpreted as behavior or as social knowledge about behavior only, is no culture at all. That is to say, analyzing it rigorously has provided a set of empirical factors of social knowledge that have been distinguished, at the organizational level, among some Western-run firms, but knowing these by themselves will do little for one's understanding of the entire cultural context in which those organizations must responsibly operate. Either social knowledge or behavior alone gives us little to go on, to improve an organization's relationship with its business market, let alone its imagined community and the wider society.

Thinking only in terms of culture at the organizational level thus provides material that is *cultural*, but is not itself *culture*, not in that holistic sense that may be accessed by the participant observation and related inquiry methods we are about to describe. In fact, such knowledge is so partial and the organizational framework so limited in itself, that it is more helpful, in applied situations of the cultural revitalization of an organization, to describe the emerging organization as a kind of ethnic group (Reeves-Ellington, 1995b).

An ethnic group fulfills the requirements of holism by existing explicitly with relationship to a wider societal area of reference. It has a feeling of culturally traceable relatedness in that the members share at least some of their normative values; but this sharing, reflecting their immersion in the larger, culturally plural context, is partial and specific—the part that is shared is more consciously recognized and voluntarily constructed. It is chosen by affiliation and identity, and it is more explicit than the cultural logic of a native social region.

Underlying ethnicity, as Reeves-Ellington (1995b, p. 250) has argued, are theoretical parameters of (1) the ethnic group as a social vessel (Barth, 1969); (2) ethnic identification and social identification (Bell, 1975); and (3) ethnicity as it relates to material goods and status (Glazer and Moynihan, 1975). Without a holistic acknowledgment of culture, which includes greater awareness of native socialized cultures, practitioners cannot achieve the fullest organization–environment integration. Responsibility, with personal agency, involves the members of a business organization as whole persons; these people will have ties to the wider society that they can reflect responsibly in their participation in the workplace.[1]

The Case, Relevance of Methods, and Plan of Presentation

Africa/Asia (A/A), a geographically dispersed, multicontinent region of Pharmco (pseudonym), an American-based multinational pharmaceutical company, provides our case. We characterize this organization's self-transformation process as organizational learning, rather than just individuals learning in an organization, for several reasons: (1) information was not developed exclusively or even primarily for management's use; (2) the deployment of information was not unilaterally directed; (3) a multilateral inquiry proceeded as an interlinked discovery process, with corrective and adjustive feedback throughout the organization; and (4) the learning was both organizational and cultural because the organization's members uncovered important cultural values and learned more about their own, as well as others', associated behavior patterns. They could then act on the information, reflecting on and adjusting their own behavior to do business more effectively in the region, regardless of their formal position or function in the organization. To make this system function in ways that permitted cross-boundary communications— across internal and external boundaries—a revised sense of organization was needed. The result was an opening of the organization from one legally defined to one that incorporated the entire customer chain. The vehicle for this organization's transformation was a guided information exchange process.

This case has special relevance to current problems of culture in business. Culture has played, and will continue to play, an increasing role as a business problematic in the globalizing economy. Although culture is frequently mentioned in the rhetoric about complexity, process, and international business issues ranging from politics and security to law, marketing, and joint ventures, it receives little attention as a shaping influence on organizational information flow and management. This may be in part due to American and western European cultural traditions that value elegance and control and, particularly in America, the propensity to recognize only senior management as the authors and voices of a firm's cultural interpretations. Ultimately, leaders try to reduce and pull away from engagement with complexity and its accompanying risks. Discussion of management in rapid organizational change (e.g., Kanter, 1996; Nadler, 1995; Vaill, 1996), the need for a knowledge-intensive workforce that has "learned to learn" (Drucker, 1992; Reich, 1993), and the rising importance of learning or "smart" organizations and systems (Argyris and Schoen, 1978; Patchell, 1993; Senge, 1994) are now almost commonplace.

In Chapter 1 ("Cultural Learning Model," p. 27), we discussed the cultural learning model for using experience in encounters to classify cultural artifacts, social knowledge, and cultural logic in an abstract way. We also discussed the general usefulness of ethnography for finding and classifying data within this heuristic model. *Ethnography*, the description of particular cultural settings, is part of the larger study of *ethnology*, the anthropology of living social and cultural systems that, among its many goals, seeks the qualitative understanding of differences in meaning and interpretation among these diverse systems. The ethnologist gains this understanding through the study of cultural theory, field and historical reports, and cultural products, but, most importantly, by conducting systematic, firsthand participant observation (PO), an experiential and interactive mode of learning in the field. We sketch some common PO methods in greater detail in this chapter.[2]

Using a continual-improvement process for information development, and applying the cultural knowledge this process afforded, the Pharmco A/A region rebuilt itself under the new vice president's leadership as a more effective product and service delivery system. This was accomplished mainly through the way information was used—more deeply and fully embedding the organization in and across multiple local contexts and largely relying on the knowledge and efforts of people. The members continually improved their communicative transparency across the entire chain of exchange. Field sales representatives were one of, but not by any means the only, practitioners with a central role in testing the results of inquiry. Members throughout the A/A region took on a greater degree and variety of social exchanges, investments, and responsibilities for the organization's business and community relations.

The ultimate goals in the Pharmco case were business–economic aims, as stipulated by its corporate home office. These globally issued business aims had to be applied locally in specific countries of the A/A region. So, there was also an externally directed action component with specified outcomes.[3] Thus, the inquiry activity overall is best characterized as *cooperative action research*. For reasons

that we describe below, the enabling objectives of the research, at both the individual and organizational levels, were (1) to develop detailed cultural and behavioral
knowledge of both the self and the organization proper and those with whom the
organization did business, then (2) to integrate, orchestrate, and apply this cultural
knowledge in business-enhancing activities throughout and beyond the organization's formal boundaries. The research therefore combined the applied paradigms
of process improvement and customer focus in business with more academic
qualitative research paradigms. Much of the important new information was collected and transformed to organizational knowledge via field strategies and frameworks of ethnology.

We present this case, first, by developing the ethnological framework for understanding and interpreting the main thrust of the Pharmco inquiry. We then introduce the elements of an applied information systems framework for understanding its organizational application to business development—its action component.
These two frameworks can be summarized as the ethnological and information
systems' aspects of the case. Finally, we describe the results of the effort, in social
and business terms, develop the insights and implications of what was learned, and
suggest directions for combined research and practice in the future.

We highlight certain departures from management convention that may be
necessary for successful reintegration of business with environment, as transcultural information systems, namely, (1) importing relevant knowledge not obviously
related to the traditional business substrate; (2) acknowledging the limitations of
emphasis on traditional personnel selection, development, and job function, for resolving organizational information-to-knowledge needs; (3) viewing culture as an
avenue for bridging discipline and interest boundaries and developing sociocultural
knowledge for business applications; and (4) expanding on the possibilities and
demands of leadership for cooperative action research.

Cooperative Inquiry, Ethnology, and Information Systems

An overarching methodological paradigm of this case is cooperative inquiry
(Reason, 1994). The premise for cooperative research is that open communication
will enable people to work together and to choose how they view others and the
environment, which all people share. It is based on experimental inquiry in specific

contexts. Reason sets out four major methodological steps for doing cooperative research.

Phase 1—Co-researchers agree on an area for inquiry and identify some initial research propositions. They . . . try out . . . some particular skills, or seek to change some aspect of their world. They also agree to some set of procedures by which they will observe and record their own and each other's experience.

Phase 2—The co-researchers then apply these ideas and procedures in their everyday life and work.

Phase 3—The co-researchers will . . . become fully immersed in this activity and experience.

Phase 4—After an appropriate period engaged in Phases 2 and 3, the co-researchers will return to consider their original propositions and hypotheses in the light of experience, modifying, reformulating, and rejecting them, adopting new hypotheses. (pp. 326–327)

The organization took on the soft and analytically difficult terrain of culture for inquiry, in part, because Pharmco A/A was a relatively peripheral outpost within the pharmaceutical industry. There were no new products in the line and no programmatic, corporatewide marketing strategies in the offing; it faced a region-specific performance challenge. The region's anthropologically trained operations vice president, Reeves-Ellington, was mindful of A/A's diverse and multicultural workforce and market, which spanned multiple continents. The A/A organization was geographically broad and economically marginal within the parent corporation, a well-known U.S. "signature" corporation with what Hofstede's group would recognize as a results-oriented, "strong culture" (Hofstede et al., 1990, p. 302). The corporate group's chief focus was a set of related product sectors, including paper, consumer goods, pharmaceuticals, and the like. While the Pharmco A/A region had more than 500 direct employees, the American parent corporation was a $44 billion conglomerate.

In 1983, the A/A region was displaying numerous symptoms of a faltering business. Its product line was aging, its market position was poor (two major brands were in a low sixth place regionally), its managers were neglected and ill-trained, and its customers had no image of the company. The region's senior company management presented a clear challenge: Pharmco A/A would become successful in key regional markets within five years. It would achieve the break-even point in three years, obtain U.S. $4 million in profits within five years, and reduce workforce size to meet fiscal challenges. Failure to achieve these goals would result in closing the regional business.

The region's new, anthropologically trained vice president, Reeves-Ellington, persuaded the region's managers to undertake a major business revitalization based on an ethnological approach to culture (cf. Reeves-Ellington, 1995b). This revitalization would involve the creation of a cultural learning organization. The organization's members began a dialogue and ultimately achieved a cultural alignment that enabled important information regarding the views and preferences of their customers to travel back and forth, with implications for behavior adjustment along the region's entire chain of exchange. This exchange was to include both traditional insiders to the organization and outsiders.

Viewing the Organization as an Extended Information System

Companies working for a more culturally aligned relationship with their partners and customers must gain a sense of "insidership" along the entire chain of exchange. The question of how to build a common working culture, how to have a business-enhancing dialogue based on shared values and expectations in a multicultural setting, comes under consideration when the organization extends to include its entire customer chain. To create an extended organizational information system requires that elements of culture and society be shared throughout the customer-supplierchain. This in turn calls for sufficient knowledge of all the culture sets involved, both national and organizational, along that chain.

Such knowledge gives the ability to predict sufficiently how each culture expresses its desires and what each expects as to social behavior. A synthetic culture of information exchange must be developed to enable information to flow through all these relevant linkages. All successful transcultural exchange involves movement from a multicultural, or mixed set, of frames of reference to a newly synthesized, interpretive framework that focuses on the commonalties. In short, it must become more integrated, harmonized, and facilitative for its members over time (Anderson, A., and Reeves-Ellington, 1995; Reeves-Ellington, 1995a, 1995b).

Emphasizing shared values, as well as expectations, in customer chains permits members to function both socially and commercially. Dorothy Lee provides a participant's subjective experience of cultural alignment in her remark: "The clarity of the structure within which I find myself—that is, the 'social constraint' . . . makes it possible for me to act . . . when I live in dialogue with this structure. . . . . It makes it possible for me to proceed in what would otherwise be a confusing jungle: It makes it possible for me to function" (1963, 63).

Figure 7 gives an impression of how the closer and localized customer chain culture and society of the marginal Africa/Asia region had to link into a larger, traditional, and formal corporate structure of the parent corporation. The nontraditional sources that were taken into the A/A, as an extended information system, were what permitted organizational learning for social responsibility.

The learning tasks facing A/A required certain radical departures from the organization's traditional information arrangements. To understand, develop, and implement this type of organization required novel research and process designs. First, the organization, through its managers, had to permit experimentation. As reflected in Figure 1, the traditional hierarchical organization had to be opened out to an extended customer chain. Centralized directives, primarily those of pure business–economic concerns, came from senior management. Throughout cultural development, the traditional business reports continued to move upward through the larger organization's channels. The regional staff, by individual country, used nontraditional methods of information gathering (discussed below) and integrated both existing customers and potential new customers into the organization. Within Pharmco, the boss of the A/A regional manager acted as a buffer between the region and the rest of the organization. One of his key jobs was to interpret the social activities of the region for the rest of Pharmco.

Cultural issues, and the interpretive content they convey, are an integral part of organizations as changing information systems and therefore have a large impact on organizational learning from a management perspective at the mid-level of organizations. Few applied examples from inside business practice directly and centrally address these practicalities of world-regional culture as an issue of information systems. Material is available on identifying certain kinds of manage-

Figure 7

Africa / Asia Region as Social Organization

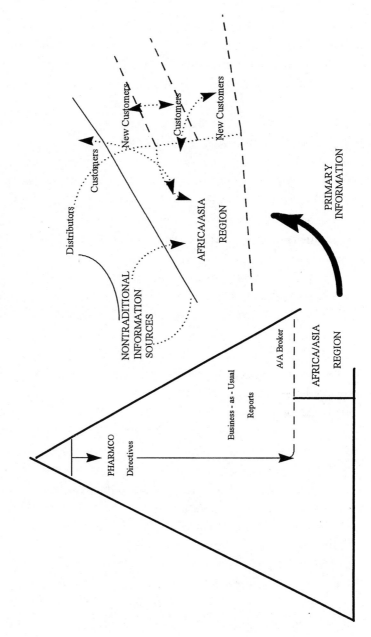

rial personnel for intercultural work (for example, Dalton and Wilson, 1996) and on general skills and attitudes that will help individuals be more successful in their intercultural encounters, but as Asante and Gudykunst (1989) point out, for reasons of the dynamic and patterned nature of cultural elements, this approach is inherently limited and can be problematic.

There is also a vast and burgeoning culture-specific literature that tries to brief managers on how to act and what to expect in specific national settings (for example, Mole, 1991). All these efforts attest to the great and continuing need to understand better how to do business in transcultural organizations and markets. But, the cultural contexts will always keep changing. Foreign organizations and partner industries will keep shifting and reinterpreting their practices. Throughout, there is little in-depth discussion of this aspect of cultural knowledge for holistic applications at the organization level.

Even less discussion exists of cultural knowledge as the driver and integrator of organizational learning and of its central role in organizational information processes. Academic ethnographic researchers' discussions of particular transcultural businesses, while generally high in quality and interest (e.g., Garsten, 1994; Hamada, 1991), lack the management practitioner's applications perspective.

Perhaps scarcest of all is material that addresses the cultural and information mechanisms bridging organizational boundaries and successive levels of inclusion. Nevertheless, this is a daily requirement of managing organizational information. Social science and management consulting discussions of learning organizations tend to adopt a clinical, internal approach, holding culture constant and discussing levels of organization serially. While they may acknowledge culture is important, they do not deal effectively with it relative to external environments (e.g., Argyris and Schoen, 1978). Other scholars, who take more interorganizational and international perspectives, usually limit their focus to structural features, which allows the development of network metrics and typologies at the whole organization level (e.g., Scott, 1991; Uzzi, 1993).

Both internal and structural approaches, while enlightening, provide limited guidance on the quality and content of intraorganizational and transorganizational links and the agents of those links. They say little about the nature of dynamic, person-to-person relationships that invite the outside social surroundings into the internal reaches of the organization. This is one of culture's most adaptive and salient features in organizations, the interplay between new information and content interpretations on the one hand, and new ways in which this information becomes processed on the other. Information flow across levels and transformation of an organization's components and levels, and its permeation of the organization's borders, are partly the result of cultural interpretation, a process that in turn affects the organization's culturally interpretive capacities.

This is a major reason why culture is a central problematic for business and why this problematic is so well suited to the theoretical and methodological orientations of field ethnology. We now turn to a description of culture and the ethnological approach as they related to the business problematic that faced the Pharmco A/A region.

The Ethnological Model and Participant Observation

We have said that cultural systems can be understood as webs of meaning that are always realized in the particular (cf. C. Geertz, 1973). People use culture in a complex and elaborate process of assignment and reassignment of socially valued meanings to the information they develop for action.

Despite its softness and notorious difficulties as a construct, culture is thus a significant and potentially very useful resource for information development and application in businesses. It continually forms, corrodes, and reforms interpreted experience. Culture's manifestations in regular public enactment between people make it accessible to learning by participation, reflection, and practice.

Participant Observation in the Field

Participant observation (PO), as traditionally employed by anthropologists (e.g., Chambers, 1985; Finan and Van Willigen, 1990; Spradley, 1980), permits the businessperson to develop and use multiple sources and channels of communication simultaneously. The primary task is to find out what is important to others (Jorgensen, 1989). This makes accessible what is normally concealed, for example, the backstage and commonsense information from another's point of view that became so important in the high-context cultural environment of Japan that we discussed in Chapter 2 (David, 1985; Hall, 1973). Businesspeople who employ PO skills better relate to those around them and learn more readily how to plan mean-ingful interactions with people of very different backgrounds.

The key modality of gaining information was through the participant observer spending time with others and doing things with them. Effective PO required a combination of direct observation and questioning techniques. This allowed the ongoing, systematic acquisition of findings about what was important to people. Gaining this needed information about others also required active listening, with two main objectives. The first is to hear what is meant by listening for the vocabu-lary chosen and voice inflections used. The second is to "listen" with senses other than hearing for nonverbal messages (as also emphasized by Covey, 1989; Hall and Hall, 1987).

Participant observers require specific plans for action that move them from that which is easily known to that which is normally concealed. Five general action strategies aided Pharmco A/A members in gaining more of this ordinarily con-cealed information. These are shown in Table 9.

A more subtle and intimate knowledge of local and organizational cultural context, gained by intensive and reflective participant observation in the field, far exceeded other methods of gaining cultural knowledge (e.g., workshops, tapes, or

TABLE 9. Strategies for Participant Observation

Appear to know to find out
This is useful because most people like to gossip and teach.

Backstage information gets more backstage information
Indicating contextual knowledge in a situation prompts others to share more of this type of information.

Use others as teachers
In order to gain information, the old journalism framework of "who-what-where-when-why" is suggested for use.

Rank others as witnesses, informants, and backstagers
Different people will provide different types of information and levels of infor-mation, e.g., witnesses confirm cultural information learned; informants teach about cultural matters; backstagers' gossip.

Claim to really need the information
This usually strengthens social bonds and provides serious information.

how-to books containing culture-specific knowledge) in its potential for understanding, response, and growth in business relationships. What was more important, unlike the preselected snapshot views, which may offer little more than packaged, secondary knowledge, learning others' cultures through participant observation will include less irrelevant material and the information that is gained will not be out of date. Applied PO opens the way for broader and deeper social relationships between people, required of any customer-centered organization. In the A/A region, it created a favorable environment for achieving mutually agreed business goals.

Ethnological Constructs for Pharmco A/A's Cultural Encounters

For the purpose of guiding the experiential learning of cultural elements that would be most meaningful and motivating for the Pharmco A/A members and customers, Reeves-Ellington began with F. R. Kluckhohn and Strodbeck's (1961) concept of central value orientations, which we discussed in Chapter 1 ("Metaphors and World View: Cultural Logic and Values Orientations," p. 23). This framework has seen further development and elaboration in the social psychological measures we reviewed by Hofstede (1980); it has been described dynamically by Schein (1985) and has been reformulated for cultural dimensions of the time orientation dimension by such writers as Boninger, Gleicher, and Strathman (1994), Roese (1994), and Strathman, Gleicher, and Edwards (1994).

The discovery of central value orientations in an unfamiliar cultural setting was necessary for a deeper understanding of the informal and underlying cultural influences of the Pharmco A/A organization and the social and national regions in which it operated. Using the three heuristics of culture—cultural logic, social behavior and artifacts—to construct their working understanding of values orientations helped the Pharmco researchers in the field to make greater sense and order of their experiences. They were able to see the direction of their social acts and what culturally shaped their partners and their organizations. All three cultural spheres were necessary to understand both the cultural contexts and the evaluation of actions within those contexts.

Pharmco's practitioners benefited from these ethnological tools in that they enhanced their ability to find an intelligible core of cultural meanings relevant to

social responsibility. This core is found in the interrelationship between the normative cultural logic and social knowledge of expected practices. Knowledge of these
cultural spheres opens the way to a better understanding of the basic ontology of a
culture set. These two aspects of value orientations form the meta-ethical foundation for all behavior in a cultural context and are often articulated as values and
principles. They are in turn reflected in the outward artifacts of custom, tradition,
and symbols. It is the core of these interrelated meanings that can be understood as
the internal "logic" of a cultural set. Such a core accommodates a range of meanings, but in the insiders' cultural construction of reality, it tends to coalesce, so that
their cultural set can be differentiated from other meta-ethical sets.

Among the basic three cultural heuristics, existential values—what we call
social knowledge—provide the moral and ethical basis for human action. Through
knowledge of what makes such a core coherent, A/A members could better understand and more accurately interpret human actions in their cultural context.

To assist A/A members in learning more about the coherence of their own
and the less familiar cultures of their regional customers and partners, Reeves-
Ellington conceptualized the learning process linking these three categories—
cultural logic, social knowledge, and artifacts—and devised a learning tool for
building three corresponding databases to be used in encounters in the field. This
learning model, which we illustrated in Figure 3, Chapter 1 ("Culture Encounter
Model," p. 28) provided a framework by which culturally important information
could be categorized and understood for specific applications in transcultural encounters. In this form, it also provided semantic cues for the lay user for appropriate kinds of information to seek in cultural encounters (what, how, who) and for
how the information is likely to be acquired and processed (i.e., seeing, hearing,
interpreting, understanding).

The categories of Figure 3 thus provide orienting assumptions for members of
a transcultural organization. They permit the user to gain information about basic
assumptions of others to interpret concrete behavior from the perspective of other
cultural frames. Visually and intellectually, the model assumes initial transcultural
contacts with outward artifacts, then the acquisition of social interpretive knowledge for better comprehending those artifacts, and finally, if possible, an understanding regarding the cultural logic that forms the basis for all of the more superficial expectations and appearances.

Cultural logic, as the ultimate set of sense-making relationships for a sociocultural system at both macro- and microlevels, answers the journalistic "why" of normative values orientations. This includes a cultural tradition's underlying assumptions about group, human nature, human relations, and relations to the environment. It offers a way to improve understanding of orienting normative values and a basis for grasping and aligning with the prescriptive ethics of social knowledge, the second term of the learning model. Cultural sets cluster in patterned ways, and any successful society—or organization—has discernible consistency in the basic value orientations that its members use to align with each other.

For this reason, once they had begun to use the ethnological tools of understanding how others' normative values orientations were expressed in social knowledge and artifacts, A/A members had to begin a process of change in their own practices that would be maximally holistic, responsive, and adaptable. For this task they had first to clarify and understand better their *own* normative values. As the "desirable," normative values are directional (invoking good or bad outcomes). They are ideological or absolute. They are applied to all people within the cultural framework under consideration. Insiders will use these norms for evaluating the degree of cultural alignment of others. No specific actions ensue directly from normative values. However, people act as if, and often believe, their ethical foundations are, or should be, universal rather than culturally specific.

Yet, cultural logic alone gives the user little information for application in the context of a social encounter. Social knowledge has more immediate behavioral implications; it reflects and interprets cultural logic for social action. It provides both the interactional "rules of the game" for behavior and their immediate interpretations for social consequences. As we have seen from the studies of social knowledge, which forms what researchers call the organizational culture, the relationship of cultural logic to social knowledge is subtle and variable. Artifacts, the most accessible information inputs, include the "who-what-where-when" aspects of getting or of "seeing" a culture.[4]

From the perspective of an ethnological field researcher, the culture model described by Figure 8 more closely reflects the participant observer's subjective reality in the field. The participant observer experiences being in the center of a given cultural milieu. All three types of cultural information are bombarding this observer simultaneously. The participant observer needs to enter this situation

Figure 8

Understanding and Predicting Culture

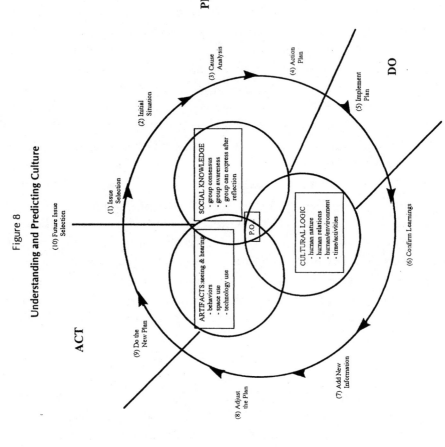

PLAN

DO

CHECK

ACT

(1) Issue Selection

(2) Initial Situation

(3) Cause Analysis

(4) Action Plan

(5) Implement Plan

(6) Confirm Learnings

(7) Add New Information

(8) Adjust the Plan

(9) Do the New Plan

(10) Future Issue Selection

SOCIAL KNOWLEDGE
- group consensus
- group awareness
- group can express after reflection

CULTURAL LOGIC
- human nature
- human relations
- human/environment
- time/activities

ARTIFACTS: seeing & hearing
- behaviors
- space use
- technology use

P.O.

with a clear understanding of the problematic at hand and begin to address interpretations reflectively and systematically. At Pharmco, a plan-do-check-act cycle, illustrated here on the outer ring of Figure 8, gave cues for continual reflective practice in members' business ethnographies. After each encounter, the participant observer makes notes about the observed and enters data into the appropriate database (artifacts, social knowledge, cultural logic). This can be reviewed, reflected on, and confirmed later. This process allows the user to understand what is culturally important in a society or organization and probe more deeply its key elements. It focuses the user on important aspects of culture that may affect personal and organizational success, to share this information with others, and to review periodically the elements for importance, further study, and understanding.

Used reflectively, social knowledge dimensions such as individualism, uncertainty avoidance, and power distance provided an entry point at Pharmco to enable a working group to identify the relative character of their own prescriptive values as an organization. They could then interrelate these identified values for a more coherent and conscious understanding of their own cultural logic.

With iterative self-study and feedback among its members, features of the social knowledge the of A/A region emerged as a common cultural set. These included (1) its intensity (the strength of the ethic), (2) the norm of the values (i.e., what principles members ought to follow), (3) choice and differential allocation of effort (a set of situational priorities), (4) deeds (to demonstrate the strength of the value and ethic), (5) relative importance within the entire cultural set (how a particular ethical dimension is ranked compared to other dimensions in the social knowledge set), and (6) its evaluation in interactive context (its affective meaning in reference to the actors' relationship to each other).

Thus far, we have described an important set of concepts and modals, with associated qualitative research strategies, that were imported from ethnology for organizational learning. This ethnological framework is based on the empirical recognition of differences in values orientations, the use of a heuristic modal of data elements for cultural learning, and a general field research strategy of participant observation. The knowledge imported to the organization by using these anthropological approaches as tools to learn, understand, and operate in and with unfamiliar cultural sets was both content intensive and process driven. It required repeated iterations and cycles of encounters, assessment, and reflection.

This chapter examines individual and systems cognition on two levels: that of the front-line manager and that of the middle and upper middle manager. The primary user of ethnographic materials, as reported in Chapter 1 ("Field Sketch: Cultural Learning Heuristics for Business in Japan," p. 29), is the practitioner. The systems developed and integrated for use at that level are primarily for self-understanding and individual cognition. However, the information gathered and categorized is useful throughout a customer chain. For cultural information to be disseminated throughout the organization (collective cognition), other, more abstract process flows are required. Within the Pharmco experience, such systems were developed by the regional vice president through collaborative actions of members of Pharmco A/A.

To understand how these tools and processes were integrated at a more inclusive organization level with other, different kinds of knowledge, we now turn to a description of the larger organizational information system and research roles they supported.

Integrating an Information System Through Collaborative Action

Conscious organizational development at the cultural level, for Pharmco, required an analytic framework, such as the cultural model we have just discussed, that all participants could understand and use. It also required a fundamental shift in the cognitive paradigms of management—from a preferred modern, Western cultural conception of business in sheer economic terms, to a broader recognition of commerce, with socially and culturally valued interpretations permeating all relationships, including business relations. This also implies shifting the cultural view of the company from the legal, strictly business entity to a more social, commercial one—with the social view being defined by the extended customer chain.

With its own further regional cultural development, Pharmco had ultimately to depart in certain respects from its American home office's monocultural business artifacts and social knowledge. This included, for example, deemphasizing company members' positions in the internal company structure, in which artifacts had been used to mark differential internal status. Pharmco A/A gave more importance to proximity and relationship as locally or regionally defined. As an extended cultural organization, the Pharmco A/A region functioned more horizontally and multilocally, rather than globally and vertically, despite its home organization's strongly influential corporate culture.

Through the cultural inquiry models, multilocal interactional linkages were effectively extended to all external customers. Members accomplished this during and integral to their regular interactions of work as a reflective and transformative act on themselves and their relationships. We now describe how the ethnology and PO models were incorporated into the larger organization as part of the information system of Pharmco A/A. Pharmco members used this process to combine traditional business information systems with the modified view of themselves as a commercial and social interaction system. This part of the Pharmco change story is one of highly pluralistic functions, research roles, and processes, driven by common underlying cultural elements and integrated through a continual improvement process.

The Cooperative Process of Extending the Organization

In Pharmco A/A, both content and process changes were achieved in the extended commercial organization. This required a shift from near-total reliance, in the existing corporation, on traditional academic, scientifically modeled research imported via consulting from the outside, to a pluralistic and continuously integrated and adjusted series of research activities. Information for the A/A region of Pharmco effort came from multiple sources: modern science, participatory action research, cooperative inquiry, and action inquiry. Research and reflective practice, and from these the creation of cultural and commercial knowledge for the organization, emerged from all along the customer chain. The traditional breakdown and application of research done exclusively by the few on the many were replaced by a series of translations exchanged between people, each operating from within a particular organizational and local situation.

Pharmco added three criteria to the general cooperative research methodology in order to refit the model's general approach for action-driven research in a commercial organization. First, the research had to meet *individual* goals for all research participants (an example of one individual's learning in this direction is discussed below). Second, it had to work in ways that also supported the *organization's* ultimate business aims. Third, within cooperative research, each of the researchers' specific products and roles had to connect via an interlocking generative process.

At Pharmco, the cooperative research team consisted of people doing three different kinds of research more or less simultaneously: (1) modern scientific research (largely by outside academics and consultants), (2) action research (by internal managers trained in the social sciences), and (3) participatory action research (by those along the value chain who were responsible for actual business and commercial exchanges). A fourth group, the practitioners, specifically put results into practice and provided feedback.

The cooperative action research operated entirely driven by the generative model of process control called Plan, Do, Check, Act (PDCA), which has since become common in industry. The region's team extended a commercial value chain based on self-identified, interlocking, and shared cultural values orientations. Each new commercial context was addressed and resolved through the application of the ethnographic and cooperative research techniques.

An Overview of Research Roles and Paradigms

The combination of such a disparate set of functions, preparations, and points of view in cooperative research clearly introduces complications for the premises of inquiry. Baskerville, Travis, and Truex (1992) have characterized the role of most academics concerning business and organizational research: They are most comfortable operating under assumptions of measured, rigorous, and objective reality, determined by using empirical positivism or postpositivism paradigms with a scientific methodology (pp. 6–7). Their reality tends to be abstract. Action researchers often start as did the Pharmco vice president in this case, importing and consuming knowledge products of academic researchers to adapt them and conduct research for their own uses. In this case, the inquiry was based on anthropological or related qualitative methods. Action researchers use an interpretive approach to the data. Baskerville (1991) has characterized this, in a more traditional information systems research context, as "radical pluralism"—the adaptation of tools developed for one purpose to new problems carrying new assumptions. The Pharmco action researcher's primary task in the collaboration was to provide information, whether it came from further up the firm's hierarchy or from the local social environment, that integrated social knowledge from sources initially external to the immediate problematic. Knowledge from these sources was then brought to bear on the pragmatic elements of the business problematic at hand. For the action research, reality was contextual (Reeves-Ellington, 1995b). A third role set, participatory action researchers (PARs), researched and reflected on what would work in their specific task areas, often taking leadership roles within those contexts. Finally, practitioners put what worked to use. They observed, recorded, and communicated back the impact of applying the new information on the business results.

While each of these roles has its own epistemological and methodological outlook, all the members of an extended cooperative research team must also share a sufficiently compatible and overarching value set. This will enable them to create and expand the knowledge and information they exchange within a common context, toward the integrated organizational aim.

The pluralistic vein in which cooperative action research was undertaken permitted each researcher to accept others in the collaboration as they were; it did not require participants first to obtain certain credentials or to mirror a single interest or type of actor. Entry into the process occurred at any point along four major stages of knowledge creation, depending on the problematic at hand. However, the vice president, as initiator of the process, did begin with a single theoretical base, from ethnology, which he imported from academic research. The PDCA model generated a flow of information with the capacity for constant review and improvement to ensure increasingly accurate and timely information.

We first describe this overall process and its four main elements in a schematic way, followed by a more detailed review of the content of the various research roles involved.

Process Guides and Elements for Cooperative Research

Figure 9 shows the general process model used to guide cooperative research for a practice integration of Pharmco A/A's cultural learning. This process of adjusting

Figure 9

Cooperative Research for Cultural Praxis Using Total Quality Generative Process

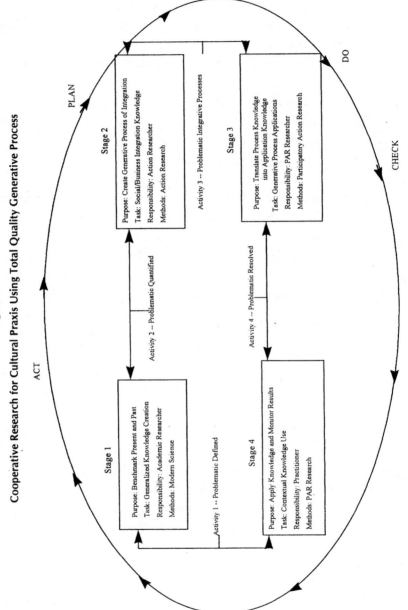

information inputs for a smoother and more precisely adaptive flow of activity bears some resemblance to the policy deployment practices described for certain Japanese firms. Imai (1986), for example, has described how notebook entries are passed along from the president's office, at the manufacturer Komatsu, and are enhanced all along the way throughout the organization, with further interpretations and specifications added at each node of passage. These entries continue down through middle management to every employee. Each successive manager adds personal and function-specific interpretations of "how" specifications will be refined to meet the president's strategic aims or the "what" of policy (Kinney, 1988). In hierarchical industrial corporations of Japan, each entry is appropriate to the position of its particular author within the organization.

The Pharmco AA region was far less hierarchical an organization and more loosely structured, yet the information exchange process along its value chain was similar in that each new exchange context called for an appropriate adjustment and translation of the information shared, toward the accomplishment of overarching common aims. The stages and activities were accomplished through the creation and translation of knowledge among each of the traditional work paradigms and methodologies. This knowledge had agreed end points and deliverables all along the way. However, the information exchange itself was based on continuous dialogue; it had no defined end point. Information continuously adapted and changed forms. It was shared formally and informally. The A/A regional personnel were applying what was recognized, at that time, as a version of the total quality process to ensure system integrity and improvement.

This generative process governed the exchange and flow of cultural information for the business problematic. Within each of four major activity stages, there were agreed purposes, tasks, responsibility, and methods. The team agreed that all knowledge would be shared throughout the network. Activity 1 establishes the problematic that needs resolution and provides acceptable end points and time lines. This is discussed largely between practitioners and academics. In Activity 2, under the leadership of the action researcher, baseline data is used to create processes that will permit integration of the surrounding societal norms and values with those of the company. Activity 3, under the leadership of various participative action researchers, inquires into social process applications that will solve the problematic. With Activity 4, practitioners, those who are responsible for performance results relating to the problematic at hand, resolve the defined issue and provide information feedback to the rest of the team.

For the process to function best, information had to flow continuously in ways that ensured ongoing learning and systemic adjustments. This type of learning has been described by Argyris and Schoen (1978) as double looped; it permits researchers of all types throughout the organization to ensure understanding, take appropriate actions, revise processes, reformulate problems, and take appropriate new actions under a newly defined situation. Similar types of systems have been identified by other management writers as total quality or process deployment (for example, Rohrer, 1990).

As a generative process model for cooperative research, PDCA functioned for the A/A personnel as a mindful emulation of a socially ideal, self-correcting learning process. It was well suited to the expectations of constant-change conditions in an organizational revitalization effort, one involving a less than fully known milieu of information seeking. Within the cycle, personnel spent more time in the planning and checking than in the doing and acting phases; this more closely resembles the Japanese use of PDCA than the usual American approach (Reeves-Ellington, 1993; Whitehill, 1991); it also reduces errors of execution. In the A/A realization, the process resulted in greater customer satisfaction and more sustained and multidimensional commercial relationships throughout the chain of exchange.

Each of the sets of research roles—academic, action researcher, PAR, and practitioner—was associated with a different approach conditioned by the requirements of the information sought and its use. No single researcher or set of researchers attempted to take on more than one primary research role within a given collaborative project. This separation maximized problem focus and epistemological clarity for the various members, who worked for their own insights and empirically tried out the implications in the field. Each had differences in underlying assumptions and approaches that best suited the individual research methodologies. Such separation of collaborating research roles is not the same thing as a separation of formal job functions in the workplace, however. It was far more fluid and general, with the role occupants arising from among action-relevant sets of overlapping and complementary job functions, especially in the case of the participative action researchers. The nature of the involvement of each depends on the problem at hand.

Academic Research Consultants

Consulting academic research team members were responsible for the traditional, modern scientific research portion of the A/A task in both qualitative and quantitative forms. Over a period of eight years, the academics A/A employed included psychologists for personal measurement skills and self-learning, anthropologists for skills related to participant observation and ethnography, information specialists to provide information systems thinking, and computer experts to aid in developing new systems for using information management technologies.

Beginning in 1983, several academic consultants were engaged to explain current theories and help A/A management develop baseline data for their organization. The consultants brought a wide-ranging understanding of existing research, the strengths and pitfalls of various theoretical approaches, and statements of the organizational problematic. The A/A region interactions with these theorists occurred on site and at academic association meetings throughout the experimental period. The bases of knowledge for these academics tended to be the products of international surveys (e.g., Hofstede, 1980), internal questionnaires (Bantigue and Reeves-Ellington, 1986), and short bursts of intensive ethnological information gathering (David, 1985). The materials were analyzed, and the data provided the region's managers an excellent understanding of where they were as an organization. However, in isolation, the data alone would provide little direction in helping the organization to change.

Action Researcher

An action researcher was needed to integrate theory and praxis for the setting and task. This role also joined the practical problems of business and social integration within an acceptable ethical framework. Further, the action researcher attempted to provide contextual assumptions, that is, purpose, aim, point of view, and construction of reality, as necessary to solve particular problems of building and shifting frameworks in the A/A region. The action researcher thus provided the basis for organization change. Finally, the action researcher acted as an inspirational specialist (Reeves-Ellington, 1995b) responsible for social and business integration.

Reeves-Ellington, the vice president, was the initiator, initial action researcher, and inspirational specialist in providing information that permitted others in the organization to attempt its transformation. He also assumed the task of training others who wanted action researcher skills. His training as an anthropologist, the experience of working with academic counterparts, prepared him to translate the knowledge of academe into shared wisdom in the practitioner's world through intensive dialogue (Reeves-Ellington, 1995b, p. 251). Throughout this period, the vice president assumed the role of fellow student, collaborator, and investigator, with equal contributory status to all others with whom he worked on this task.

A feature supporting his role as action researcher was that the vice president was relatively marginal in status both to the persons to whom he reported and to those who reported to him. Apart from Japan, the A/A region was not central to sales and profits for the multinational Pharmco. The vice president's immediate supervisor acted as protector of the region while it was in its experimental phase, and the vice president was marginal even to the region, primarily due to geographic distance: The closest country was a 10-hour plane ride away. This marginality was critical to the success of his work as action researcher and as inspirational specialist to the organization. Also, his geographically remote location from the home office allowed him more room to innovate in nonconforming ways without presenting to the company at large a disproportionate image of risk, which might otherwise make the senior corporate management uneasy.

As action researcher, the vice president's focus was on three activities: (1) a shift in business paradigm from an anonymous and impersonal producer/consumer, or "business" model, to a more intensively and socially embedded customer/supplier, or "commerce," model; (2) development of a business vision through a process that permitted all A/A region personnel the opportunity to self-initiate beneficial change through information exchange and knowledge creation; and (3) interpretation and integration of the organization's cultural logic and social knowledge across the customer-supplier chains within the region. The vice president's main process-analytic contribution was the second item, visioning.[5] This was designed to allow all employees in the region to develop a shared vision of what they wanted from a personal point of view, both from and for the business. The process also permitted the recognition and integration of shared customer visions all along the chain of information exchange.

Figure 10 illustrates how this visioning process worked:

1. Managers and executives outside the region established the business objectives and goals for the region. The vice president set the format of a paradigm shift from a business focus to a more socially embedded commerce focus. A time line and agenda for both the business and paradigm shifts were set outside the A/A region.

2. All individuals in the region, working alone, developed their own personal visions of their social roles in the revised organization and how business needs would fit into the social needs.

3. Individuals joined work teams that decided the underlying values and ethics they needed. They then selected the core elements from each individual vision that would be shared by the team. Differences were ignored.

4. A common vision was developed and consensus was achieved—everyone on the team had to agree to the common vision.

5. The vision was "reality tested" against six specific criteria to ensure that the original intent of the drafter was intact and that the vision was clear enough to provide a basis of action. The membership found that the vision was sufficiently clear for others in the customer chain to understand and support it.

A vision checklist employed by those developing a vision contained six criteria: Did the vision identify the uniqueness of the entity being developed? Did it provide sufficient rationale for adoption? Is it compelling? Does it address mutual self-interest (important for alignment of cultural norms)? Does it identify external customer chains? And, finally, does the vision identify internal customer chains? The purpose of the checklist was to ensure that the vision created added customer and supplier value to the broader organizational value chain.

The A/A region's management, when envisioning what they wanted, consciously established a goal of wanting to develop an "ethnic organization" (Reeves-Ellington, 1995b) that would provide a basis for broader organization change within Pharmco. The idea of ethnic organization provided the uniqueness

Figure 10

Visioning Process for Social Integration

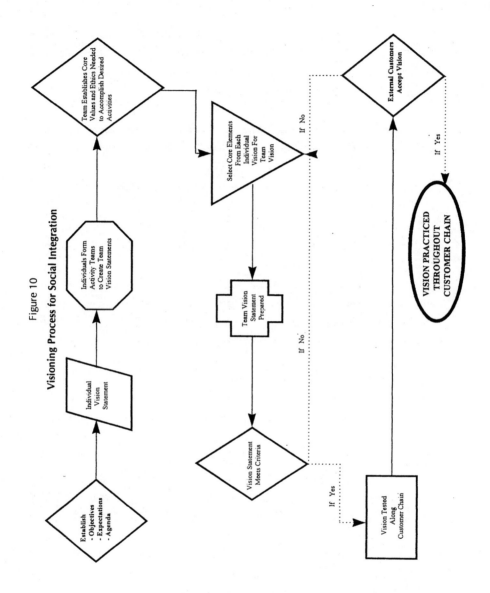

position, satisfying the first criterion. The rationale for adoption was clearly to meet the home office profit requirements within the parameters given. The parameters were compelling, and, as the concept of an ethnic organization unfolded, that idea also became intrinsically compelling to the entire region. Two levels of self-interest were addressed. First, of course, there was survival of employment, but of more interest was the challenge of learning and increasing one's self-worth and the challenge of creating worth for the entire organization. Within the A/A's revised concept of organization, value chains, both internal and external, had to be identified and developed. Project management software was used to track and maintain these chains.

In more traditional conceptions of organization, unsuccessful visions often fail on the "compelling" criterion, on "provides sufficient rationale for adoption," and on "addresses mutual self-interest." Numerical measures such as "we will be market leader in our four top brands" usually lack a rationale for adoption by all the organizational members. For example, A/A support staff could not identify with and work in any focused way toward such function-specific measures. A secondary reason for failure of corporate visions is often a lack of resonance (i.e., not "compelling") for all the organizational members. Anything with "world class" or "global" appeal, for example, failed to compel Pharmco A/A members. These may have resonated with some organizational members, but many others failed to see how they addressed mutual self-interest.

Participatory Action Researchers

The participatory action researchers (PARs) also acted as inspirational specialists, or charismatic leaders, in their several A/A regional organizations. Their responsibility was the awakening of all people within their local-to-regional organizational customer chains. Their primary task was twofold: (1) to produce knowledge and action directly useful to a group of people and (2) to establish an environment and a process in which all people could empower themselves (i.e., self-initiate beneficial change through their own agency) through the construction, use, and sharing of their own knowledge. The PARs were leaders who confirmed the validity of the generative models and processes developed by the academics and action researcher when applied in their social contexts.

The PARs used the PDCA knowledge-generative model to effect visionary changes within their customer chains, thus extending the organization to those who would traditionally be considered outsiders. The PARs self-selected naturally into this research role as the generative model was introduced; they were found throughout the region and at all levels of organization. They were not always the senior managers, but in each case they were knowledgeable about the problematic, or wanted to learn, and always desired the role. Thus, a PAR might be a sales manager for participant observation skills companywide, a new sales supervisor for a particular country's business, or, as in one case, a secretary, who acted as the PAR for a particular country's cost reduction program.

Participative action research produced much more finely calibrated knowledge of customer desires within each local region. By benchmarking what was important to customers and developing strategies and programs to learn what customers wanted, PARs were also able to deliver services that customers defined as desirable. The A/A PARs developed these innovative benchmarks with a series of customer satisfaction measures that (1) were systematic, (2) were defined by customers in terms of their definition of satisfaction, (3) compared both products and social services to those of A/A's competitors, (4) related to a predetermined time schedule, and (5) were actionable. Key customers were benchmarked against these standards every six months, after which new standards were negotiated with these customers. In keeping with total quality principles, these standards were expected to be improved for each cycle.

To ensure that all these criteria were met, an overall customer measurement process was developed by the PARs. The purpose of measurement was to ensure that Pharmco's test brands and social activities were meeting the needs of those customers most likely to participate in social and business interaction with the A/A region companies. The process developed for measurement also highlighted the need to provide services for key customers that would cause them to want to work with Pharmco. Competitive analysis on these points was necessary to ensure continual improvement of targeted areas that Pharmco customers considered important. Conceptually, the process measured all aspects of field selling, relations with government authorities, and distributors—all interactions along the customer chain.

Practitioners

The practitioners using participatory action research processes for enhanced exchange were heavily represented, in the Pharmco case, by field sales representatives. They adopted the process in order to gain greater control over their work with outside customers and, as they themselves put it, "to drive management in customer development." For these practitioners to succeed, the participatory action research processes had to be adopted by all persons along the customer chain, hence all practitioners working with Pharmco products developed and agreed on these measures for success.

Once they understood and accepted the new processes and underlying paradigmatic change, practitioners worked to develop specific measurements to ensure that implementation of dialogue and interaction occurred along the customer chain. Salespeople led in this effort. They worked with various other functions in the company and other customers to develop meaningful measurements.

A formal reporting form was used by a customer receiving goods and services, and another was used by the field representative as a compilation of territorial data. (These data collection tools are described in more detail in Reeves-Ellington, 1995a.) The measurements were taken every six months for every major customer in the chain. The form completed by the external customer reported on the brand, related services, and competitors. A second form was also developed to measure overall customer satisfaction levels in ways permitting practitioners to understand differences between Pharmco and its competitors as seen through the eyes of the key customer. From this data, individual practitioners could adjust their relationships with particular customers. Forms were developed jointly by those completing them, working in consultation with the field sales team. In this way, information collected was that which was considered important to all the people who would use the data.

Other, less formal measurements were also developed. For example, in the Philippine sales force, one salesperson identified that improvements in three key uses of time would improve effectiveness and efficiency. The improvements desired were less waiting time in the doctor's office, more time in conversations with doctors, and an increase in the annual number of visits. The sales team jointly developed baseline data for each of these variables, a control range for each activity, and a new standard they desired.

Results of Collaborative Action
Research and Development

As a result of cultural praxis through the cooperative research strategy, the A/A region of Pharmco surpassed its goals. Profit was achieved in three years. By the fifth year, the region led its division in profit as a percentage of sales. Regional customers recognized Pharmco as an innovator and responsible community citizen. An early project phase of turnover and, later, vigorous recruitment of region personnel by competitors brought and kept the region workforce at the size levels required. (Other business outcomes are described in detail in Reeves-Ellington, 1995b). Toward the end of the revitalization period, managers outside the region began reviewing the program to learn what the region was doing and how to adapt it to their own operations.

A view of the way individual, social, and cultural content and knowledge informed the organizational changes within and beyond Pharmco A/A's boundaries can be illustrated in one individual's story of professional development. This account also illuminates how learning proceeded through the organization.

Self-Learning as a Basis for Social Learning: One Participatory
Action Researcher's Experience

The program for cross-cultural learning to bring about transboundary cultural inclusion in the Pharmco A/A customer chain began with staff development at the individual level. This development helped individuals first to understand themselves, in terms of what is important to them and their various social and business contexts, and then how to relate to others. The underlying premise was that social responsibility comes only after personal responsibility. Within cross-cultural contexts, "knowing oneself" is doubly challenging. The self must be placed in both domestic and multicultural settings. The A/A personnel attempted to create habits of responsibility to self and to others. By habit, we followed Covey's definition: "A habit is the intersection of knowledge, skill, and desire. Knowledge is the theoretical paradigm, the what to do and the why. Skill is the how to do. And desire is the motivation, the want to do" (1989, p. 47). Success in personal responsibility was built on proactivity (making things happen), knowing where one wants to go (vision), and focus on the important. Social responsibility, built on personal responsibility, required personnel to think in terms of success for all, understand others, and maximize social interactions.

The experience of a Filipino janitor provides an example of socially responsible activity resulting from the self-learning of personal responsibility. After staff development training, using Covey's and related models, the janitor requested to learn to use computers. He was thus proactively pursuing a personal vision. He argued that the knowledge would aid in his keeping down janitorial costs and thereby make him more valuable to the company. Thus, he brought his personal vision to focus on what was important to Pharmco A/A while also improving himself.

He did receive the training, and after he finished, he inventoried all janitorial supplies, kept comparative prices, and reduced costs (what management consultants like to call a "win-win" situation). His skills using spreadsheets caused others within the traditional organization boundary to come to him for training. Materials managers, marketing managers, and others approached and interacted with him, and he listened and responded to their needs. The exposure at close quarters to company professional staff gave this janitor an opportunity to do participant observation to learn this sector of corporate and occupational culture and society as he watched Pharmco professionals interact with each other in the customer chain.

When physicians and others later asked A/A Philippines for help in setting up accounts, learning computer spreadsheets was part of the required training. The janitor accordingly received the training assignment—with an appropriate computer trainer's salary increase. He was subsequently sought as a trainer by more physicians and thus achieved further synergy with A/A's customers based on the collective investments that had been made in his own development.

Reflections

In this qualitative study, we described how the theoretical frameworks and learning methods of field ethnology were applied for business results in a multinational firm using process improvement tools for managing the organizational information. The resulting business turnaround was achieved through people; it centered on the application of enhanced cultural skills. The leader of this organization's culture and information expansion was also the principle integrator of the processes involved. He used guided, cooperative, experiential inquiry rather than relying on more traditional, unilateral management interventions.

Several observations can be made regarding the case:

1. To work at the cultural level, knowledge needs to be imported that is not obviously related to the business substrate as traditionally conceived. This was particularly so in the A/A region, which was not in a position to market new products as a relatively minor extension of the larger company, itself an asset of a large consumer products conglomerate. The A/A region was in immediate trouble and needed to generate more sales and a better market position as soon as possible. The business performance issue was very specific to the A/A region as an organizational component.

2. There is often an urgent need, at the midrange business level, for more responsive, motivated, and creative people, yet it is not practical to meet this need using restructuring interventions. The region vice president was new, Pharmco's home office wanted fewer total personnel, and the region was scattered across several continents. It is also clear that, in a such a multinational setting, relying on wholesale training packages may well give guidance that is too monocultural, single shot, and unresponsive to local differences to be effective. Active, field-based learning methods such as PO, for use during the workday encounters, are critical.

3. Better knowledge of how cultural systems work results in knowing ways to apply this knowledge to the self, as well as to the customer and market. This entails what to analyze, how to discover what is important, what people want and will work for in the organization, and, by extension, who "our" customers are from organization members' points of view. In Pharmco, the revitalized organization's new awareness of a cultural self-identity prepared Pharmco people to identify those customers who would prefer Pharmco people and their products over those of the competition. From Pharmco's perspective, these were "our" people, those whose values most closely matched Pharmco people's values. The informational content of culture, appropriately directed, transformed the way further information was sought and used.

4. Alignment of organization members on the basis of agreed cultural values breaks the deadlock of workplace difference. Such a deadlock can be seen often in American workplace identity politics. The quantum leap in the quality of informa-

tional exchanges that this allowed in Pharmco A/A released what Fals-Borda (1991) has called pent-up organizational knowledge. It encouraged a more fluid division and complementarity of labor in the inquiry process. With respect to customers, it also represented a more genuine alternative—desirability—to the exercise of rational and impersonal marketing principles of "attracting," "motivating," and "serving" the target market segment. This traditional approach is the stripped-down business paradigm that assumes manipulation of a passive and depersonalized consumer, rather than entering humanizing dialogue with an active and respected customer. Cultural alignment allowed organization members both to retain their personal integrity and to find trading partners who shared meaningful portions of their view of the world.

Several traditional cultures in Mexico, India, and China have done similar things with success. Ellington has demonstrated the power of ritual kinship in bonding villagers and city people in both trade and politics (1966, pp. 25–31). Karve (1965) has documented cultural alignment among subcontinent Indian kinship systems working within that country. Kotkin (1992, pp. 27, 67) demonstrates how the Indian and other diaspora use kinship for commerce. Ellington (1976, pp. 47–50) has discussed cross-cultural use of kinship and ethnicity between Indonesian pribumis and Chinese for successful commerce in Indonesia.

5. A leader-integrator in a midrange organizational effort like this one must assume overlapping organizational roles (task manager, information coordinator, normative leader, inspirational specialist), but must not attempt plural research roles. The Pharmco action researcher's primary research function was to import and link information and to oversee its transformation to knowledge for action. This required cross-disciplinary and cross-functional knowledge for the needed interpretations and a solid foundation in the social sciences. It was critical to perceive shifts in context so that the appropriate interpretations could be made. We can speculate that such a role might well be difficult for managers who are deeply socialized, as are many in America, to look "up and around" for "the main chance" in the internal organizational hierarchy, as Jackall (1988) puts it, valuing only the most reductive and elegant solutions in management information, directed at an audience of senior executives. Any comfort to the participants in a transforming multicultural organization, whether members or managers, will not be one of elegance or the emulation of a monocultural hierarchy.

6. It is also clear in this case that the ethnology and information systems aspects of Pharmco did not fit a neat dichotomy of content and process. Not only was the one transformed by the other, the two were highly interdependent, especially as cooperative action research got fully under way. The action researcher, as initiator and integrator did begin with general ethnological theory and knowledge of process tools. He then acted to awaken new networks of information flow, with a clear directive for applying the new and emerging knowledge. The emergent circuits of information, in the hands of those who built and used them for organizational learning, could then become circuits of power.

We believe one important reason for the scant attention paid to culture in direct business information applications, apart from problems of internal human resources and general marketing strategies, may be that acknowledging culture from a management position immediately forces the leader to acknowledge the inherent limitations of structural power and predictive control. The appearance of mastery of these elements is highly prized in American business organizations (Jackall, 1988). The practical limitations that culture underscores regard how people will interpret and normatively evaluate the information they receive, rather than how they may be ordered or manipulated to behave per se—an older, Hobbesian notion of power. The further away a traditional manager is from day-to-day interpretive scenes in which culture is enacted, the more multicultural the workforce is and the more worrisome this lack of predictive control becomes. Exclusively resorting to structural methods for achieving control such as restructuring and right-sizing may be appealing, but these methods quickly reach their sustainability limits. Competition grows, markets mature, niches become filled.

Managers have choices in the kinds of power they apply in organizations. They could contribute to further turbulence through unilateral and structural interventions, or they could seek to discover new ways to amplify their organization members' inherent response capacities through the software of culture.

To grand strategists, cultural inquiry for business at the midrange level might appear a mere matter of tactics in the field, at most a local or regional strategy. Once individual members reopen negotiations with customers, business plans and corporate portfolios become crowded with complexity. Greater information support of reflective processes needed in the field, toward greater communicative transparency, will greatly aid the expansion of organizations as information systems. Culture will probably continue to be most fruitfully addressed as a matter of individual development but public interpretation and enactment. Certainly, the variety of cultures facing business managers will only become more complex. They will not be identified only by national boundaries, but in addition by self-defined groups. These might be ethnic groups as traditionally conceived (e.g., Rommi, Blacks, Serbs) or such "tribes" as academics, practitioners, or medical professionals. As the mix of cultural types continues to shift, managers in business operations must constantly learn, adopt, and respond to complex social material. Social sciences and cultural education will undoubtedly become increasingly important. This education will reveal that the manager's desire for certainty, clarity, and risk avoidance must be replaced with an ability to handle ambiguity, fuzziness, and social responsibility, while systematically orchestrating the incorporation and mutual feedback of new processes and content.

The successful manager, in this milieu, is an information ethnologist capable of identifying and creating new social and cultural contexts through the identification and harmonizing of interests and meanings. Such managers can vision alternate realities in which the focus is on discovery and commonality rather than control and difference. Within this paradigm, power tends to be relational rather than structural. Managers in the middle will have to learn to interpret and leverage systemic power through dialogue rather than to legislate it. The study of management in this situation will undoubtedly grow in an interdisciplinary direction. Management practice, as well as management scholarship, will only be furthered in these circumstances by knowledge of a variety of bodies of research and levels of analysis and a willingness to import and adapt the findings of others.

Organizations and leaders that provide opportunities and process guidance for information sharing, acknowledging the mutual feedback of information content and process, should find more competitive advantage in and near the multicultural localities in which they operate. Future research for practice applications might include continued emphasis on the development of information applications and on communications infrastructures that to support the integration of multiple perspectives in organizational inquiry.

If, as research and scholarship suggest, cultural communications are constantly evaluated and reinterpreted, if they are grounded in shifting contexts among the regional, organizational, and diverse personal histories of an organization's members, then focusing on the unilateral control of difference, or simply the awareness of it, as much of American management and diversity training has in the past, will be missing the point. If this case is illustrative, learning culture through systematic participation and ethnological knowledge, then applying what works well in negotiation (cf. Pruitt, 1983)—a search for commonalties and new opportunities—may bring responsible business closer to the mark. Careful inquiry into the social knowledge of alternate cultural values sets, with continual adjustment of approach and behaviors to identify and reach areas of greatest commonality and mutual agreement, is a promising avenue for exploring ways to enhance transcultural business relations and the complex organizations through which they take place.

Notes

1. In this context, the term *diversity* refers to the variation brought to the organization through personal agency rather than simply as defined by quotas, rights, program goals, or entitlements. While we do not address issues of policy per se, we see mere reliance on policy as a basic difference between socially responsible and agenda-based organizations.

2. Garsten (1994), examining Apple Computers, and Hamada (1991), reporting on American and Japanese working relationships in a Japanese-American joint venture, rely on ethnographic methods. Their work is holistic and addresses mainly questions of regional cultures and how organizations do or do not deal with them successfully. We think these approaches provide more insight to social reponsibility than the more Western-centered and traditional organization work by Deal and Kennedy (1982) or Imai (1986). These last two works intertwine total quality improvements, culture, and leadership in ways that indicate a lack of understanding of their distinct purposes.

3. The business aims were global in intent. The company had specific global earning objectives, expressed in percentage of market share, earning as a percentage of sales, and so forth. However, plans to obtain the global objectives were not global but rather customized for specific countries and markets.

4. Reeves-Ellington (1996b), building on work by C. Kluckhohn (1951, pp. 11–14), Boninger et al. (1994), C. Geertz (1966), Roese (1994), and Strathman et al. (1994) has used the categories of human nature, human relationships, relationships to the environment, and time orientations to differentiate regionally influenced organizational cultures in eastern Europe. However, in these applications, too, such dimensions enhanced understanding of workplace behavior only in relationship to the social knowledge of the particular context.

5. In more mundane language, Reeves-Ellington's role was to broker thoughts, ideas, and actions among all other players. The desired outcome for such brokering is integration of ideas and actions that are desired by all participants (Reeves-Ellington, 1994 pp. 213–215).

6
Responsibility and Commerce:
A 1970's Land Purchase in Java

Commerce, as a kind of exchange that extends beyond the economic, is often informed by diverse and unobvious ethical interpretations. These include how the people involved at the level of field operations interpret social responsibility for their particular situations. In the most extreme and incommensurate transcultural encounters, responsible interpretation is often left to those at the first line of contact. This is where the impact of diversity is greatest and where interaction for the fitting response can be crucial. Accordingly, to illustrate such diversity in closer detail, this chapter provides the perspective of a general manager in field operations (Reeves-Ellington) in an account of the context and events that transpired during a Western multinational company's investment in a developing country—Java, in Indonesia. Even the most rapid transcultural encounters, which have become increasingly characteristic of late modern business, offer ample opportunities for more or less responsibility and the chance to either minimize or amplify cultural responses that can materially affect human adaptation.

Discerning what is fitting for the situation can help practitioners identify the events and processes in which they can influence the possibility of attaining better consequences for business and community alike. The unreflective (and, some would add, incipiently coercive) use of economic power, or power used as if reified in a set of principles viewed from a particular standpoint, cannot automatically deal with transcultural issues without the need to appeal to the very Western legalistic institutional frameworks that may have created translation problems in the first place.

The Java land purchase narrative illustrates an approach to social responsibility that was for an operation with modest means: The business was a subsidiary subject to both corporate and local political constraints, and it exercised its discretion largely through relational, rather than reified, power. This kind of response to a complicated situation assumes a basic loyalty to the goals of business. It also works within the constraints presented by the immediate social context. The approach of loyalty is more sensible for the vast majority of business practitioners than either of two other possibilities of engagement that have been framed by the economist A. O. Hirschman (1970). He indicates that the alternatives to institutional loyalty are either exit, a kind of principled withdrawal (that is, personal or institutional exit), or, alternately, voice—the vocal advocacy of particular social or political agendas at one or another institutional level. Indeed, in certain social regions at particular times, political voice is barely tolerated at all. Java in the early 1970s certainly was, and largely still is, one of those places.

The story recounts various circumstances and arrangements associated with buying land, building a pharmaceutical manufacturing plant, and starting up manufacturing operations in what was at the time a rural area. Many business case narratives are, from a cultural viewpoint, stripped down; in them, the interest in context mainly reflects problems of market entry or legal and political trade barriers. This story views the local social and cultural contexts, within the larger contexts defined by the national and global political circumstances and the corporate presence in the area, as the defining ones for responsible action fitting to the situation.

Specific features of this context included the nature and requirements of the project itself, the purchased land's traditional use, the complicated political situation of this region in the early years of Suharto's policies of import replacement development and foreign investment, and the political, social, and cultural aspects of everyday life that figured importantly in doing business there. During the entire land purchase and subsequent activities, Pharmco management in Indonesia had to work with and within three national cultures—Javanese, Chinese, and corporate American. There was a constant need to integrate the three into common and agreed strategy. Each phase of the transaction brought up its own particular issues of commerce, yet the whole—if indeed it is judged as responsible—must be seen as both relatively economically successful and as culturally coherent for its participants.

Under a severely and multiply constrained context, the most viable and responsible action is what occurs when all possible information for commerce is maximally apprehended, translated, shared, and brought to bear within the resources and time frames that are feasible. Indeed, active inquiry and responsive interpretation were necessary for the investors just to discover what the viable and optimal choices might be.

In this land purchase, there were a number of considerations operating together at various levels and from various perspectives. The staging of events begins with the initial requirements of land purchase. The details of the sale negotiation, the methods and form of the payment, and the alternate and multilayered circuits of power that were involved presented the project team with a diverse set of requirements. At each point, cultural differences and institutional frameworks interacted in specific ways. To ignore any of these would be to endanger the project, the people, or both.

The considerations involved not only realizing the project at the point of engagement with the holders of the land, but also coming to terms with discrepancies between government policies and internal political and regional actors at various jurisdiction levels. Tasks affected by this included the site selection, plans for community employment, the immediate use of the site, and the more frequently encountered details of starting up the factory project proper, namely, the site development, construction, worker recruitment, and work conditions.

The chapter ends with some brief reflections on short- and long-range outcomes of the project in the context of business development in Indonesia in general. The authors suggest that attention and preparation of practitioners for responding to intercultural interactions at this very small scale, especially in developing country locales, are important for maximizing the chance for a positive outcome of business. They may also minimize any negative effects of social change to a developing area.

Background and Context: Pharmco's Project

In this particular project, Reeves-Ellington was a business practitioner whose general managerial responsibilities included the region in which the new plant was to be located. The plant's purpose was to produce powdered and injectable pharmaceutical products and tableted pills. The time frame involved was 1972–1974. The place, Indonesia, was and still is world-famous for both its difficulties and its promise of opportunity—a large and culturally diverse population, concentrated wealth among the top stratum of elites, a repressive and volatile polity, lengthy and intensive development efforts, rapid international investment, an actively developing infrastructure, extremely low labor costs, and, finally, a place of historically deep and persistent bureaucratic corruption.

In 1972, Pharmco (pseudonym), an American pharmaceutical company and subsidiary of a major American multinational company, had obtained approval from the Indonesian government for plant construction in East Java. This project would require that land be purchased from several peasant families so that the plant could be built within the Indonesian government's designated development area.

Island of Java and Environs [1]

At the time, the investment policy of the Indonesian government emphasized import substitution in manufacturing, with pharmaceuticals an important consideration. A rush of pharmaceutical investors had already begun into the area, led in the mid-1960s by the Pfizer Corporation. In the early 1970s, all the major pharmaceutical companies from around the world had already arrived or were trying to get in. By the time of Pharmco's arrival, 16 pharmaceutical companies were already active in the area.

Other foreign investment industries included at least five food companies; other consumer products firms (among them Unilever, Brylcreem, Gillette); paint (Imperial Chemical Industries); vehicles for complete knockdown assembly (Toyota, Dodge); and, most important, foreign oil companies. The oil investors were obliged to operate under the auspices of Pertamina, the national oil company. There was also a high level of activity in timber, nickel, and other natural resource extraction.

During that period, Indonesia was experiencing the same pattern that more recently became familiar in former Soviet bloc countries and China, the arrival of multitudes of international business and investment consultants and advisors, government and private, all of whom were offering their advice to foreign investors. Advisors were present in the area under sponsorship of the Ford Foundation, the U.S. government, the World Bank, the International Monetary Fund, and UNESCO (United Nations Educational, Scientific, and Cultural Organization), among others.

This consulting environment spanned the full social and ideological range. At the same time, many of the Indonesian government's officials had become expert in identifying and overcoming internal barriers and, occasionally, in creating further ones that were most conveniently remediated through the right payments to the right people. The Western commercial sector was working most intensively on oil development, but all American businesses were encouraged to come. International political and intergovernmental advisors were concerned to reduce what they then perceived as the Communist threat through the creation of a popular Rostowian concept widely known as economic takeoff.

Within the U.S. embassy, the lead of the military attaches, Col. Benson, on his third or fourth assignment there, was familiar with Indonesia's new military leaders. He cultivated these military connections and was instrumental in gaining substantial U.S. military aid to the area. The embassy's economics department worked on increasing the World Bank's and International Monetary Fund's involvement.

Other agencies were worried about the effects that the push for rapid investment and development would have on already impoverished members of the civil society. The Ford Foundation, the World Council of Churches, and Population Planning were among those prominent in expressing social concerns about development. The Ford Foundation, in particular, provided a powerful counterbalance to government and industry investment advice.

Until 1972, all pharmaceutical investment had been located in the Jakarta area. Initially, there were no minimum investment or product line requirements. After 1972, however, the government closed Jakarta to small industry. Any new investor would have to go either to the outer islands (where there was virtually no market, transportation, or other infrastructure) or to east Java. This second alternative was the one chosen by Pharmco for its pill factory project.

All foreign investors worked on a cost-plus basis until the later 1970s. After 1969, any new foreigners were required to set up joint ventures with local partners. The locals had to have a minimum 5% investment, with a recommended entry level of 10%. Virtually no one had any money to invest, and partner selection was a difficult issue; most who wanted and could afford to invest were ethnic Chinese. The partner Pharmco eventually found was a Chinese, a doctor whose family had lived in Java for a long time. (He spoke no Chinese and had never been to China, but he had been to Singapore and Hong Kong.)[2]

Other stipulations for investors had been added by the Indonesian government by this time. Any new pharmaceutical plant had to have a sterile area, to make at least one raw material within five years, and to produce only products that had been approved by the Ministry of Health. This approval was prerequisite to overall approval of the investment. These additional requirements added substantial cost; at the time of Pharmco's entry, the minimum sterile facility cost alone was U.S. $300,000, whereas the total costs of earlier investment projects had run no more than $500,000. There were other, institutional background issues. What a raw material facility was, for example, had never been clearly defined. This left open opportunities for additional consulting by Indonesian government officials, such as those in the Ministry of Health. Pharmco's plant would be making tablets, sugar-coated pills, ointments, liquids, and sterile injectables. By the time the project was ready to begin, the minimum investment would come to $1 million.

Politics

From the point of view of midlevel business, the politics of the times presented anything but a straightforward picture. First, elections in Indonesia were never of any practical consequence once Sukarno had fallen. Suharto and his national party, Golkar, remained in firm control of all external trade issues at the national level. The United States, as a major player among foreign oil investors, dominated investments in general. This augured well for would-be American pharmaceutical investors, even though German pharmaceuticals, with their highly valued equipment, had been actively present since World War II. Throughout the late 1960s and early 1970s, under David Cohen, the American embassy's trade section in Jakarta gradually became even more important than its economic section, a first in U.S. official memory there.

The dominant American military and economic presence in the world virtually guaranteed potential American investors open access to important host government officials. Yet, this access guaranteed very little in the way of assuring conditions for practical operation on the ground. While these circumstances might imply great ease of potential investment by American companies, they came nowhere near an adequate description of the complications posed by this developing nation's postcolonial background institutions, especially for foreign investors who wanted to operate responsibly.

The national government maintained a putative one-stop central Investment Board, then under the direction of Barli Halim, a colleague of Suharto. The realities for Western investors, however, were anything but one stop: Halim's board would hand out the forms, but the investors had to find, cultivate, and collect a multitude of signatures from appropriate government agencies. A partial Jakarta-level list of such government agencies, for Pharmco's intended project, included the following: for the site, the city planning board; for the equipment and design, the Ministry of Light Industry; for financial aspects, the Central Bank and Ministry of Finance (the respective financial officers of which reputedly did not get along); for duty relief, Customs; and for all employee matters, the Ministry of Labor. At each ministry, there was a minimum of 12 signatures from given departments and

levels—in Reeves-Ellington's notes, this included 115 signatures for the central
Jakarta portion alone. There was, in addition, a regional counterpart for each of
the central ministries at the region's offices in Surabaya.

Tea Money

These Indonesian government office signatures had often been the source of an ethical
dilemma for foreign investors. As has been the case in some other national business
settings, foreign business people in Indonesia often found that providing a gratuity for
services—cash, gifts, or business opportunities—seemed to make it easier to get the
relevant administrative gatekeepers to expedite their shipments, applications, or requests. From this arose the concept of tea money (that is, a little extra money to buy
tea, a custom described in more detail elsewhere by Ellington, 1980).

Tea money had long been integral to the Indonesian circumstances of political
and cultural emphasis on minute negotiations and mutual social obligation. As an
artifact of subtle accommodation among the potentially competing interests of different social groups, the roots of tea money lay deep in the country's often bitter
and quietly ambivalent relations between rulers and ruled, from the times of the
early southeast Asian kingdoms to their colonial and modern military successors.
Multiple layers of social hierarchy persisted, reflecting both continuities and se-
quences of contact with Asian northerners, the Dutch, and the Japanese military.

The elaborate system of ritual exchanges and customary expectations of mutual help extended through all areas of life. They could clearly be seen in the social
institutions of sharing resources during wet rice irrigation and in the hierarchical
prerogatives of the *prijaji*, the gentile, customary ruling class (Anderson, B., 1972,
p. 38), who became the civil service class in modern times, and whose familial-
based aristocratic status extended historically to traditional Javanese court society.[3]

In the tea money system, help returned was viewed as commensurate with the
help rendered. Status and ritual obligation, rather than the preference of impartial
fairness of law or duty that lies at the basis of Western business ethics, formed part
of the cultural logic for a social knowledge of business relations. The cultural ethic
of *rukun*, which has been well described by H. Geertz (1961), prescribes an appropriate demeanor and etiquette—the emphasis is on dignity, pleasant composure,
and avoidance of direct confrontation with peoples' differences. This has sup-

ported a patient working out of minute and complex interdependencies in this hierarchical framework.

In the cultural context of American multinational businesses multinational at that time, the popular and politically correct view was that virtually any informal or personal compensation lay beyond the pale of ethical business relations. Many Westerners interpreted tea money gratuities entirely from within their agenda-driven ethic: It was corrupt bribery, no matter in what scale or form, and, besides, it would add to costs. Americans in particular often responded to tea money requests with righteous anger, impatience, and arrogant outbursts regarding services they felt entitled to demand. For the most part, this only resulted in higher payments of tea money being demanded and less help and service being extended. Both sides, affronted, could see their business relationship spiral upward in dollars and downward in respect, and respect was another very high priority in the regional values orientations, a quality absolutely necessary for continuing successful business relations in Indonesia.

An alternative response was to flout the rules of Western business ethics and buy cooperation with copious amounts of American money. This too would result in resentment and a heightened distrust between Western business partners and local people, with the added result of further inflation in payoff expectations. Neither of these two options yielded social responsibility.

It is virtually certain that all Western companies that stayed to do viable business in Indonesia did from time to time pay some type of gratuity Indonesians would have seen as tea money. The tea money concept spanned the entire range of statuses, functions, and amounts. Did all pay tea money in circumstances and amounts that would look, from the American business standpoint, like corrupt bribes? No, but it is safe to say that most did, on the report of multiple sources Reeves-Ellington considered reliable at that time. This was also highly plausible in light of the fact that most Western businesspeople, particularly Americans, believed they had little time to invest in the complicated task of learning and responding appropriately to local cultural interpretations. Economic drivers were the only ones of importance in most business investments at the time. Without a commensurate investment in cultural learning for the fitting response, they would not have begun to see and maximize mutually responsible opportunities in the relations of this highly compromised and culturally complex setting. If they had done so, the many pitfalls of payoffs might have been avoided.

The option of righteous refusal was also generally unsuccessful. Some righteous scenes of American confrontational outbursts did occur; these were received by Indonesians,[4] at least in Reeves-Ellington's experiences, as unseemly and disrespectful. (According to a local saying, The empty barrel makes the most noise.) The complainant would either end up out of business or pay more anyway, and for poorer assistance.

To learn a more culturally responsive ethic for this context took time, tenacity, and astuteness. It also took the cultivation of relationships with persons who could both tolerate the investors' lack of social knowledge and guide them toward more successful interpretations for action. Pharmco's foreign managers, at length observing how irritated objections to requests for service gratuities only made things worse, set about discovering Indonesian equivalents to business gifts and relationships that would be both respectful and culturally acceptable for both sides. The process necessarily involved mistakes, recoveries, approximations, small compromises, and continual and persistent information gathering and verification.

Building good faith among area officials eventually obviated the need for bribes in most cases; greater and cultural astuteness provided ways to avoid them in others. In one typical example among many, the demand of a Jakarta health department official for a bribe to obtain his signature was overcome by social relationship building and culturally appropriate demonstrations of respect. The Pharmco management staff, which included Javanese, learned of the official's wife's birthday. They arranged to take the right gift and flowers to the man's house at the right time in the evening. While such touches came to typify many so-called customer-driven American firms in the 1990s, especially at the high-end customer and executive partnership levels, in the 1970s and in a foreign country they were unusual. This was particularly so in that it occurred on Indonesian terms in an Indonesian context. In the case in question, without paying a bribe, Pharmco had obtained the official's signature within days.

Many other instances like this one arose during the project. Hosting *wayang*, the area's traditional and highly esteemed shadow-puppet play performances[5] and inviting local guests, as well as company people, to participate in ritual occasions worked against the foreigners' inevitable social mistakes and helped to counteract somewhat the artifacts of excess and disrespectfulness in foreigners that would be likely to attract demands for bribes. This sort of thing also was not widely done in the early 1970s in Indonesia. American firms were only forced to consider personal relationships and response to alternate cultural contexts beginning in the later 1970s in the face of competitive examples of manufacturing and international trade success established by the Japanese.

Negotiating the Land Purchase

The regional administrative center for Pharmco's intended project was located in Surabaya. This center represented yet another site of required signatures and added some new features to the social and political context. Pharmco's advance work on the institutional background had revealed only that there was a lack of clarity of the relationships between the national and the regional authorities. These were unclear not only to the expatriate business consultants, but also to the firm's U.S. government contacts.

When Pharmco pursued signatures at this level, as necessary for approval of the company's offer to purchase the government-designated land, this vagueness of linkages was made clearer: While the target site of Pharmco's interest had been officially designated by the Jakarta office as an industrial location, it was still listed as farmland under the jurisdiction at the regional Surabaya level and was found to be under the purview of the Ministry of Agriculture. Furthermore, it was left up to the investors who wanted to obtain the required government approvals for the intended purchase under the new purpose to arrange for the entire transfer of use themselves. Thus, the regional government operated under Jakarta in theory, but not according to the practices of the legal infrastructure and the behavior of the officials.

So it was that Pharmco discovered that the central government at Jakarta had no practical control over the disposition of the land they were offering. Nor would Jakarta want to coerce the local inhabitants. If such reluctance seems uncharacteristic of the Suharto government, it may be revealed to be less so when considering that the land in question was located in the heartland of the late communist partisan Aidit, a popular leader who was alleged by Suharto's government to be the key communist coconspirator in the failed 1965 alleged coup attempt.[6]

Indeed, Aidit's home village was not far away. It was here that his popular support was said to have been strongest, and also here that some of the worst of the civil-military bloodbath had taken place in the aftermath of the coup attempt. Local context, therefore, included several complications: the strong and yet peculiarly Indonesian influence of reform Islam, the constraints of an authoritarian national government with an an unarticulated array of national and regional institutions, and a local history of opposition to the side currently in power. The peasants' background was also infused with an older, syncretic mix of animism (a tradition known as *abangan*), overlain by the region's previous Hindu-Buddhist tradition and by the more recent influence of Islam. The local peasantry were strongly land centered and were said to have been staunch supporters of the deposed Sukarno. Thus, in East Java of the early 1970s, even a national government that has been described as notoriously repressive faced certain practical limits in the exercise of its power—notwithstanding its reification by some areal scholars, such as B. Anderson (1972), for example.[7]

Given this local history and access to several insiders' knowledge of this area, it was Pharmco's strong impression that the regional Surabaya bureaucrats would be as wary of causing local offense as they were fearful of Jakarta's wrath. This was not only consistent with the area's recent political experiences, it was also culturally consistent with the rukun ethic of conflict avoidance and the social knowledge stressing implicit rather than explicit communication of differences. Furthermore, from either a political or an economic standpoint, why would the regionally based authorities go out of their way to break local rice bowls for foreigners?

These were not the last of the difficult considerations involved. There also arose the issue of a large tea money payment being demanded by an agricultural ministry official whose approval was involved. We return to this issue below.

While such regional conditions left the entire purchase agreement responsibility up to each company that wanted to build in East Java, and while the conditions were certainly anything but ideal, it was the Pharmco opinion that this was still the best location available to investors, in an area widely deemed to have great long-term economic growth potential. The gap in background institutions had left the local communities open to a wide range of possible ways of dealing on the part of those wanting to buy land, and it was here that stories of corrupt foreigners had found their most fertile ground.

When it had become clear that Pharmco would have to make and negotiate its own offer for land at the village level, microlevel issues and face-to-face commercial relationships brought social responsibility issues to the fore. Pharmco's Javanese employees were worried about their fellow country people, and so the firm's lawyer in this transaction, who was from a nearby village and known in the hamlet where the purchase offer would be made, became centrally involved in the negotiation process. Other involved people, beyond the families themselves, included the local *dukun* (the curer and spiritual advisor, who also headed the local mosque) and the hamlet's traditionally elected *lurah*, or village head. (Again, H. Geertz, 1961, provides a good description of these roles.) The terms and conditions of the offer would have to be acceptable to all parties for the deal to succeed.

The village setting presented a complex array of procedural traditions, but *adat* (traditional indigenous) legal conventions prevailed regarding land tenure and inheritance. It would be of major importance that all the transactions be done publicly, and that they have the participation of all the parties, including the landowning families involved. But the real surprise, at least from the Western multinational company's perspective, would be the entry into this process of the more modern religious influence, one with social prestige implications—specifically, the valuation the peasants placed on the *hadj*, the Islamic pilgrimage to Mecca.

Making an Offer

The land purchase and subsequent activities involved a large cast of players. Those primarily involved in the purchase were the Pharmco employees located in Java (who included Javanese, Chinese, Americans, and Danes), the Pharmco attorney (Javanese), the sellers and their families (Javanese peasants), Pharmco's partner (Chinese), the local lurah (Javanese), and the dukun (Javanese). A secondary cast of players also was extensive and multinational: the Minister of Religion (a Javanese aristocrat), the Minister of Education (a Javanese aristocrat), the Director of Pharmaceuticals (Miningkabau), the Investment Board director (Javanese),

Pharmco's Hong Kong business associate (Chinese), and Pharmco's regional office personnel (Egyptian, Swiss, and Swiss-Indochinese).

The purchase also involved several social and legal systems: Indonesian law (based on Dutch law), American law, Muslim law and religious prescriptions, and Javanese adat, with its infusion of local animism and social customs.

Pharmco's research in the area gave a fairly clear idea of the commercial value of the land. Company representatives initially checked their perceptions by reviewing the firm's intended offer with the two local village officials. This took place before the representatives made their initial approach to the peasant families involved. The company's intended offering price was confirmed as being fair by both the lurah and dukun. Since the lurah was selected by the villagers themselves and the dukun was locally powerful and influential, the input of these persons would be important to the foreign investors' achievement of sufficient initial cultural alignment for a respectful approach to the families.

The actual land negotiations excluded any officials other than these two local ones. The company's own locally knowledgeable staff (including their Javanese personnel officer and the Pharmco lawyer, who also came from a neighboring village and was known to the principals) verified that the lurah and dukun were the persons the landowners could be most expected to trust.

The initial approach consisted mainly of polite social introductions, in ways traditional to local Javanese, between the peasant owners and Pharmco's Javanese representatives. Pharmco's personnel person and lawyer had spoken initially with the lurah and dukun. The purpose was to "introduce" Reeves-Ellington as Pharmco's American manager (he was not present at the initial meetings) and to bring up the matter of Pharmco's interest in purchasing the land. After proper introductions, Reeves-Ellington followed, observing appropriate local conventions of indirect approach. For example, he brought flowers, drank tea with the local officials, and joined polite conversation about wayang.

During a series of meetings that followed, the three Pharmco representatives—two Javanese, one American—heard the lurah out as he described the families and their hardships on the land. He told them that over the generations, the division of inheritance of land in some large families was "breaking up vast holdings." On follow-up investigation, Pharmco learned that the actual size of the largest holdings approximated 1.5 hectares, or 2.25 acres, and some of the current plots were down to meters square in size. About half were too small for the use of a water buffalo. (The families did not own these animals, but they would have had access to them during plowing season.)

The local officials eventually introduced the Pharmco representatives to the landowners themselves. These initial meetings went quite well from Pharmco's viewpoint. After several meetings, however, no deal had been struck, and Pharmco officials began to be frustrated. The peasants had shown interest and were not asking for more money, yet they continued to indicate that they did not want to sell for the stated offering price.

In those early years of the 1970s, apart from What westerners could see as the large gap between their own and the Indonesians' economic status, health, and standards of living, and apart from the Western optimism about the positive potential of foreign investment, there was considerable underlying concern. Among the intergovernmental groups, this concern centered on peasants losing their land and livelihood in the process of too-rapid foreign investment and development. The World Bank was interested and worried, as were some members of the Ford Foundation group. At the village level, it emerged that the peasants were conscious of gradually losing the viability of their long-term livelihood from the land through the successive breakups of inheritance among their children. Family planning groups were using this as an argument for increased family planning activities. The peasants pointed out that they needed their large families for support. This was a pragmatic view based on their cultural experience of systemic interdependence of work, land, and cash economy—a system that generations had carried forward in that particular locality.

The peasants of this particular land had been long integrated into the cash economy; they purchased much of their food and paid cash for the schooling of their children, for clothes, for personal items like glasses, and for farm implements. Above-subsistence economic relationships and dependencies had also existed with the ethnic Chinese, who controlled the milling system and would keep some of the rice as payment. The Chinese would also purchase rice produced should farmers need to sell it. Often, the woman of the household, and in some cases both husband and wife, would supplement family income by running a *warung* or small market stall, turning over extremely small amounts of money by Western industrialized standards. (H. Geertz's 1961 study of family economic roles and Alexander's 1987 study of rural Javanese market traders give valuable ethnographic details relevant to these local systems.)

Seeing the apparent impasse that had developed, Pharmco consulted separately with the local village officials, who in turn approached the landowners themselves; the landowners still did not budge. Reeves-Ellington then met separately with the lurah. He asked him if he would be willing to inquire about the possibility of other, nonmonetary issues that might be blocking progress in the negotiations. Of particular concern to Pharmco was whether pressure for payoffs was being applied to these peasants from the level of the regional government offices. If the regional investment or agricultural offices were demanding substantial payment from the peasants, perhaps Pharmco could help in resolving some of the needs. The lurah assured him that there were no issues of any consequence in this regard.

Then, within two weeks, the lurah returned, relaying two concerns from the peasant families. Before reviewing these, he confirmed to the Pharmco representative that the price itself was satisfactory; it was not more money that the landowners wanted. Rather, one of the issues was that the peasants wanted to use their land sale money to buy tickets to go on hadj, the pilgrimage of purification to Mecca. Throughout Muslim society, *hadjis*, those who have made the pilgrimage, gain significant status, both religious and social. In Java they were titled, wore special clothes, and if contemporary Muslim connotations of the hadji's piety and honesty are any indication, the status had some potential for enhancing the person's chances of business success. This would have occurred through a higher general appraisal of trust and social expectations of piety on the part of a hadji within the community.

While the opportunity for people as poor as this to go on hadj was rare, and it was potentially compelling as an attraction of selling, the lurah reported that the peasants had not been able to gain access to the means for its arrangement, even with their prospects of having a cash windfall from a land sale in the offing. Not only was the number of hadj tickets limited, but the Ministry of Religious Affairs was not responding to their requests for tickets. The lurah said they saw no need to close the deal for this amount of money if they could not use it to go on hadj. Without the purpose of investing in the pilgrimage, the mayor explained, from their perspective they "had no use for so much money."[8]

The Pharmco staff speculated that the peasants were worried that an unprecedented amount of undedicated money could attract extortion or theft. If this representation against the need of "so much money" seems incredulous to an outside businessperson, in the local context it might also be interpreted as an indirect statement expected to cause further questions that could then be answered. This was how Pharmco staff decided to receive the message, and this is exactly what happened. Pharmco responded with further questions, and the local intermediaries uncovered further answers. Direct questions from outsiders would not have been seemly or an appropriately Javanese way to do business.

The lurah's second issue blocking the sale, viewed in retrospect, was related. At the time, Reeves-Ellington discussed it with Pharmco's Javanese staff and other Javanese professional contacts for the area; however, at the time it was construed in Western terms as a psychological need. The peasants still felt reluctance, Pharmco staff speculated, notwithstanding their awareness of the new opportunities and of the practical diminishing returns of their agricultural land. They were bound to the land in a deeper, moral way. It had been in their families' possession for many generations. Viewed in local animistic context, the land represented a spiritual tie. According to the lurah, while the peasants wanted to sell, they were struggling with this idea of breaking ties to the land.

Pharmco representatives took these issues back to the Pharmco home office. First, as to the issue of hadj tickets: What if Pharmco attempted to obtain the tickets on behalf of the peasants? The initial Pharmco home office response was, of course, negative; the idea was viewed as "crazy." Rationales given for this view hinged on everything from American ideals of separation of church, state, and business, to comments on the folly of a secular, non-Muslim organization trying to obtain tickets for the high holy Muslim pilgrimage. For some time this view prevailed, not only in the U.S. home office, but (except for one manager, who was Swiss) at Pharmco's Hong Kong office as well.

After persistent arguments on the part of the Java team, but particularly those made by Pharmco's Javanese lawyer,[9] who told them the idea was a stroke of genius and should be done, the home Pharmco managers finally relented. Pharmco's senior management agreed to approach their government contacts in Jakarta for advice. Such guidance would not have been available to the peasants. Not unlike Pharmco's long trek downward through the hierarchy of officials' signatures, the peasants would have had a long climb upward through successive layers of regional and district religious offices before being able to approach the Jakarta offices.

As it turned out, Pharmco's efforts proved quite successful. Going through the National Investment Board, Pharmco managers began a dialogue between Investment Board officials and senior officials in the Ministry of Religion. This began indirectly. One of the Pharmco managers was on the local international school's board of education and had made friends in the Indonesian Ministry of Education; these friends had friends in the Ministry of Health and Pharmacy and Ministry of Investment, in which further links existed to the Indonesian partner of a Western multinational company headquartered in Hong Kong. At the end of this network was the Minister of Religion in Jakarta.

Why all the parties helped is a matter of speculation. Pharmco staff knew for certain that the regional religious ministers were not involved. (Indeed, Reeves-Ellington was told by a reliable source that the officials at this level would have been terrified to say anything.) The outcome might have been influenced by the gradual buildup of goodwill that had gone on throughout the business relationships Pharmco had cultivated earlier in Jakarta: socializing, birthday flowers, letters of support for college-bound children, the odd pair of tennis tickets in Jakarta— things that are little different from corporate business networking in America.

Whatever the influences, they did not involve anything like bribes. Perhaps the partners looked favorably on the Pharmco manager's support for young puppet carvers and dalang, or perhaps these particular officials liked Americans. Commercial actors do not always keep score objectively; they make relationships intuitively. Thus, without ever approaching directly, and therefore without broaching certain tensions of Muslim-Christian sentiment that might have negatively influenced the results, Pharmco managed to gain access to the Minister of Religion himself. The required number of tickets was obtained to enable the peasants to go on hadj.

Pharmco had decided to pay for the tickets as a premium, in addition to the initial purchase price offered to the peasants. This was done for two reasons. First, the cost was minimal, less than 10% of the purchase price. Second, Pharmco members believed that the impact of putting actual tickets on the table would be a greater incentive toward closing the sale than would offering a letter or merely a verbal confirmation that tickets would be available. This reasoning proved accurate for additional reasons. The tickets were concrete; they had the name of a ship, they were usable, and they could not be mislaid by an official or their existence denied, as was often the case with other kinds of official documents. That the tickets came through the Minister of Education directly from the Minister of Religion was not only clear to the principals negotiating the deal, but it became common knowledge at the regional government level, and no one would have dared interfere with the minister's tickets. Putting the tickets on the table up front was indeed a gamble. But it was also a concrete gesture that made Pharmco's good faith clear, and no doubt also signified the strength of their relational power.

This gesture proved auspicious in other ways. Pharmco later learned they had achieved another unexpected bonus with their peasant sellers by providing the tickets up front. In getting them directly, Pharmco learned they had avoided the obligation to pay a large sum of tea money to the Ministry of Religion and Transportation. This sum would certainly have been required of the peasants. If there had been only a letter, it would have been passed to many hands along the way before being received by the peasants. Even if Pharmco had delivered the letter, it would have had to pass to still more hands on the way back to the tickets. All these hands would have been extended for tea money. This amount, Pharmco learned, could have taken as much as 30% of the total payment for the land. The peasants, understandably, would appreciate being able to keep this money for themselves.

The second issue, of the peasants' animistic bonds to the land, was perhaps even thornier than the bureaucratic arrangements for purchasing hadj tickets. The Pharmco side initially suggested to the lurah that, as the firm did not require all of the land in the initial stages of their commercial activity, they should allow the peasants to continue to farm the sections the company did not immediately need. Others better versed in adat legal conventions, including the lurah, said no: This would make it impossible to claim the land for use later. Pharmco and local lawyers, in consultation with other area lawyers and ministry officials, confirmed that allowing the same people to continue to use land they had formerly owned would give them de facto squatters' rights. Pharmco then might well lose any access to the land when they eventually wanted it.

After still further consultation with both the lurah and the dukun, another solution was reached. Pharmco agreed to make some of the lands available for public use, with a gradual reduction of land availability over several years. The arrangements for the use of this land would be managed by the lurah. It was agreed that land availability would rotate among all the peasant families that were selling and would start with those who did not own the particular blocks that were being made available for public use. This would allow the peasants to wean themselves away from the land. According to the local lawyers, it would also avoid the establishment of squatters' claims.

The Pharmco field management accordingly brought this second proposal to their Java headquarters. They argued that, while peasants were at least nominally Muslims, they were also syncretic animists. From the Pharmco team's perspective at the time, the underlying cultural logic involved the argument that the spiritual bonds between people who had been the acknowledged owners and their former land were not easily or automatically broken; this separation would require some time. Their held beliefs in bonds to the land must receive some respect, and these bonds must be allowed to be relaxed in a more gradual manner. On the other hand, allowing original owners to remain on their former plot would only work in the direction of maintaining those bonds.

Finally, the plan also allowed use of available land that would otherwise have been abruptly put out of production. Because these peasant families were selling their total holdings, the mayor and Pharmco manager agreed that they would be given priority consideration for employment opportunities in the new Pharmco plant. This was prompted by the concern that the sellers might have no immediate means of support after selling their land. Headquarters agreed, and the purchase offer, including the land use proposal, was put to the peasant families at the same time that the hadj tickets were put on the table. Within a week, a purchase deal was struck.

Thus, a Western transaction evolved that incorporated significant cultural elements of non-Western origin. While not easy to achieve, the land purchase agreement offered some advantages for all sides. Peasant families stood to gain status by being able to go on hadj. They had some access to traditional lands over a number of years. Their greater psychological and spiritual comfort with this transition was enhanced by the endorsement and subsequent ritual participation of their dukun. The involved parties also stood to gain community status through the multinational company's efforts to make the land available for public use.

In the area during that time, there were ample numbers of other prospective foreign land purchasers, including several who came offering more money. In the case of another company Pharmco managers knew about that did go through all the regional and central ministry offices, the amount left to the peasants by the end of that deal was reported, by local people, to amount to only 20% of the negotiated proceeds of their land sale. In Pharmco's case, the villagers kept all the proceeds.

Pharmco obtained the land they needed to carry out the factory project. They gained strong local support in their later efforts at local employment. The increased prestige of the dukun and the lurah were also of immense value to Pharmco throughout the plant's construction and in the hiring of employees over the next three years. During this time, these officials were instrumental in assuring a protected work site, a good workforce that came to work on time, and some of the best-educated people in the village. The immediate outcome reinforced Pharmco's intuitive impressions of the rightness of the way they had conducted business. No complaints emerged as the project moved forward, and the American manager received attention as a Western practitioner who was knowledgeable of Javanese concerns both locally and in the international business press. The lurah was admired for his wisdom in mediating the matter, and, significantly, Pharmco subsequently had no owner problems or strike problems. The local officials not only gained prestige through helping to finalize the sale, they also continued to play roles as the plant project progressed. The dukun officiated with plant siting and later at plant-opening ceremonies and was paid for these services.[10]

Payment and Land Use Registration

Even with the deal struck, payment for the land in the Pharmco project was not going to be easy. Pharmco offices were in Jakarta, and the peasants were in East Java, a distance of five hours' travel. The drive took two days due to the bad roads. The peasants were accustomed to operating in cash and had never used banks. For them, payment had to be made in cash. The total for the roughly 10 hectares was U.S. $55,000 (in 1970s dollars). At the time, the exchange rate was about 275 rupiah to the dollar, and per capita income was roughly $100 annually. In rupiah, the largest Indonesian bill was equivalent to about U.S. $0.50, necessitating the transport of approximately 135,000 paper bills. This transport of cash was a physical problem for Pharmco. At best, it would be four reasonably large suitcases of currency.

The peasants wanted to assure that there would be no recriminations among themselves after payment for the land. For such assurance, they wanted their extended families and the lurah to be present at the counting. This would involve some 50 or more people. In short, the activity was going to be reasonably public and well known. Further, the counting would take at least eight hours, so a meal had to be organized for the participants. This made the payment even more of a public event. A site needed to be organized and a caterer found to provide food. (Pharmco was expected to pay, but the peasants would be the food vendors.) Because of the heat, some cover had to be provided.

The Pharmco home office had assumed that the payments would be made by bank transfer. They automatically approved payment by check should a bank transfer be difficult. Readers can imagine the consternation created when the request was made for transporting payment in the equivalent of paper 50-cent pieces. If that were not enough, the highly public nature of the event put the transfer at risk of robbery. Finally, the money was going to be counted individually to each of the landowners—an event that would take all day. The home office said, "No." They then relented and said it would be approved with cash in transit insurance and under the control of the company's bank. There was no insurance, and the bank declined on the basis that the entire event was too uncontrolled and therefore too risky for them.[11]

After at least two trips by Reeves-Ellington to Singapore just to correspond by phone and a further trip by a senior Pharmco finance officer to Indonesia, the payment method was reluctantly approved. The money would not be transferred by auto, but rather by air, with the last leg of transport by car. The bags would not be checked but would have to be hand carried. This entailed buying a seat for each of the bags. Three local managers, including Reeves-Ellington, would be responsible for the transfer. The company did indemnify them in case of robbery (although they were not bonded if any of them had decided to abscond with the money).

Purchase of airline tickets was no problem, but explaining to the boarding agent that each bag had a ticket, and therefore a seat, was a problem. There were standby passengers who wanted the seats, and they too did not agree that bags had precedence over people in the seats. The Western logic that Pharmco managers had purchased the tickets and could therefore put in them what they wanted did not prevail. At the time and place, people prevailed over property rights. The suggestion was made that the bags be checked so people could have the seats. Three two-suitors plus briefcases were hand carried by the Pharmco managers. Each bag was stuffed with money. The managers did not want to broadcast that the bags were stuffed with money, and that for that reason they could not be checked. Finally, the bags were taken and checked. The team was told that if this was not satisfactory, they would be taken off the flight. With the closing at stake, the bags were checked, and the team boarded the aircraft. All arrived safely at the Surabaya airport.

The remainder of the trip and the money counting event itself went uneventfully. All the families stayed until all the money was paid. Eight family farms were settled in that closing. It was unclear (and pointedly not the foreigners' business to ask, according to the local officials and staff) how many people were involved from each family. Pharmco staff suspected that, in some cases, one of the selling families actually represented more than one owner; that is, that the eldest sibling represented others. This may have been one reason why so many people were at the closing. The entire economy was coming out of a modified state-owned system and was cash poor. Everyone carried their cash.

Beyond hadj, there were a number of speculations possible regarding the peasants' needs and uses for this money. Pharmco and the local negotiating team worried about the insecurity of the payment after delivery to the sellers. This led to queries to the local officials, who said, "Don't worry, it is not your problem, besides we are friends here." Certainly, if Surabaya had been involved, its officials would have been more than happy to assist—they would promptly have relieved the peasants of some, and perhaps a good portion, of the money. Reeves-Ellington remembers the sight of seven of the family parties walking barefoot down a dirt road, each carrying a rice sack full of money. (The eighth family, apparently, left by a different direction.) The Westerners wondered what the families would do with the money, but had been warned not to ask. Within the week, as it happened, all the sellers did host a party in the village with a well-known dalang. Someone told Reeves-Ellington that the surplus probably was buried somewhere for safe-keeping. With the money's ownership public, officially and religiously recognized, Pharmco hoped there would be some assurance of considerable social or perhaps even religious repercussions for anybody who dared steal someone's hadj stake.

Just before boarding a plane at the Surabaya airport for the return trip to Jakarta, one of the managers was approached by a peasant who had sold land. He said that he did not have all of his money. He was short one bundle. The manager replied in typical Western business manner, "I have yours and the lurah's signatures on paper that you received all your money." "Yes [you do]," said the peasant, "but I don't [have it]." The manager looked in his case. There was one bundle of money—the amount the peasant was missing. The money was handed over, and the matter was settled. The peasant was very happy that he had the money.

With the bills paid, the next step was to get the regional land registration changed from agricultural to industrial. Construction could then begin. Pharmco assembled the necessary documents and submitted them to the regional Ministry of Agriculture office in Surabaya. The Jakarta officials had assured the company that this was nothing more than formality and would not take much time. However, nothing happened. The documents remained on the senior Surabaya official's desk.

Informal contacts with the official indicated that there were no serious problems with the paperwork, but that he was busy and it would take a while to get to the matter. Pharmco's Indonesian ethnic Chinese partner, who lived in Surabaya, checked into the matter. He learned that this official had the reputation of living an extravagantly high lifestyle with an expensive gambling habit. The partner indicated that money would have to change hands for the land registration change approval to surface on this man's desk. From the perspective of U.S. law at the time, such a payment might be construed as legal: The company was not asking the official to do anything illegal, only to perform his job in a timely manner. (In this connection, Elfstrom, 1991, provides a helpful discussion of international customs of gratuity.)

Under this interpretation, the local manager asked the partner to see what it was that the official wanted: The answer was U.S. $20,000. This was far too much money. It elevated the payment from the potential range of gratuity to a clear bribe of significant proportions, and the amount could not be paid. Furthermore, it was a high percentage of the money paid for the land. Worse, if the company paid this amount, other hands would be held out for similar amounts of money. The project would then be in jeopardy. So, the documents sat.

Further inquiry about this official revealed that his gambling habit was severe. Indeed, he had lately gambled away all the office's money. This was of particular concern as *Labaran* (also known as *Idul Fitri*, the major Muslim holiday after the Ramadan fast) was approaching. On this holiday, government offices were expected to provide food for all employees and new work uniforms for the next year. All civil servants were furnished with khaki work clothes. There was no central supply source, so tailors made them, with some variation. Anyone seen dressed in work clothes at that time would likely be assumed to be working for the state, and so the matter of the work clothes was one involving social status. This regional minister's office was not going to be able to fulfill this obligation as it had no money.

Pharmco's partner and its Javanese employees saw the official's predicament as an opportunity. They proposed that Pharmco, by providing the money for the food and uniforms for the office's 40 employees, would save face for this official, and thus they might get him to sign the land documents. The cost of this undertaking would be no more than U.S. $300. The immediate question arose about the risk of giving this official the money and then seeing him gamble it away. Also, how would Pharmco be certain to get him to do his job and obtain the signature in exchange for a payment to cover these holiday provisions?

Several ethical questions arose. The American Pharmco manager was not comfortable providing cash to the official. He argued that the person was corrupt, and Pharmco should not support or encourage his behavior. The Chinese partner argued that this was just a necessary cost of doing business. The Javanese employees offered a third perspective. They argued that the people who would suffer were the employees, who would go without new uniforms and holiday food. They suggested that Pharmco arrange to have the food and uniforms produced under Pharmco's auspices and only then allow the Surabayan Agrarian Office to distribute them. In return for the ministry chief's signature on Pharmco's documents, Pharmco would allow him to take credit for the holiday distribution. The Javanese Pharmco employees were certain they could make all necessary arrangements.

This last plan was approved. Within a week, Pharmco had the documents, the Agrarian office employees and their families had their uniforms and holiday food, and the regional chief did not have to face public embarrassment. While Pharmco kept their word not to mention their role in the food and uniform arrangement, rumors nonetheless circulated in Surabaya and in the village where the Pharmco plant was to be built, crediting Pharmco with "saving ordinary people's holidays." The company gained further respect for understanding how to solve problems Javanese style. The goodwill this solution generated would be invaluable in the months and years to come.

Dedication, Hiring, and Opening

With the land purchased, the authorization for industrial use obtained, and the building plans approved, construction on the Pharmco plant was to begin in 1973. Local leaders advised the observance of traditional rituals to gain maximum alignment and acceptance within the community. This would also aid in worker recruitment when the plant would be ready to open. Local Pharmco management agreed and invited senior U.S. company officials to join in the laying of the building's cornerstone. To his subsequent dismay, Reeves-Ellington, the American general manager, did not ask specifically what activities would be carried out or what kind of participation would be expected.

On the day of the opening ceremony, the local dukun, as master of ceremonies, led a water buffalo calf into the center of the area where the plant would be erected. Then, in the middle of a downpour (during Chinese New Year and a very good omen), the assembled group, including four foreigners, watched the dukun lop off the head off the buffalo with a single blow of his ceremonial knife. The head was carefully wrapped in a shroud and buried in the proper cornerstone (as determined by means not understood by any of the foreigners, but only the dukun). The rest of the buffalo was divided among the peasant spectators for eating later.

The next part of the ceremony was a feast of delectable Indonesian foods. However, before all could begin filling their plates, the head of the company, at first identified as the senior foreign visitor, was invited to eat the head of the mound of rice and then to eat the head of the first chicken served. This visitor readily consumed the rice, but balked at the chicken head. He quickly pointed out that the local American manager (Reeves-Ellington) was president of the company and should be the one to have this honor. Besides, the president was also an anthropologist and would not mind eating chicken heads. Reeves-Ellington put the head of the chicken in his mouth and broke for the outdoor toilet, chased by the dukun, who had some inkling of his intentions. With the outhouse door shut and the dukun pounding on it, Reeves-Ellington reconsidered spitting the chicken head down the hole. Company and personal honor prevailed. He opened the door, showed the dukun the chicken head, chewed quickly, and swallowed. Peasants and government officials cheered, Reeves-Ellington choked, and the other foreign visitors laughed with great relief. It was the Americans' impression that this event strengthened the bonds between the company and its peasant neighbors.

There were other adjustments in the initial operation of the plant, including particularly the significance of work uniforms. When the first employees were hired, they received uniforms, including sneakers, distributed by Pharmco. Pharmco management discussed with employees the necessity of wearing both uniforms and shoes at all times in the plant. The employees were to be responsible for the cleaning of both, and neither the uniforms nor the shoes were to be worn outside the plant other than coming to and going from work.

Within a week of their distribution, there were almost no uniforms or shoes to be seen on the employees working in the plant. When asked about where they were, the employees responded, *"Tidak tahu Tuan"* ("Don't know, Boss"). After several replacements, the plant manager knew something had to be done. Company employees were wearing street clothes and walking around the plant barefoot. Both were against company and government regulations.

The solution Pharmco adopted was to build a small section onto the employee section of the plant. Separate locker areas for men and for women were placed immediately inside the door. All employees entered the plant through the showers—all took a shower—and then put on the uniforms and shoes, which were located in lockers on the other side of the showers. The reverse was practiced on leaving the plant. The company assumed responsibility for laundering the uniforms and keeping the shoes clean.

Epilogue and Reflections

The plant's impact in general was surely extremely modest. At the time of opening, annual sales approximated about U.S. $1 million, about equal to the initial investment. Prices in Indonesia at the time were roughly 60% of the parent corporation's outside-U.S. prices, and these in turn were about 70% of U.S. pharmaceutical prices. Price by product varied, of course, but the target market was internal to Indonesia following the national import replacement strategy.

The investment payback period of the plant had been estimated at 10 years, and this was achieved. At opening, the plant employed 120 people, with all but the plant manager Indonesian. After the first three years, the plant manager was also an Indonesian. There were 20 to 30 persons in the sales force at various times, about 15 other nonproduction positions, and the remainder were in the plant production workforce. In all, three expatriates were present during the first three years; thereafter, one-half of an expatriate person's time was assigned. The plant was quite marginal in the parent corporation's worldwide operations, constituting not even 1% of international sales and far less of its total pill business.

Wage and salary equivalents now would be meaningless, for the exchange rate was 200 to 1 at the time and has since undergone revisions. Pharmco paid rates that were considered competitive at the time and also at the upper limits imposed by the Ministry of Trade and Ministry of Pharmaceuticals. Pharmco could not pay what it wanted. Most workers in the bottling, machine pill bottle filling, and tube filling areas were women, as was the case with factory workers that D. Wolf (1994) studied in the Indonesian foreign-export light assembly industries of the 1980s. Men worked in the yards, worked security, and operated the generator. The few kitchen staff were women.

At the time of writing, the plant was still open. It still had the two major shareholders, the corporate and the regional partner who began the joint venture. However, it was also listed on the Indonesian Stock Exchange. Proceeds from the operation earned by the original Indonesia-based partner not only paid off the debt, but sent his two children to the university in the United States. Also, at the time of writing, the plant had still never had a strike—the only plant Reeves-Ellington knows in the vicinity that can make that claim. The parent company rated the operation one of its best in terms of profit to sales, and two expansions have taken place since the opening.

There are clearly limits to any conclusions that can be drawn from a purely business standpoint in reviewing this one plant's establishment. Also, from outcome-driven views of social or political agendas, the insights to be gained are modest. Much has changed, yet much has remained the same in Indonesia over the 25 years of the plant's operation. The import substitution pursued in the early Suharto era to industrialize the country has evolved into a much greater regional and global economic integration, with the consequent crowding of Java by factories, construction, and other effects of urbanization and industrialization. But, the greatest wealth creation remains confined to a privileged network closely connected to the government head, there is considerable continued emphasis on resource extraction, and there is, above all, continued government suppression of what has become an increasingly vocal civil political dissent (*Economist*, 1993; Laber, 1996; Schwarz, 1994; Winters, 1995).

Indonesia's standard of living and per capita income rose through the period, but it still lags far behind the affluent industrialized world, and economic takeoff, at least in the sense widely imagined by developmentalists during the years Pharmco's plant opened, has not been realized in so dynamic a way.

Many other things have changed little. As a 1993 review in *The Economist* notes, "Last August Sony had to stop its production line for six days because components were held up in customs—a galling experience for the just-in-time Japanese" (p. 7), and, "Sane businessmen do their utmost to steer clear of the Indonesian courts" (p. 11). As for land purchasing,

> One foreign company in Jakarta, looking to expand and noticing a vacant site next door, made inquiries about buying the land. It discovered that the plot it was interested in appeared to have three owners. Two of the land titles, it was explained, were "genuine but false"—the paperwork had been issued by the right people for the wrong reasons. It took 11 years to sort the purchase out. (p. 11).

Increasing attention has been given in recent years to the conditions of work and living on the now-crowded island of Java, and new government programs of relocation have been implemented to place residents on the outlying islands of Indonesia, such as Kalimantan, where there are less crowded conditions but also few of the amenities of urbanized living. The transmigrants to these areas most often work for private plantations, logging companies, or the government's reforestation programs (Mydans, 1996, August 25, p. 22). The visions of either those who advocated a purely business agenda or those who advocated a largely redistributive social agenda have for the most part not been realized, even though there has been improvement in some of the conditions associated with each.

Even from the point of view of a successful plant opening at the local level, many questions of causality can be raised but not answered definitively. Luck was certainly involved; but response to opportunity was critical. Luck was with Reeves-Ellington, the American general manager, when on the third night in Indonesia, and still staying in the Hotel Indonesia, he heard of a dance practice group nearby. On going to see it, he was one of two Americans who had been there. At this event, he met one of two brothers who were Indonesian anthropologists; the elder brother was keenly interested in the craft and performance arts of wayang. From this contact, Reeves-Ellington obtained tickets to a National Radio monthly performance. At that performance, Reeves-Ellington suggested the character of one of the puppets. Luckily, he was correct, establishing a spiritual affinity.

Commercial exchange involves listening and responding, to align action at the level at which the impact is going to occur. Practitioners cannot build on something that is not there already and cannot expect the details to be automatically worked out from a programmatic scheme. Likewise, business cannot expect the multitude of ethics of social knowledge and artifacts of capitalism or of Western liberal democracy to appeal automatically to everyone as the best way to do things. For example, it is clear that in a situation such as Java posed then, arm's length relationships did not necessarily result in either greater efficiency in reducing transaction costs or in upholding an agenda-based notion of ethics: Foreigners refusing to learn and respond to the inner workings of Javanese social knowledge would only be subjected to increased cost, either in monetary or ethical terms.

Social responsibility as conceived in terms of personally adaptive, responsive, and inclusive decisions may proceed entirely independently of business success in particular ventures, but it operates from many of the same underlying approaches to a new situation. Reeves-Ellington and his Pharmco colleagues may well have been simply lucky in their participation in a small succession of improbable events. But without as complete an exchange of cultural dialogue as possible at the local level, without the construction of a synthesis of practice and meaning that acceptably fits the needs of each side of the transaction, the authors believe that pessimistic outcomes will always exceed auspicious ones. Commercial actors maximize the likelihood of joint successes, with options for future successes. Socially responsible commercial actors do this with a constant awareness of belonging to and imagining an expanding moral community.

Luck is improved by using the listening ear and hearing the music. A University of California musicologist, Mantle Hood, once suggested that gamelan music is like a babbling brook, constantly changing and never ending—the life rhythms of Indonesia. A foreign businessperson's responsibility is to learn to understand the music and teach others his or her music. In the Javanese context described here, it may be that commercial actors assumed wayang roles at the table, for example: Modesty, older brother, not god. To those who insist that only controlled economics matter and that only American management negotiations are correct, we can only suggest that they have not sat in someone's house, drunk tea with them, and have not had gamelan music played for them. Try to insist on acting in an American way. Impossible—unless you cannot hear the music.

Notes

1. Map adapted by Adele Anderson (1″ = 280 mi.).
2. The historical relationships between ethnic Chinese business people and natives of the Indonesian islands have at times been ambivalent and even hostile, but historically deep and always closely intertwined. Both heads of Indonesian government since its independence in 1945 have had close ties with Chinese associates (Schwarz, 1994).
3. The benefits of tea money compensated for significant shortfalls in salary, for example, among civil servants and military officials, to support themselves and their families in a culturally normative fashion. Trade functionaries anticipated tea money to augment their incomes for children's school fees, books, and clothing and to stretch the family food budget. They saw their services—handing out visas or work permits, advising on their proper completion, or seeing that mailed packages were not stolen—to be rightly compensated in some small way. Some of the added cost of services was regulated, such as the requirements to use an agent, who then charged anywhere from 0.5% to 5% of invoiced value to clear goods through customs in a given time period. Timely clearance avoided spoilage, extra hiring fees or lost production time. Javanese stories of foreign corruption grew as they circulated; foreigners were said to provide large overseas bank accounts, expensive trips

abroad, or high payment for officials' houses, all bribes to get local people to sell land. The result was more hands extended for more money, more Indonesians assuming they had been cheated and most likely insulted by the foreigners, and a buildup of bad will rather than good. The initial motivation to enhance status markers grew in some cases to an expectation of opulent lifestyles comparable to those of very top foreign executives. One area sales applicant said, when asked his job requirements, "I must have an air-conditioned Ford Galaxy, a home in Kabajoran [the most expensive part of town], $40,000 a year and guaranteed repatriation to the U.S. in two years to a senior manager position." At the time, the manager of the company drove a Volkswagen Variant, made $10,000 a year, and lived in a middle-class Indonesian neighborhood.

4. Their anger could be quite visible. On one occasion, Reeves-Ellington was at the port attempting to clear some goods, but the port customs official needed some tea money that was more than the total value of the shipment. When Reeves-Ellington became angry and raised his voice, the official's eyes looked as though shades had been drawn behind the irises. He started picking his teeth with a long, manicured little fingernail. It was obviously time to leave.

5. The *wayang-kulit* or shadow-puppet play is not merely a folk entertainment, but has deeper meaning, in both the moral attitudes and the magico-religious life. It includes delicate and fine leather works of colorful puppets, played by the dalang on the screen, music and poetry by the songster and the gamelan orchestra, and the funny and wise stories narrated by the dalang, bearing moral and virtual education, depicting the scenic beauty and culture of the region. Wayang requires the skills of the artist, sculptor, poet, playwright, musician, dramatist, craftsperson, and instruments (Josodharnodjo, 1967).

6. The debate continues as to whether this coup attempt was in fact Communist led (Laber, 1996), but under the present government it is treated with the assumption that it was.

7. Benedict Anderson's (1972) well-known analysis of Javanese state power was somewhat modified for Reeves-Ellington, who at one point in his residence there was reading an article in the *International Herald Tribune*. Joseph Kraft was lamenting the power of the Suharto government by commenting on the jackbooted army troops terrorizing the rest of the population. While reading, Reeves-Ellington noticed a platoon of Indonesian capital crack troops shuffling by—barefoot, no two weapons matching, and looking generally miserable. For those who might question such a unitary and reified power analysis as Anderson provides, we recommend reading at least one of a quartet of political and historical novels written by the dissident Indonesian novelist Pramoedya Ananta Toer and translated into English by Max Lane (1990). Toer's polylingual and variegated cast of characters, whether high class or lowly born Natives, Eurasians, ethnic Chinese, Dutch, French, or Japanese, give a much fuller and more pluralistic picture of the power interpretations that have been operating in Java for over a century.

8. According to Nugroho, the Pharmco attorney who had gone on hadj with his wife, the bare minimum cost of the pilgrimage trip, after tickets, would have been around $1000.

9. Reeves-Ellington always considered Mr. Nugroho, the Javanese attorney, as a Javanese key informant and colleague first, and only secondarily as an attorney. But, the home office legal staff saw him primarily as a Western-trained attorney; for them, this is what certified

his reliability, particularly as he was educated in the Dutch tradition. They relied on him from the point of view of this expert status, just as Reeves-Ellington relied on his advice in cultural matters.

10. In order to assure the plant was protected from evil spirits and that good ones would enter, a prime ritual job of the dukun was to determine the siting of the plant on the property. Westerners assume a plant front should face and be parallel to the road, but the dukun's determination was spiritual. Of course, Reeves-Ellington was assured the plant would face the road, sort of, and it did—about 15 degrees off center to the road. Obviously, there was some spiritual flexibility here. When the Western architects and engineers from the United States learned of this, one said, "No damned witch doctor is going to tell me where my plant will be sited." But the dukun did. The village head acted as a plant hiring consultant and was also paid by Pharmco for his services. As an official, he received great local respect and most likely economic benefit, as is common among officials and military personnel in Southeast Asia. With rural areas not institutionally integrated (a point on which Peacock, 1978, concurs), locals may have felt this moderate personal enrichment less onerous than outsiders taking their money. Did these local leaders extort people for work opportunities? We cannot know for sure, but Reeves-Ellington heard from field informants was that they did not. Such extortion has been reported at a number of other localities and foreign investment projects, both at the regional level and among local financing partners. Such deals were reported to include both money and sex for jobs. It is likely that both the village head and dukun, having mediated the successful deal, benefited from the social obligations they incurred and could call on the villagers for support in other matters. But how different is this from the situation of politicians in the United States? There also came with the Pharmco plant construction opportunities for local suppliers of workers' food (paid for by Pharmco) and, later, for the plant's canteen. Other locals contracted to do laundering on site for the plant.

11. One of the Reeves-Ellington's distributors regularly checked a Samsonite suitcase full of money on Garuda airline to Singapore—he was not worried, he said; he tipped the staff to take care of the bag. The author also remembers standing in line at a Chase Manhattan bank in Jakarta, behind a man with a full rice sack. When the man got to the counter, he tipped it upside down and it was full of dollars and rupiah. Later, the author heard it was more than U.S. $100,000.

7
Beyond Agenda

In this book, we have approached social responsibility in business from the combined point of view of anthropology and business practice. We have described some differences between informal, though often strongly traditional, cultural interpretation and more formal bodies of programs, rules, and principles that now pervade late-modern organizations. Agenda is the name we have given to these more formal and rationalized principles. We have argued that their proliferation has combined with the general breakup and reorganization of older forms of social-knowledge-based behavioral expectations, forms with more homogeneous cultural origins. This turn of events has permitted many people to abandon their efforts to respond personally, exercising their own active cultural interpretations of responsibility. Indeed, the development of successive layers and versions of imposed and rationalized legalisms has even seemed to discourage attempts to respond actively.

We have defined responsibility following an older usage, as mutual acknowledgment and response for a social context or the fitting action. This kind of response requires that people have an image of a moral community. Such a community sometimes must be reconstructed or discovered anew in unfamiliar cultural contexts. Social responsibility in business involves a commercial entity's integration within all the wider sociocultural contexts in which it operates. Business that is an organization of reality for its economic aims alone, that is not also an organization for the variant social realities of the wider society, cannot be socially responsible.

Within a personal context of power, we view responsibility as reflexive with freedom. In this sense, responsibility is the fulfillment of preexisting social obligations that are based in cultural logic and social knowledge. Individual variance occurs as an expression of rights based on the concept of freedom. The two are in tension, one with the other, but both are necessary if commercial dialogue is to occur. At the organizational level, this reciprocity is expressed between commercial dialogue and social responsibility.

Culture and Agenda

Within a holistic anthropological framework, knowing the difference between culture-based ethics and agendas can facilitate a more socially integrative organization. Viewed holistically, culture is not simply composed of shared meanings, but of complex and patterned interrelationships among the sets of meaningful elements used by members of a sociocultural system. Social knowledge interprets the commonly understood behavioral prescriptions of a setting in use. Normative values orientations and worldview together form the integrative compass by which people symbolically orient their apprehensions of themselves, others, and the world. Observing and experimenting with knowledge of these elements, the newcomer can discern, construct, and interpret a cultural logic of action for a particular setting.

Artifacts, the most easily accessible and visible products and expressions of cultural activity, are only an extract of the knowledge and context in which symbolic cues are used. They include human products such as rituals, material culture, and, notably in late modern times, the rationalized, formulated and communicated bodies of codes, rules, and purposes that, collectively, we have been calling agenda.

Cultural contrasts appear most vivid when comparing different countries and world social regions. The patterned shift of meanings between sociocultural systems at such comprehensive scales is the most visible evidence of cultural holism. Ethical interpretations also vary across cultural traditions and across peoples' statuses and circumstances within them. Yet, coherent and responsible exchange between persons from these different regions is possible if what is mutually important and valued can be made intelligible and workably coherent to both parties within the logic of their respective cultures. At the same time, responsible commerce and communication will not always mean precisely the same thing to all the parties involved.

Awareness of the different types of cultural elements and of the process for cultural learning can greatly facilitate the task of integrating business organizations into the wider society. Especially in times of change, the need to learn and interpret the unfamiliar is continual. It must take place in persons and at the same time in organizations, which are devices for gathering power, resources, and authority to direct, control, and organize people. Social responsibility for practitioners involves the discovery, deciphering, and matching of correspondent understandings and then responding to what is important to people in and across environments. What can be mutually established as important, shared, and agreed defines its content for commerce.

The concept of organizational culture, viewed in isolation, largely fails to provide adequate information to make organizations more responsible, either internally or externally. It is only part of a much broader, holistic context within which people have to orchestrate their business activities. That which becomes culturally common to an organization's members, especially if they are from diverse native social settings, is the setting-specific social knowledge, the expected practices and behavioral predictions people make from day to day. All organization members must, however, map these expectations and interpretations into their own native cultural logic. Historical circumstances may well imprint, and organizational founders and leaders formally institute, many elements of meaning imported from a particular native social region. But, over time and depending on their perspectives and opportunities, the workforce will always dynamically reinterpret and reinvent them.

In the context of a commercial organization, agenda is a special kind of social knowledge extract, a written or verbally repeated set of artifacts largely derived from the social knowledge of some people, preponderantly founders and leaders. Agenda is a useful invention for formalizing and quickly and efficiently spreading specific social knowledge extracts that answer particular procedural needs. It helps reduce efforts in areas in which individual or local decision making is judged unnecessary or takes up too much time, or where doubt and delays are felt to introduce unacceptable risks to the organization.

Agendas from the larger society similarly reflect a desire to reduce inefficiencies and the frequency of occurrence of undesired outcomes. These agendas, too, are rationalized extracts of the social knowledge of some people. Whether or not they are written down, agendas often come to acquire a stability comparable to other artifacts—a structure and internal consistency that holds its general shape even when taken and viewed out of context. It is when following this consistency becomes foolish in the operating context that the usefulness of agenda, regardless of its source, should be questioned.

Successful agenda relies on the reification of obligation and therefore power. Further, agenda assumes organizational actors to be compliant and not active moral agents, as is the case for social responsibility. The individual actor's response to the reification of power and obligation is opportunism. This in turn is controlled through exact laws, rules, and regulations in agenda companies. This is why *pure business organizations are also pure agenda companies.*

Business and Commerce

For making business more responsible, we have identified certain contrasts between purely business approaches and wider commercial ones. Two priorities are implied by these terms. Pure business as an ideal type overemphasizes the economic; it includes such basic wealth-creating, wealth-accumulating demands as growth, viability, and profitability. Commercial priorities include a range of additional social benefits, direct or indirect, internal or external. They might be economic, safety, health, education, and information or a host of other benefits that accrue to the wider society, and the people employed by the business and their families.

Purely business concerns form the basic primary defining context of a commercial organization in which social responsibility takes place. Commerce, which we see more broadly as the exchange of things and ideas beyond purely business concerns, is the integrative context for socially responsible behavior. Practitioners who are not overdependent or overconstrained by internal business agendas or external social ideologies can consider and incorporate social issues as integral to their commercial activities and make responsible business possible. The business-economic aim cannot responsibly be neglected or obscured behind a social agenda rhetoric, and neither can social responsibility be realized through economic considerations alone. Neither of these exclusive positions is integrative or responsible for commercial practitioners.

The provision of leadership, support, and fostering of personal agency for social response can promote and facilitate social responsibility in business. These actions can take place by acknowledging and maximizing the power of cultural interpretation. Agenda alone will not take care of social responsibility. As an artifact and partial extract, agenda well used can be a wonderful device for facilitating paths of routine communication, assessment, and empirical evaluation, and for focusing members as they work together on novel and difficult interpretive tasks. Beyond its procedural usefulness, it must be recognized as inherently limited and limiting. Substituted for cultural interpretation and laden with social prohibitions that are ill fitting to context variation, agenda shrinks personal agency and tends to keep pent up the adaptive variations of social knowledge. Its application should therefore be subjected to careful consideration. It is best suited for those limited uses in which leaders, managers, and workforce can clearly identify and demonstrate a compelling benefit.

In the illustrations of commerce and culture that we have provided, we have tried to focus on the elements most broadly susceptible to cultural analysis and interpretation across many kinds and scales of commercial organizations. Our main aim has been to turn the focus on the kinds of agency and social responsibility situations that affect members at midlevel and field operations. The issues have been relatively soft, human interaction focused and widely prevalent among different localities of workforces, markets, and workplaces.

Other kinds of business responsibility problems, such as those primarily concerned with decisions about allocation and use of scarce technological infrastructure, of proprietorship of large quantities of unequally globally distributed natural resources, or of access to exclusively or highly specifically trained workforces, have not been at the center of our focus. While these problems require a similar process of interpretation with the input of a variety of intersecting stakeholders, they involve sociocultural system complexity at such a large scale that most are properly the subject of transsectoral activity. To deal adequately with these kinds of issues without simply taking the view of a particular agenda would have taken us from issues of business operations to a different ecological level of social institution. It would also require us to address a more technically specialized set of concerns.

Alternate Perspectives on the Case Material

There are many ways practitioners and students can think about and utilize the case examples and arguments provided in this book. They might be interpreted and assessed quite differently depending on the viewer's perspective. Sometimes the rise of new conditions abruptly eclipses preexisting agendas. A sobering example, related to the 1970s controversy over infant formulas discussed in Chapter 2 ("Agenda Interpretations: The Nestlé Controversy," p. 56), was a recent finding in studies of the AIDS pandemic that mothers infected with the AIDS virus could transmit it through breast milk. At the time of this writing, the United Nations had estimated that one-third of all infants with HIV got the virus through their mothers' milk. Thus, the formulas once blamed for Third World infant deaths due to misuse might prevent the life-threatening infection (Meier, 1997).

Readers might ask themselves how the development of vision and values guidelines at Pharmco Africa/Asia (A/A) was distinct from the production of other kinds of agenda. This process bore some similarities to more traditional management guidelines. What might have happened if the Pharmco A/A region leadership had demanded closer adherence to the U.S. parent company's artifacts? Could the sales force, which from a corporate perspective occupied the bottom of the social hierarchy, have led the revitalization as they did?

It could be questioned why A/A's management, under an uncertain future, undertook extensive workforce development. Competitors inside and outside the parent company eventually lured away some of the staff to higher paid positions elsewhere. Which outcome is more compelling, limiting investment that will result in someone else's success or the propagation of skills and knowledge beyond the firm's borders into the wider social environment?

A number of questions have already been raised regarding the Body Shop's marketing with the use of a wider social change agenda, while its own activities were probably limited in substance to public information and charity. If viewed from an economic development perspective, would the firm have been justified if it had succeeded in founding a competitive local business in rain forest commodities? When, if ever, does advocacy of a social and political agenda become exploitation?

The many unknowns remaining in the Java land purchase case raise other interesting questions. What elements might account for the peasants' decision to sell their land? Given the significance of hadj in many parts of the Muslim world, as a pilgrimage of purification undertaken later in life, could it be that this purpose would have been the only acceptable way, in local social knowledge, to sever traditional spiritual bonds to the land? Given that Islam has occupied a significant role in Indonesia as a political counterweight both within and beyond ruling regimes, might hadj participation have been for the sellers more than just a religious rite and means of possible social mobility—perhaps also a veiled expression of resistance?

Some specialists interested in social aspects of development might well question the peasants' use of a substantial fraction of their land proceeds to help finance such a trip. They might view it, for example, as a waste of scarce resources. Either a purely economic or a socially managing orientation could lead in this direction. We would only caution that this kind of interpretation arises from Western social knowledge, by a tradition that often imbues cultural activity of all kinds with the characteristics of a commodity, much as we have come to make commodities of time and education.

From the above examples, we can see that each potential assessment implies a particular context for the viewer, as well as for that which is viewed. Viewer standpoints in turn imply particular arrangements of social and cultural priorities. To be maximally socially responsible, it is necessary to gain as much insight as possible into what these priorities might be.

Doctrinal Context for Alternate Perspectives

The view of social responsibility we have adopted in this book implies a particular philosophical position with respect to business as a Western social institution. In accord with the kind of reflexive approach we have advocated for responsible action, we have an obligation to try to articulate our position clearly as a doctrine among others that are equally possible, though as we will argue, not equally useful, for business practitioners working from the Western institutional framework.

We illustrate this doctrinal context by means of an exercise of taking alternate perspectives; an ecological model well suited to this need has been offered by the economist A. O. Hirschman (1970). Hirschman suggests that people will act on their perceptions of any organization or institution's declining performance by selecting from among three basic options: exit, voice, or loyalty. We can use this general framework to classify our perspectives. The normative standpoint we adopt influences where we look and the kinds of conclusions we are apt to draw.

The author's claims and methods indicate that our basic position is one of loyalty, a faith in the ability of existing business institutions to achieve a measure of social responsibility, largely through the agency of their practitioners. At either large or small scale, commercial organizations are a source from which human good can come. It is valuable to understand in just what ways and by what assumptions this view differs from the other two alternatives, exit and voice. We can illustrate this better by describing some typical responses that we would expect the rival positions' advocates to make regarding social responsibility in business. We can extrapolate imaginary responses they might offer to the case we presented in Chapter 6, the 1970's Java land purchase.

Exit

A strict exit doctrine with respect to social responsibility in business would be expected to involve the rejection of business, and possibly the rejection of capitalism altogether, as a moral and economic institutional arrangement. Most advocates in the exit category have adopted somewhat modified versions of this position, however. They may predict or propose collapse or major overhaul of existing government or intergovernmental systems that regulate or influence business or major change in its other formal institutional aspects.

Exit or near-exit proponents have generally stopped looking for solutions from within business itself. They tend to look instead for social and ethical effectiveness to interventions that come from beyond business, from other types of social institutions and authorities. If they assume a political economy perspective with conflict between collective interest groups, there is a need for social change at a larger scale to *make* business more responsible. This typically includes some kind of political agenda.

Bodley (1996), for example, addresses large-scale finance capital and its associated outcomes of inequality in business and financial globalization as real and imminent threats to small-scale cultures. He finds the root of the problem to be a cultural one. He concludes that: "Political power must regulate the commercialization and financialization processes." Yet, he also goes on to say: "The primary obstacle to such change will [be] . . . the ability of elites to control the cultural symbols that motivate human beliefs and behavior for their own interests" (p. 214). This is an interpretation he makes at the cultural level. He recognizes the difficulty of directing cultural change by agenda, so he is left hoping that global information and communication networks will provide an adequate cultural response capacity and, particularly, that they will not become "commercialized." In other words, he has largely given up on social responsiveness from within existing late modern business institutions due to the way their inherent nature, as he sees it, has evolved with finance capital and large scale.

O'Connor (1994a), from a more thoroughly politicized perspective, declares that radical greens, deep ecologists, socialist biocentrics, green anarchists, and ecological feminists all agree that global capitalism is not sustainable (p. vii). His interpretation of economic interests and activity is more explicit: They are immoral; for example: "Private vice does not sum to public virtue" (p. 16). His preferred remedy is also political ("Socially too all this freedom becomes a trap" p. 17), and he argues, in a later chapter, that the word "sustainable" is ideological and political and not an ecological or economic question (O'Connor, 1994b, pp. 152–153).

Extrapolation 1: Exit Java

Given what has been presented in the case of land purchase in Java, if a viewer chose exit as a doctrinal position, one conclusion might be to dismiss the value of the case and, possibly, at the pragmatic level of action, to suggest that Pharmco and other foreign investors did not belong in Java at all. The exit advocate might claim, for example, that Reeves-Ellington's account is inherently biased and in all likelihood unrepresentative; in any event, both the case and his role in it were of extremely modest importance. The vast preponderance of similar cases will show that corporations in general have acted conjointly with governments to maximize their own incomes, even if it it involves coercing people in small-scale communities out of their land in morally and economically asymmetric deals. Even if Reeves-Ellington's case were demonstrably accurate, balanced, and generally representative, such deals offer the peasants little of value. The only long-term effect is to destroy traditional livelihoods and, with them, the local ecology and cultural system.

The above imagined response carries a number of implicit assumptions with which not all exit advocates would necessarily agree: It includes assumption of conflict of interests, distrust of large scale, advocacy of environmental and cultural preservation, and a preference for certainty and control of social outcomes through modern scientific demonstration. The case itself cannot answer these objections, in part because a commercial venture of this kind, at this level, is not in an ecological position to influence, anticipate, or control outcomes to the extent that would satisfy these challenges. The interventions suggested are not fitting to this context at this level of analysis.

It is important to note that there are many variations, possible and existing, of the doctrinal position of exit, and in this short space, our imaginary response scenarios are necessarily oversimplified. As alternate views, however, they begin to suggest how doctrinal viewer stance, as well as the context of the material itself, affects both methods and analysis.

Many exit advocates in Western society see pragmatic limits to the actions they can legally and nonviolently take at the present time. Their approaches and methods, therefore, often exist mainly at theoretical and philosophical levels. They pursue and test their theories through historical, economic, ethnographic, and a variety of other studies. Their exercise of speech and academic freedoms to advance these agendas often places them, for practical purposes, in another of Hirschman's categories—that of voice.

Voice

Voice as a basic doctrine actively questions how well business or their social institutions are really working as they now exist, but does not necessarily include the immediate intent to leave, to fundamentally restructure them, or to replace them. Voice advocates are often more pragmatic about proposed method and actions at smaller levels of inclusion and impact. They will often appeal to outside authority and public opinion to try to effect changes and reforms within existing institutions. As Hirschman (1970) points out, while voice does not include imminent plans to leave the entity that is perceived not to be meeting expectations, it does propose to influence change and reform through a mobilization of the effective *threat* of exit.

From a social responsibility perspective, many social activists of the 20th century, such as Ralph Nader, Cesar Chavez, and others in consumer and labor movements, have exercised voice to obtain business reforms at a variety of levels. Customers and investors may be encouraged to take their business elsewhere through the kind of journalistic exposé that Jon Entine used on The Body Shop or through the kind of publicity campaign that The Body Shop itself waged in 1996, urging consumers to boycott Shell Oil (Wallace and Brown, 1996). Exercisers of voice may simply call for greater public scrutiny of an organization or industry, hoping in this more diffuse way to affect its market share or stock prices. Alternately, they may make more concrete attempts to mobilize direct exit threats at the operational and market level, organizing boycotts and strikes or engaging outside interventions such as legislative and regulatory reforms, international sanctions, or class action suits.

Within an organization, threats to leave by influential members rarely succeed in influencing organizational practice, for obvious reasons relating to power and authority, as our discussions in Chapters 2 and 3 suggest. In rare cases, the parties are prepared to follow up by engaging heavily in strategic battles for their own positions within the organization. But, from inside late modern business itself, voice is an extremely difficult doctrinal position from which to initiate change for most practitioners, as the real physical conflicts of past unionization movements can attest. At the same time, the presence of strife in such movements is a clear indication that the fitting action has not been realized for a wider context engaged by the particular business in question.

Extrapolation 2: Voice in Java

If the viewer adopts voice as the doctrinal position from which to view the Java land purchase, the argument bears a certain basic resemblance to the one above on exit, but it is also somewhat modified. For example: The Java case is interesting because it offers a glimpse of different collective interests that were and still are at odds in the Indonesian, regional, and global political economy. Reeves-Ellington's self-portrayal as business practitioner is of limited importance except as an inside witness to events that would have been inaccessible to most neutral observers. As a manager, he can only act as an agent of the corporate interests he has been hired to represent. The preexisting power relations consist of foreign military and capital in support of a nationalist military despot, who pursued the kind of statist program of import replacement then fashionable. These factors together determine the outcome, the sell-off of local farm land to majority control by foreign investors.

The complications of this case mainly involve how this is done. They include manipulations of native cultural symbols and of the existing and colonially entrenched civil aristocracy. They also mirror the inequalities in the Southeast Asian regional trade hierarchy, which was then and is still, in many localities, dominated by ethnic Chinese. Finally, they involve a reluctant peasantry who had been among the principle targets of the mass civil violence in 1965. The despot's power, extant foreign policies, and the dominant American presence virtually guaranteed the outcome.

The peasants may not have been privy to the larger significance of what they were doing in agreeing to alienate their land. If any benefited, it was probably male heads of families, and to a lesser degree their wives, if they did manage to ascend to the social status of hadji traders as a benefit of the pilgrimage. The status and input of women, who later did the majority of the factory production work, and of other workers may have been little improved or not improved at all in the long run.

This individual case, even if locally successful or beneficial to some people, could not have set a precedent of any significance, as is demonstrated by the long-term influx of exploitative and often predatory subcontracting factory development throughout Indonesia up to and through the mid-1990's. In a Third World situation like this one, social responsibility can only be effectively pursued through organized advocacy and pressure for sociopolitical reform at the national level, through pressure applied at the level of trade, for tighter and better enforced codes of international business conduct, and through the pressure of other international sanctions.

Like exit, the voice position is generally compatible with a political economy and agenda approach to social responsibility. Both positions generally assume conflict, and advocates of voice, like those of exit, claim that a business or industry cannot carry on the way it has and be socially responsible. They may, like exit advocates, further assume that businesses and their leaders must always be forced to be socially responsible through power brought to bear from the outside. As with the exit view, voice proponents may view most businesses as generally and inherently untrustworthy, or they may hold this view toward a more selective subgroup of businesses, as defined by the industry, scale, or institutional arrangement under which they operate. Voice advocates under this second category may view voice as necessary mainly to round up outliers or reform surrounding institutional arrangements in what to them is normally and otherwise a responsible business arena. In other words, voice proponents can span a conceptual range that shades into an exit position at one end of the spectrum or for some parts of business and assumes a basic loyalty position for others.

Loyalty

As we have said, the third group, loyalty, is the basic doctrinal stance the authors take in this book. We find in the loyalist group many other mainstream business practitioners and educators. Most of those would address social responsibility in business primarily within the scope, initiative, and power of business institutions as they now exist. The prevalent approach to social responsibility from this position is the one we have already described at some length in Chapter 2. American business ethics textbooks reflect this outlook when they implicitly stake the claim of ownership and the adequate authority and expertise to determine their own occupationally based moral community.

The loyalist canon of normal business that has been created in business higher education well accommodates this interpretation of business ethics. Stories of firms that erred, usually through flawed decision making or communications, provide cautionary tales for the modern rational and scientific discipline of management. The principles that well-run business is inherently ethical and that ethics is eminently rational have great appeal in business popular wisdom. When ethics are badly handled, this reflects a lack of control and this condition describes the statistical outliers rather than the norm. At the same time, it reflects badly on the reputation the entire business community. Most loyalist rhetoric is based on agendas extracted from within the Western tradition. They are usually couched in terms of the socialized, disciplinary power of peer surveillance—even though, as we have pointed out, a kind of Hobbesian power of the executive, filtered through a chain of immediate bosses, is the power that holds pragmatic sway at the cultural level once a practitioner becomes the employee of a specific organization.

Extrapolation 3: Java Land Purchase from a Loyalty Perspective

While in many respects an exercise in extrapolating from the loyalty position will closely resemble the account we have already given for the case in Chapter 6, there remains ample room for variations and for questioning our approach. Many loyalist Western readers, looking for evidence such as time efficiency to confirm the effectiveness of the Pharmco field interpretations, might ask questions such as the following: How long did the negotiations take? How long did it take to learn cultural insidership for doing commerce in the business environment of Indonesia? While we could answer that the project was accomplished within a year or two, depending on the criteria, we would have to add that such linear time questions are not relevant in the Javanese perspective. The overriding question is whether to learn culturally or not. Once the affirmation is made, learning is ongoing.

In the field, we portrayed management and specialist teams seeking ways to meet the company's and their own culture's ethical requirements, while they also imagined and reality tested potential impacts of the business on the local people involved. They relied on a mutual process of response and exchange of information about local interests to form an appropriate approach by the buyers and to negotiate the details.

We portrayed the people involved as simultaneously maximizing their own interests and responding to wider moral communities—or, more correctly speaking, to an expanded moral community composed of an interdependent chain of local, organizational, and international communities. From a traditional corporate headquarters point of view, much about the approach might be, and was, at least on some points, viewed as risky. Had corporate headquarters been privy to more details, it might have been even less pleased with the time spent on the approach and the arrangements, especially the potential of embarrassing and alienating regional officials in case the Labaran festivity scheme had backfired. Senior corporate leadership might have put up with this general approach for a limited period of time only because their priority was the assurance of bottom-line business goals. Also, the segment of the organization involved was very small—it made up less than 1% of total world operations.

What Lies Beyond Agenda?

The positions of exit and voice as we see them correspond closely to methods of study and action involving conflicts between collective interest groups and the formal institutions of governance, including those of business. They do not present a complete or accurate recipe for social responsibility, and they do not tap the enormous potential that lies beyond agenda for responsible commerce at a cultural level. On the whole, as regards the preponderance of business practice, we view their objections as unnecessarily pessimistic. In part, our response reflects our own loyalist doctrine and concurs with our ecological point of view from within the operations of business.

At the same time, we are skeptical that there is any necessary connection between ethical behavior and business success, either long term or short term, as has been predicted by many business ethicists. Such a proposition represents the opposite point of view to that which predicts the preponderant social and environmental harm that business success, especially if short term, will cause (e.g., O'Connor, 1994b, p.170). While we have witnessed positive and negative social impacts in business, we find no conclusive evidence that these impacts are necessarily related in a particular way to economic results.

The vast majority of those who work in business have more modest, but real, means of being socially responsible, but this does not necessarily indicate that they occupy a particular political position with respect to business as a social institution at large. From a humanistic perspective, organization leaders can ask themselves if they have demonstrated their faith in the responsive capacity of their workforce through support of personal responsibility. For practitioners throughout business organizations, they can ask themselves if they have demonstrated faith in transcultural partners' ability to act on their own behalf, and whether they have pursued and persisted in joint efforts of information sharing and mutual cultural learning, rather than attempts to control the outcomes of social life.

Where the authors have differed from the normal business ethics pproaches and the rational science of management is in our basic definition of what social responsibility is and in our emphasis on culture as important to the methods for achieving it. Sole reliance on rational management agendas can do no more than political agendas can do to bridge cultural boundaries, respond to localities, and facilitate practitioners' learning of a fitting response. We urge practitioners and educators not to adopt approaches that will preclude discovery of the myriad opportunities that exist for exercising social responsibility while also engaging in successful commerce. Ultimately, in a climate of uncertainty, we ask those now in business to consider what they have to lose in keeping their options open, in seeking and discovering, for any given context, the fitting response.

Inferences

There are several things that can be inferred from the foregoing discussion of commerce, culture, and social responsibility. For communications, it is clear that a more holistic cultural approach leverages the same richness and symbolic redundancy as can be seen reflected in the human use of language. Cultural interpretation relies on multiple sets of interrelated meanings. Unlike an agenda of control, unitary modeling, or prohibition, cultural inquiry releases the potential of stored wisdom from varying contexts. It helps to facilitate better understanding, using polyphonic channels of expression. It does not need to prohibit expression, but, pursued systematically, leads to discovery of key points of agreement and mutually acceptable ways to make commerce work.

A culturally interpretive approach to socially responsible commerce does not require the arbitration of how relationships are defined between social and economic valuations. As with many other features of culture, we would expect these to vary from place to place.

Working at the cultural level also does not require a unitary sovereignty to control all areas of activity. Rather, it allows for integration of different types of leaders and specialists as suitable for fitting tasks in the organization. It requires no assumption of a single, monolithic culture within the organization, but only that people work toward the building of a more facilitative and organizing joint vision, one that has personal, as well as organizational, benefits. More formal institutional arrangements work best when significant parts of cultures are already shared.

Cultural interpretation can become a supportive foundation for, but does not always change predictably as a result of, the imposition of artifacts of formal institutional arrangements.

There are several direct implications in this view for education, organization development and training, and leadership and management of business organizations. Leaders, wanting a purely business-driven organization, will be apt to educate through instruction by experts on the assumption that any expert can give instruction. Cultural experts may include consultants and technicians, but these roles are primarily adopted by the organization's leaders in terms of organizational development and organizational morality. Instruction is often preferred because it is delivered in controlled ways and in controlled places through transfer of information from instructor to students. Up to the present time, this tendency has been mirrored in institutions of higher education in business, as well as in practicing business organizations.

It is clear that learning for social responsibility through a cultural approach cannot rely on these and other agenda-related modalities any more than organization members can rely on their superiors' promulgated codes and rules to ensure social responsibility. Cultural learning ultimately has no gurus. It requires the engagement of active and participative learners. Organizations can support an environment in which this learning can take place more thoroughly and richly, in which the pent-up, stored wisdom based on experience can be released.

There are many helpful methods but no permanent guidelines for such development. Practitioners at any level of organization can only raise questions for themselves, as fitting to the contexts in which they work. Only by continual effort to develop cultural insights and self-knowledge of a cultural home base will they come to fit their actions to the occasion in ways most integral to them. Awareness of habits of reification, suspicion of events in which they seem to extract, receive, or make something for free or in exchange for nothing, and a healthy skepticism of reliance on unattainable perfection in communications, or on a set view of what is natural, are all helpful skills to cultivate. The challenge for those who trade and dwell at the margins between worlds and world views is to create responsible activity within the constraints of life as lived there. They will co-create responsibility not by drowning out other sources of light with their own, but by reading wisely, adding their illumination to the wisdom of the community.

References

Ackerknect, E. (1943). Psychopathology, Primitive Medicine, and Primitive Culture. *Bulletin of the History of Medicine*, 14, 30–67.

Advertising Age. (1994). Roddick Skewers Critics. 65(44), 31.

Alexander, J. (1987). *Trade, Traders and Trading in Rural Java*. New York: Oxford University Press.

Anderson, A. (1993, March). *Culture, Total Quality, and the Information Age*. Paper presented at the annual meeting of the Society for Applied Anthropology, San Antonio, Texas.

Anderson, A., & Reeves-Ellington, R. H. (1995). *Toward a Global Paradigm for Praxis Research*. Paper presented to the Academy of Management conference, The Organizational Dimensions of Global Change, Cleveland, OH, May 3–7.

Anderson, B. (1972). The Idea of Power in Javanese Culture. In C. Holt (Ed.), *Culture and Politics in Indonesia* (pp. 1–69). Ithaca, NY: Cornell University Press.

Argyris, C., & Schoen, D. (1978). *Organizational Learning: A Theory of Action Perspective*. Reading, MA: Addison-Wesley.

Asante, M. K., & Gudykunst, W. B. (Eds.). (1989). *Handbook of Intercultural Communications*. Newbury Park, CA: Sage.

Bantigue, W., & Reeves-Ellington, R. H. (1986). *Understanding Physician Values*. Manila, The Philippines: Norwich Eaton Pharmaceuticals.

Barth, F. (1969). *Ethnic Groups and Boundaries: The Social Organization of Cultural Difference*. Boston: Little, Brown.

Baskerville, R. (1991). *Philosophical Autonomy and Radical Pluralism in Scientific Pratice*. Unpublished manuscript, State University of New York at Binghamton, School of Management.

Baskerville, R., Travis, J., & Truex, D. (1992). *Intervention: Researching Information Technology in Postmodern Organizations*. Binghamton School of Management Working Paper Series, 92-214. Binghamton: State University of New York at Binghamton.

Bass, B., & Avolio, B. J. (Eds.). 1994. *Improving Organizational Effectiveness*. Thousand Oaks, CA: Sage.

Bass, B. M. (1985). *Leadership Beyond Expectations*. New York: Academic Press.

Bauman, Z. (1987). *Legislators and Interpreters*. Cambridge, England: Polity Press.

Bell, D. (1975). Ethnicity and Social Change. In N.Glazer and D. Moynihan (Eds.), *Ethnicity: Theory and Experience* (pp. 141–174). Cambridge, MA: Harvard University Press.

Berger, P., & Luckman, T. (1967). *The Social Construction of Reality*. New York: Doubleday (cited in Harmon, 1995).

Bodley, J. (1996). *Anthroplogy and Contemporary Human Problems*. Mountain View, CA: Mayfield.

The Body Shop. (1992, May). *The Green Book*. West Sussex, England: The Body Shop International.

The Body Shop. (1994, October). *Company Profile* [Broadsheet]. West Sussex, England: The Body Shop International.

The Body Shop. (1994). *Values and Vision 94*. West Sussex, England: The Body Shop International.

The Body Shop. (1996, May). *Annual Report and Accounts*. West Sussex, England: The Body Shop International.

The Body Shop. (1995, November 24). *Press Release* [On-line]. Available: http://www.the-body-shop.com/prar.html.

The Body Shop. (1996, January). *Measuring Up: A Summary of The Body Shop Values Report 1995*. West Sussex, England: The Body Shop International.

Boniger, D. S., Gleicher, F., & Strathman, A. (1994). Counterfactual Thinking: From What Might Have Been to What May Be. *Journal of Personality and Social Psychology*, 67(2), 297–307.

Boulding, E. (1991). The Old and New Transnationalism: An Evolutionary Perspective. *Human Relations*, 44(8), 789–805.

Brannen, M. Y., & Sanyal, A. (1993, October 15). *Bicultural Alienation in Japanese-Owned Companies: A Preliminary Study in Scale Development*. Paper presented at the annual meeting of the Academy of International Management, Maui, HI.

Brown, R. M. (1991). *No Duty to Retreat: Violence and Values in American History*. New York: Oxford University Press.

Buber, M. (1958). *I and Thou* (R. G. Smith, Trans.). New York: Charles Scribner's Sons.

Bulletpoint Communications. (1996, March). *Building a Visionary Organization*. [Brochure]. New York: Leo Burnett Advertising.

Burlingham, B. (1990–1991, Winter). More than Skin Deep. *Best of Business Quarterly*, 38–47.

Business Ethics. (1994, September/October). Interview: Ben Cohen. 8(5), 18–21.

Campbell, J. (1960). *The Masks of God: Primitive Mythology*. 2nd ed. New York: Viking.

Campbell, J. (1968). *The Hero with a Thousand Faces*. Princeton, NJ: Princeton University Press.

Campbell, J. (1973). *The Hero with a Thousand Faces*. Bollinger Series VII. Princeton, NJ: Princeton University Press.

Chambers, E. (1985). *Applied Anthropology: A Practical Guide*. Prospect Heights, IL: Waveland.

Chesher, J. E. (1992). Business: Myth and Morality. In R. W. McGee (Ed.), *Business Ethics and Common Sense* (pp. 45–107). Westport, CT: Quorum.

Clark, M. (1995, March). Socially Responsible Business Brawl. *Progressive*, 14.

Clegg, S. R. (1989). *Frameworks of Power*. Thousand Oaks, CA: Sage Publications.

Coleman, J. S. (1982). *The Asymmetric Society*. Syracuse, NY: Syracuse University Press.

Covey, S. R. (1989). *The Seven Habits of Highly Effective People*. New York: Simon & Schuster.

Cowe, R. (1995, November 1). Body Shop Buy-Back Depends upon Mr. 28 Percent. *Guardian*, 1(3), 1.

Cringeley, R. X. (1992). *Accidental Empires*. Menlo Park, CA: Addison-Wesley.

Dalton, M., & Wilson, M. (1996, August). *Choosing and Developing Managers Who Can Work Across Borders*. Paper presented at the annual meeting of the American Psychological Association, Toronto, Ontario, Canada.

David, K. (1985). *Participant Observation in Pharmaceutical Field Selling*. Norwich, NY: Norwich Eaton Pharmaceutical.

Davis, K. (1990). Five Propositions for Social Responsibility. In W. M. Hoffman & J. M. Moore (Eds.), *Business Ethics* (2nd ed., pp. 165–170). New York: McGraw-Hill.

Davis, R. (1994, September 19). The Body Shop Plays Hardball. *New York*, 27, 16–17.

Deal, T. E., & Kennedy, A. A. (1982). *Corporate Cultures: The Rites and Rituals of Corporate Life*. Reading, MA: Addison-Wesley.

DeGeorge, R. T. (1993). *Competing with Integrity in International Business*. New York: Oxford University Press.

Doi, T. (1990a). *The Anatomy of Dependence*. Tokyo: Kodansha International.

Doi, T. (1990b). *The Anatomy of Self*. Tokyo: Kodansha International.

Dreifus, C. (1996, July 7). The Maxims of Esther Dyson. *New York Times Magazine*, Sec. 6, pp. 16–19.

Drucker, P. F. (1955). *The Practice of Management*. London: William Heinemann.

Drucker, P. F. (1992). *Managing for the Future: The 1990's and Beyond*. New York: Truman Talley/Dutton.

Economist. (1993, April 17). Indonesia: The Long March, p. 3 (14 pp.).

Economist. (1994, September 3). Storm in a Bubble Bath, p. 56.

Elfstrom, G. (1991). *Moral Issues and Multinational Corporations*. New York: St. Martin's Press.

Eliade, M. (1964). *Shamanism: Archaic Techniques of Ecstasy.* Princeton, NJ: University of Princeton Press.

Ellington, R. (1966). *Compadrazgo and Padrinazgo in Middle America.* Unpublished master's dissertation, Wayne State University, Detroit, MI.

Ellington, R. (1976). *Business Elites in Indonesia.* Unpublished doctoral dissertation, City University of Los Angeles.

Ellington, R. (1980, January/February). Pitfalls of Payoffs in Indonesia. *ASIA,* 6–9, 46.

Entine, J. (1994). Shattered Image. *Business Ethics,* 8(5), 23–28.

Entine, J. (1995). No Whales Were Killed in Writing This Paper: Is "Socially Responsible Business" Greenwashing? In St. John's University (Ed.), *Proceedings of "From the Universites to the Marketplace: The Business Ethics Journey"* (pp. 260–270) New York: St. John's University.

Etzioni, A. (1961). *A Comparative Analysis of Organizations.* New York: Freepress.

Fals-Borda, O. (1991). *Some Basic Ingredients.* In O. Fals-Borda & M. Rahman (Eds.), *Action and Knowledge* (pp. 3–12). New York: Apex.

Fatsis, S. (1992, December 28). An Original at Corporate Xerox. *The Daily Messenger,* Canandaigua, NY, p. 7A.

Fatsis, S. (1993, January 4). Razing the Pyramid. *The Daily Messenger,* Canandaigua, NY, p. 7A.

Finan, T. J., & Van Willigen, J. (1990). The Pursuit of Social Knowledge: Methodology and Practice of Anthropology. In J. Van Willigen & T. J. Finan (Eds.), *Soundings: Rapid and Reliable Research Methods for Practicing Anthropologists* (pp. 1–9). Washington, DC: American Anthropological Association.

Foucault, M. (1977). *Discipline and Punish: The Birth of the Prison.* Harmondsworth, England: Penguin.

Frank, J. (1985). Therapeutic Components Shared by All Psychotherapies. In M. Mahoney & A. Freeman (Eds.), *Cognition and Psychotherapy* (pp. 49–79). New York: Plenum.

Garsten, C. (1994). *Apple World: Core and Periphery in a Transnational Organizational Culture.* Stockholm: Stockholm Studies in Social Anthropology.

Geertz, C. (1966). *Person, Time, and Conduct in Bali: An Essay in Cultural Analysis.* Cultural Report Series No. 14. New Haven, CT: Yale University, Southeast Asia Studies.

Geertz, C. (1973). Thick Description: Toward an Interpretive Theory of Culture. In C. Geertz (Ed.), *The Interpretation of Cultures: Selected Essays* (pp. 3–32). New York: Basic Books.

Geertz, H. (1961). *The Javanese Family: A Study of Kinship and Socialization.* Prospect Heights, IL: Waveland.

Gellner, E. (1992). *Postmodernism, Reason and Religion.* London: Routledge.

Gelman, E., & Rogers, M. (1985, January). It's the Apple of His Eye. *NewsWeek*, 54–57.

Giscard d'Estaing, O. (1995). Evolution of the Market Economy: The Responsibility and Contribution of Business. *Futures, 27*(2), 246–252.

Glazer, N., & Moynihan, D. (Eds.). (1975). *Ethnicity: Theory and Experience*. Cambridge, MA: Harvard University Press.

Goodman, N. (1978). *Ways of World Making*. Brighton, England: Harve Press.

Gregory, K. (1983, September). Native-View Paradigms: Multiple Cultures and Culture Conflicts in Organizations. *Administrative Science Quarterly*, 361–382.

Griffin, G. R. (1991). *Machiavelli on Management*. New York: Praeger.

Grubb, M., Kock, M., Thomson, K., Munson, A., & Sullivan, F. (1993). *The "Earth Summit" Agreements: A Guide and Assessment*. London: Earthscan Publications.

Halifax, J. (1978). *Shamanic Voices*. New York: Penguin Books.

Hall, E. T. (1973). *The Silent Language*. New York: Anchor. (Original work published in 1959)

Hall, E. T., & Hall, M. R. (1987). *Hidden Differences*. New York: Anchor Press.

Halliday, D. (1983, February). Steve Paul Jobs. *Current Biography, 5*, 204–207.

Hamada, T. (1991). *American Enterprise in Japan*. Albany: State University of New York Press.

Hamayon, R. N. (1994). Shamanism in Siberia: From Partnership in Supernature to Counter-Power in Society. In N. Thomas & C. Humphrey (Eds.), *Shamanism, History, and the State* (pp. 76–89). Ann Arbor, MI: University of Michigan Press.

Hanna, D. P. (1988). *Designing Organizations for High Performance*. New York: Addison Wesley.

Harmon, M. M. (1995). *Responsibility as Paradox*. Thousand Oaks, CA: Sage.

Hayashi, S. (1988). *Culture and Management in Japan*. Tokyo: University of Tokyo Press.

Heinze, R.-I. (1988). The Multiplicity of Being, an Investigation of the Relationship of Multiple Personality and Possession. In R.-I. Heinze (Ed.), *Proceedings of the Fourth International Conference on the Study of Shamanism and Alternate Modes of Healing* (pp. 2–18). Berkeley, CA: Independent Scholars of Asia.

Heinze, R.-I. (1991). *Shamans of the 20th Century*. New York: Irvington Publishers.

Hirschman, A. O. (1970). *Exit, Voice and Loyalty*. Cambrige, MA: Harvard University Press.

Hobbes, T. (1972). *Man and Citizen* (B. Gert, Ed.). New York: Anchor Books.

Hofstede, G. (1980). *Culture's Consequences: International Differences in Work-Related Values*. Beverly Hills, CA: Sage.

Hofstede, G. (1991). *Organizations and Cultures: Software of the Mind*. New York: McGraw-Hill.

Hofstede, G., Neuijev, B., Ohayv, D., & Sanders, G. (1990). Measuring Organizational Cultures: A Qualitative and Quantitative Study Across 20 cases. *Administrative Science Quarterly,* (35), 286–316.

House, J. R., Spangler, W. D., & Woycke, J. (1991). Personality and Charisma in the U.S. Presidency: A Psychological Theory of Leader Effectiveness. *Administrative Science Quarterly,* 36, 364–396.

Hugh-Jones, S. (1994). Shamans, Prophets, Priests, and Pastors. In N. Thomas & C. Humphrey (Eds.), *Shamanism, History, and the State* (pp. 32–75). Ann Arbor: University of Michigan Press.

Humphrey, C. (1997). Shamanistic Practices and the State in Northern Asia: Views from the Center and Periphery. In N. Thomas & C. Humphrey (Eds.), *Shamanism, History and the State.* Ann Arbor: University of Michigan Press.

Imai, M. (1986). *Kaizen: The Key to Japan's Competitive Success.* New York: Random.

Ishida, E. (1974). A Culture of Love and Hate. In T. S. Lebra & W. P. Lebra (Eds.), *Japanese Culture and Behavior* (p. 27–36). Honolulu: University Press of Hawaii.

Jackall, R. (1988). *Moral Mazes.* New York: Oxford University Press.

Jacob, R. (1992, January 13). Body Shop International: What Selling Will Be Like in the '90's. *Fortune,* 125, 63–64.

Jeter, K. (1989). The Shaman: The Gay and Lesbian Ancestor of Humankind. *Marriage & Family Review,* 14(3–4), 317–334.

Jorgensen, D. L. (1989). *Participant Observation: A Methodology for Human Studies.* Newbury Park, CA: Sage.

Josodharnodjo, S. B. (1967). *The Aspects of the Javanese Wayang Kulit.* Djakarta, Indonesia: Kosgoro Institute of Art and Culture.

Kanter, R. M. (1996). *The Change Masters: Corporate Entrepreneurs at Work.* London: International Thomson Business Press.

Kanungo, R. N., & Mendonca, M. (1996). *Ethical Dimensions of Leadership.* Thousand Oaks, CA: Sage Press.

Karve, I. (1965). *Kinship Organization in India.* New York: Oxford University Press.

Keesing, R. (1974). Theories of Culture. *Annual Review of Anthropology,* 3, 73–97.

Kepos, P. (Ed.). (1995). The Body Shop PLC. *International Directory of Company Histories,* Vol. 11, pp. 40–42. Detroit, MI: St. James Press.

Kim, U. (1996, August 11). *Relational, Extended, and Contextual Self in Korea and Japan.* Paper presented at the annual meeting of the American Psychological Association, Toronto, Ontario, Canada.

Kinney, J. (1988, November 29). *Policy Management: A Beginner's Perspective.* Paper presented at the American Supplier Institute Conference on Policy Management, Cincinnati, OH.

Klimo, J. (1988). The Emergence of a New Paradigm. In R.-I. Heinze (Ed.), *Proceedings of the Fifth International Conference on the Study of Shamanism and Alternate Modes of Healing* (pp. 394–402). Berkeley, CA: Independent Scholars of Asia.

Kluckhohn, C. (1951). Values and Values Orientations in the Theory of Action. In T. Parsons & E. Shils (Eds.), *Toward a General Theory of Action* (pp. 409–410). Cambridge, MA: Harvard University Press.

Kluckhohn, F. R., & Strodbeck, F. L. (1961). *Variations in Values Orientations*. Westport, CT: Greenwood Press.

Kotkin, J. (1992). *Tribes*. New York: Random.

Krackhardt, D., & Kilduff, M. (1990). Friendship Patterns and Culture: The Control of Organizational Diversity. *American Anthropologist, 92*, 142–154.

Krippner, S. (1988). The Use of Dreams by Tribal Shamans. In R.-I. Heinze (Ed.), *Proceedings of the Fifth International Conference on the Study of Shamanism and Alternate Modes of Healing* (pp. 294–310). Berkeley, CA: Independent Scholars of Asia.

Laber, J. (1996, January 9). Smoldering Indonesia. *New York Review of Books, 44*(1), 40–45.

Law, J. (1986). Editors Introduction: Power/Knowledge and the Dissolution of the Sociology of Knowledge. In J. Law (Ed.), *Power, Action and Belief: A New Sociology of Knowledge?* (pp. 1–19). Sociological Review Monograph 32. London: Routledge & Kegan Paul.

Lebra, T. S. (1976). *Japanese Patterns of Behavior*. Honolulu: University Press of Hawaii.

Lee, D. (1963). Freedom and Social Constraint. In D. Bidney (Ed.), *The Concept of Freedom in Anthropology* (p. 61–92). The Hague: Mouton.

Le Vie, D., Jr. (1988). The "Significant Experience" as a Mnemonic Device in Shamanic Symbolism. In R.-I. Heinze (Ed.), *Proceedings of the Fifth International Conference on the Study of Shamanism and Alternate Modes of Healing* (pp. 161–167). Berkeley, CA: Independent Scholars of Asia.

Levitt, T. (1958). The Dangers of Social Responsibility. *Harvard Business Review, 36*(5), 41–50.

Levy, S. (1984). *Hackers: Heroes of the Computer Revolution*. New York: Dell Publishing.

Lukes, S. (1974). *Power: A Radical View*. London: Macmillan.

Machiavelli, N. (1990). *The Prince* (P. Bondanella, Ed.; P. Bondanella & M. Musa, Trans.). Oxford, England: Oxford University Press.

Mahon, T. (1996, January 11). The Spirit in Technology. *The Wall Street Journal*, p. A23.

Margolis, H. (1982). *Selfishness, Altruism and Rationality*. Cambridge: Cambridge University Press (cited in Wilk, 1996).

Marshall, L. (1997, March). The World According to Eco. *Wired*, 144–196.

McClelland, D. (1961). *The Achieving Society*. Princeton, NJ: Van Norstrand.

McKechnie, J. L. (Ed.). (1983). *Webster's New 20th Century Dictionary of the English Language*. (2nd ed., unabridged). New York: Prentice-Hall.

McKeon, R. (1957). The Development and the Significance of the Concept of Responsibility. *Revue Internationale de Philosophie*, 11, 3–32.

Meier, B. (1997, June 8). AIDS Spread Reopens Baby Formula Battle. *TimesFax from The New York Times*. [Online]. Available: http://www.nytimes.com.

Mintzberg, H. (1970). *Power In and Around Organizations*. Englewood Cliffs, NY: Prentice-Hall.

Mintzberg, H. (1973). *The Nature of Managerial Work*. New York: Harper & Row.

Mintzberg, H. (1979). *The Structuring of Organizations*. Englewood Cliffs, NJ: Prentice-Hall.

Mintzberg, H. (1983). *Power In and Around Organizations*. Englewood Cliffs, NJ: Prentice-Hall.

Mole, J. (1991). *When in Rome—A Business Guide to Cultures and Customs in 12 European Nations*. New York: AMACOM.

Moody's International Manual. (1996). Body Shop International PLC, p. 10,145. New York: Moody's Investors Service.

Moran, E. T., & Volkwein, J. F. (1992). The Cultural Approach to Organizational Climate. *Human Relations*, 45(1), 19–47.

Morris, D. (1995). Mondragon: The Cooperative Alternative Meets Free Trade. *Earth Island Journal*, 10(1), 38.

Mydans, S. (1996, August 25). Resettled Indonesians Find Hard Life. *New York Times*, International Sec., p. 22.

Nadler, D. (1995). *Discontinuous Change: Leading Organizational Transformation*. San Francisco: Jossey-Bass.

Nelson, D. (1980). *Frederick Taylor and the Rise of Scientific Management*. Milwaukee: University of Wisconsin Press.

New York Times. (1994, September 23). Body Shop Again Criticized, Sec. D, p. 4.

New York Times. (1994, July 11). Stake Reduced in Body Shop, Sec. D, p. 7, c. 6.

Niebuhr, H. R. (1963). *The Responsible Self: An Essay in Christian Moral Philosophy*. New York: Harper & Row.

O'Connor, M. (1994a). Introduction: Liberate, Accumulate—and Bust? In M. O'Connor (Ed.), *Is Capitalism Sustainable?* (pp. 1–21). New York: Guilford Press.

O'Connor, M. (1994b). Is Sustainable Capitalism Possible? In M. O'Connor (Ed.), *Is Capitalism Sustainable?: Political Economy and the Politics of Ecology* (p. 152–175). New York: Guildford Press.

Ohmann, O. A. (1989). Skyhooks. In K. R. Andrews (Ed.), *Ethics in Practice: Managing the Moral Corporation* (pp. 58–69). Boston: Harvard Business School Press.

Ottman, J. (1993). *Green Marketing*. Lincolnwood, IL: NTC Business Books.

Overling, J. (1990). The Shaman as a Maker of Worlds: Nelson Goodman in the Amazon. *Man*, 25, 602–619.

Patchell, J. (1993). From Production Systems to Learning Systems: Lessons from Japan. *Environment and Planning*, A25, 797–815.

Pattee, R. (1989). Neo-Shamanism: A Source of Creativity for Our Time. In R.-I. Heinze (Ed.), *Proceedings of the Fifth International Conference on the Study of Shamanism and Alternate Modes of Healing*. (pp. 136–155). Berkeley, CA: Independent Scholars of Asia.

Peacock, J. (1978). *Muslim Puritans*. Berkeley, CA: University of California Press.

Pelzel, J. C. (1974). Human Nature in the Japanese Myths. In T. S. Lebra & W. P. Lebra (Eds.), *Japanese Culture and Behavior*. Honolulu: University Press of Hawaii.

Perry, J. (1986). Spiritual Emergence and Renewal. *ReVision*, 8(2), 33–40.

Peterson, M. F., & Smith, P. (1996, August). *Implications of International Comparative Studies for Cross-Border Manager Selection and Development*. Paper presented at the American Psychological Association annual meeting, Toronto, Ontario, Canada.

Pfeffer, J. (1981). Management as Symbolic Action: The Creation and Maintenance of Organizational Paradigms. In L. L. Cumming & B. N. Staw (Eds.), *Research in Organizational Behavior* (Vol. 3, pp. 1–52). Greenwich, CT: JAI.

Pruitt, D. (1983). Achieving Integrative Agreements. In Max Bazerman & Roy Lewicki (Eds.), *Negotiating in Organizations* (pp. 35–50). Beverly Hills, CA: Sage.

Raghavan, C. (1995). *Ever Increasing Biopiracy by TNCs*. [Online]. Written 6:58 PM October 18, 1995, by twn in igc:twn.features. Third World Network. Available by E-mail request to apc-info@apc.org. For further information, contact A. Anderson, SUNY Empire State College, 8 Prince St., Rochester, NY 14424; E-mail address axanders@sescva.esc.edu.

Reason, P. (1994). Three Approaches to Participative Inquiry. In N. K. Denzin & Y. S. Lincoln (Eds.), *Handbook of Qualitative Research* (pp. 324–339). Thousand Oaks: Sage.

Reeves-Ellington, R. H. (1993). Using Cultural Skills for Cooperative Advantage in Japan. *Human Organization*, 52(2), 203–215.

Reeves-Ellington, R. H. (1994). Corporation Anthropologist at Work in the Third World. In H. Serrie (Ed.), *What Can Multinationals Do for Peasants? Studies in Third World Societies* (p. 213–240). Williamsberg, VA: William & Mary Press.

Reeves-Ellington, R. H. (1995a). Anthropology and Total Quality Management: Improving Sales Force Performance in Overseas Markets. In J. F. Sherry, Jr. (Ed.), *Contemporary Marketing and Consumer Behavior* (pp. 169–208). Thousand Oaks, CA: Sage.

Reeves-Ellington, R. H. (1995b). Organizing for Global Effectivnesss: Ethnicity and Organizations. *Human Organization*, 54(3), 249–262.

Reeves-Ellington, R. H. (1996a, March 27–31). *Integrating the Sacred and the Profane: Corporate Leader as Shaman*. Paper presented at the annual meetings of the Society for Applied Anthropology, Baltimore, MD.

Reeves-Ellington, R. H. (1996b). Liberal Arts Education in Bulgaria: A Vehicle for Change. *International Education*, 25(2), 5–33.

Reich, R. B. (1993). *The Work of Nations: Preparing Ourselves for 21st Century Capitalism*. London: Simon & Schuster.

Robbins, S. P. (1983). *Organizational Theory: The Structure and Design of Organizations*. Englewood Cliffs: Prentice-Hall.

Roddick, A. (1991). *Body and Soul*. New York: Crown Publishers.

Roddick, A. (1995, January–Feburary). Who Judges the Judges? *Utne Reader*, 67, 104.

Roderick, K. (1993). Searching for Sustainability. *Omni*, 16(2), 26.

Roese, J. J. (1994). The Functional Basis of Counterfactual Thinking. *Journal of Personality and Social Psychology*, 66(5), 805–818.

Rohrer, T. C. (Ed.), (1990). *A Continuing Series for Implementing Total Quality*. Cincinnati, OH: Procter & Gamble.

Rose, F. (1989). *West of Eden: The End of Innocence at Apple Computer*. Harmondsworth, England: Penguin Press.

Runes, D. D. (Ed.), 1960. *Dictionary of Philosophy*. Totowa, NJ: Littlefield, Adams, & Co.

Sackman, S. (1992). Culture and Subcultures: An Analysis of Organizational Knowledge. *Administrative Science Quarterly*, 37, 140–161.

Sartres, J.-P. (1956). *Being and Nothingness* (H. E. Barnes, Trans.). New York: Philosophical Library. (Cited in Harmon, 1995).

Schein, E. H. (1985). *Organizational Culture and Leadership*. San Francisco: Jossey-Bass.

Schein, E. H. (1987). *Organizational Culture and Leadership*. San Francisco: Jossey Bass.

Schultz, E. A., & Lavenda, R. H. (1995). *Anthropology: A Perspective on the Human Condition*. Mountain View, CA: Mayfield.

Schwarz, A. (1994). *A Nation in Waiting: Indonesia in the 1990s*. Boulder, CO: Westview.

Scott, J. (1991). Networks of Corporate Power: A Comparative Assessment. *Annual Reivew of Sociology*, 17, 181–203.

Sculley, J., with Byrne, J. A. (1988). *Odyssey. Pepsi to Apple . . . A Journey of Adventure, Ideas, and the Future*. New York: Harper & Row.

Senge, P. M. (1994). *The Fifth Discipline*. New York: Doubleday.

Sethi, S. P. (1994). *Multinational Corporations and the Impact of Public Advocacy on Corporate Strategy*. Boston: Kluwer.

Sherry, J. F., Jr., McGrath, M. A., & Levy, S. J. (1995). Monadic Giving: Anatomy of Gifts Given to the Self. In J. F. Sherry, Jr. (Ed.), *Contemporary Marketing and Consumer Behavior: An Anthropological Sourcebook* (pp. 399–432). Thousand Oaks, CA: Sage.

Siikala, A. (1978). *The Rite Technique of the Siberian Shaman.* Folklore Fellows Communication Communications No. 220. Helsinki: Soumalainen Tiedeskaremia Academia.

Siler, C. (1994). Body Shop Marches to Its Own Drummer. *Advertising Age,* 65(43), 4.

Sinha, J. B. P. (1990). A Model of Effective Leadership Styles in India. In A.M. Jaeger & R. M. Kanungo (Eds.), *Management in Developing Countries* (pp. 252–263). London: Routledge.

Sinha, J. B. P. (1995). *The Cultural Context of Leadership and Power.* New Delhi: Sage Publications.

Smith, P., Peterson, M., Leung, K., & Dugan, S. (1996, August). *Individualism— Collectivism and the Handling of Disagreement: A 23 Country Study.* Paper presented at the American Psychological Association annual meeting, Toronto, Ontario, Canada.

Smith, P. B., & Peterson, M. F. (1988). *Leadership, Organizations and Culture.* London: Sage.

Soros, G. (1997, February). The Capitalist Threat. *The Atlantic Monthly* [On-line] 279(2), 45–58. Available: http://www.theatlantic.com/atlantic/issues/ 97feb/capital/capital.html.

Spradley, J. P. (1980). *Participant Observation.* New York: Holt, Rinehart & Winston.

Springette, P. (1994, July 9). Roddicks Get £8 m in Shares Sell-Off. *The* [Manchester, England] *Guardian,* p. 30+.

Stogdill, R. M. (1974). *Handbook of Leadership: A Survey of Theory and Research.* New York: Free Press.

Strathman, A. F., Gleicher, D. S., & Edwards, C. S. (1994). The Consideration of Future Consequences: Weighing Immediate and Distant Outcomes of Behavior. *Journal of Personality and Social Psychology,* 66(4), 742–752.

Thomas, N., & Humphrey, C. (1994). *Shamanism, History, and the State.* Ann Arbor: University of Michigan Press.

Toer, P. A. (1990). *This Earth of Mankind* (M. Lane, Trans.). New York: Penguin. Original copyright P. A. Toer, 1975.

Turner, T. (1990). *The Disappearing World of the Kayapo: Out of the Forest.* Chicago, IL: Granada Television International Films.

Turner, T. (1992). *Invasion of the Body Shoppers: London, September 17-18, 1992.* Unpublished manuscript. Chicago, IL: University of Chicago.

Turner, T. (1995). Neoliberal Ecopolitics and Indigenous People: The Kayapo, the "Rainforest Harvest," and the Body Shop. In G. Dicum (Ed.), Local Heritage in the Changing Tropics: Innovative Strategies for Natural

Resource Management and Control (pp. 113–123). Bulletin Series #98, Yale School of Forestry and Environmental Studies. New Haven, CT: Yale University Press.

University of Bristol. (1996). *Body Shop—FAQ's* [On-line]. Available: http://bizednet.bris.a...act/bodyshop/body9.htm.

Utne, E. (1995, January–February). Beyond the Body Shop Brouhaha. *Utne Reader*, 65, 100–102.

Uzl, D. J. (1992). Corporate Social Responsibility. In R, W. McGee (Ed.), *Business Ethics and Common Sense* (pp. 137–144). Westport, CT: Quorum.

Uzzi, B. (1993). *The Network Effect: Structural Embeddedness and Firm Survival.* Unpublished manuscript. Evanston: IL: Northwestern University School of Management.

Vaill, P. B. (1996). *Learning as a Way of Being: Strategies for Survival in a World of Permanent White Water.* San Francisco: Jossey-Bass.

Vander Weyer, M. (1996, January). Only Fools and Masochists. *Management Today*, 26–30.

Vernon, R. (1986). Ethics and the Multinational Corporation. In W. M. Hoffman, A. E. Lange, & D. A. Fedo (Eds.), *Ethics and the Multinational Enterprise: Proceedings of the Sixth National Conference on Business Ethics, Oct. 10–11, 1985* (pp. 61–69). Lanham, MD: University Press of America.

Vogel, D. (1992, Fall). The Globalization of Business Ethics: Why America Remains Distinctive. *California Management Review*, 30–49.

Wahid, A. N. M. (1993). The Socioeconomic Conditions of Bangladesh and the Evolution of the Grameen Bank. In A. N. M. Wahid (Ed.), *The Grameen Bank: Poverty Relief in Bangladesh* (pp. 1–21). Boulder, CO: Westview.

Wahid, A. N. M. (1994). The Grameen Bank: Poverty Alleviation in Bangladesh: Theory, Evidence, and Limitations. *American Journal of Economics and Sociology*, 53(1), 1–15.

Wall Street Journal. (1996, March 5). Body Shop Chief Plans to Take Firm Private, Sec. A, p. 6.

Wallace, C. P., & Brown, E. (1996, April 15). Can The Body Shop Shape Up? *Fortune* [On-line]. Available: http://pathfinder.com/@@i@izAAcAwa-4ggIDU/fortune/magazine/1996/960415/managing.html.

Walsh, R. (1990). *The Spirit of Shamanism.* Boston: Shambhala.

Walsh, R.. (1994). The Making of a Shaman: Calling, Training, and Culmination. *Journal of Humanistic Psychology*, 34(3), 7–30.

Watson, F. (1993). *Notes from Visit to A'Ukre.* London: Cultural Survival. (Cited in Entine, J., 1995)

Weedon, C. (1987). *Feminist Practice and Poststructuralist Theory.* Oxford: Blackwell.

Wesson, W. H. (1964). Management. In J. Gould & W. L. Kolb (Eds.), *Dictionary of Social Sciences* (pp. 403–404). New York: Free Press.

Wheeler, D. (1992, Winter). Environmental Management as an Opportunity for Sustainability in Business—Economic Forces as a Constraint. *Business Strategy and the Environment*, 1(4), 37–40.

Wheeler, D. (1993, October). Two Years of Environmental Reporting at the Body Shop. *Environmental Auditing*, 23, 13–16.

Whitehill, A. M. (1991). *Japanese Management: Tradition and Transition*. New York: Rutledge.

Whitmont, E. (1982). *Return of the Goddess*. New York: Crossroad.

Whyte, W. F. (1991). *Making Mondragón*. Ithaca, NY: Cornell University Press.

Wilk, R. R. (1996). *Economies and Cultures*. Boulder, CO: Westview Press.

Wilkins, A., & Ouchi, W. (1986). Efficient Cultures: Exploring the Relationship Between Culture and Organizational Performance. *Administrative Science Quarterly*, 23, 464–481.

Winkelman, M. J. (1992). *Shamans, Priests and Witches: A Cross-Cultural Study of Magico-Religious Practitioners*. Arizona State University Anthropological Research Papers. No. 44. Tempe: Arizona State University.

Winters, J. (1995, December). Suharto's Indonesia: Prosperity and Freedom for the Few. *Current History*, 420–424.

Wolf, D. (1994). *Factory Daughters: Gender, Household Dynamics and Rural Industrialization in Java*. Berkeley: University of California Press.

Wolf, G. (1996). Steve Jobs: The Next Insanely Great Thing. *Wired* [On-line] 4.02, Wired Ventures. Available: http://www.hotwired.com/wired/4.02/features/ jobs.html.

Wolin, S. S. (1960). *Politics and Vision*. Boston: Little, Brown.

Womack, J., Jones, D., & Roos, D. (1990). *The Machine that Changed the World*. New York: Rawson.

Xerox Corporation. (1993, May). *The Xerox Quest for Quality*. Staff presentations at the annual conference of the New York Sate Association of Rehabilitation Facilities, Albany, NY.

Young, J. S. (1988). *Steve Jobs: The Journey Is the Reward*. Glenview: Scott, Foresman & Company.

Yukl, G. A. (1989). *Leadership in Organizations*. Englewood Cliffs, NJ: Prentice-Hall.

Author Index

Subject Index